NÝJA ÍSLAND

NÝJA ÍSLAND

Saga of the Journey to New Iceland

by

Guðjón Arngrímsson

Translation:
Robert Christie

TURNSTONE PRESS

Turnstone Press
607–100 Arthur Street
Artspace Building
Winnipeg, Manitoba
Canada R3B 1H3
www.TurnstonePress.com

Originally published in Iceland by Mál og Menning (1997) 𝗠
ISBN: 9979-3-1627-6

Turnstone Press gratefully acknowledges the assistance of the Canada Council for the Arts, the Manitoba Arts Council and the Government of Canada through the Book Publishing Industry Development Program for our publishing activities. Turnstone Press acknowledges the support and assistance of the National Museum of Iceland.

Cover photograph: *Lady of the Lake*. Photographer: J.H. Clarke, West Selkirk, 1896 or 1897. Courtesy of Nelson Gerrard, Eyrarbakki Icelandic Centre.

Printed in Canada by Friesens for Turnstone Press.

Canadian Cataloguing in Publication Data
Gudjón Arngrimsson, 1955–
Nýja Ísland: saga of the journey to New Iceland
Translation of: Nýja Ísland.
Includes bibliographical references.
ISBN 0-88801-255-1

1. Icelanders—Canada—History. 2. Icelandic
Canadians—History.★ 3. Iceland—Emigration and
immigration—History. 4. Canada—Emigration and
immigration—History. I. Title.
FC106.I3 G82123 2000   971'.0043961   C00-920148-3
F1035.I2 G8213 2000

CONTENTS

No. 12

O. Wathne

Eg undirskrifaður ~~umboðsmaður Sigfúsar Eymundssonar~~, agents Allan-línunnar, hef tekið á móti Kr. *480*

gegn því að neðanskrifaðir vesturfarar verði fluttir með téðri línu á vanalegan hátt frá Íslandi via Granton til Winnipeg samkvæmt þeim skilyrðum, sem tekin eru fram í lögum um tilsjón með flutningum á þeim mönnum, sem flytja sig úr landi í aðrar heimsálfur, 14. janúar 1876.

No.	Nöfn vesturfara.	Aldur.	Staða.	Síðasta heimili.
1.	Einar Þorkelsson	38	bóndi	Húnavatns
2.	Sigurlög Pjetursdóttir	30	kona hans	sama
3.	Árni Einarsson	4	barn	sama
4.	Björg Einarsdóttir	2	barn	sama
5.	Sigríður Einarsdóttir	½	barn	sama
6.	Oddbjörg Pjetursdóttir	24	vennukona	sama
7.	Þorkjæll Einarsson	½	barn	sama
8.				

Politi-skrifstofu Norður-Múlasýslu.

12 júlí 1887.

O. Þunaskun

Lögreglustjóri.

sett

Á ÍSLANDI.

Seyðisfirði *12* júlí 1887.

~~Umboði Sigfúsar Eymundssonar~~
~~authoriserade Emigrations Agentr~~

O. Wathne

6

...no matter what opinion one may have of the emigrants, I am utterly convinced that all men of sense would agree that of all the movements which have arisen in Iceland since the Reformation, the emigration movement is the most significant. Without doubt, it has captured the public imagination to a greater extent than any other popular movement of the last 300–400 years, and has directed the people of Iceland onto a path that they could never have known before. Every nation on Earth views the emigration to the New World as a deeply momentous event in its history. Wherever one looks, it has brought with it new wealth, new labour practices, and new ideas, in a word, new life. But because our nation is the smallest, poorest and most isolated of all the world's nations, and because as a people we have been at greater risk of becoming stubborn, eccentric, narrow-minded cranks, whose national ambience is that of the farmhouse living-room, where the invigorating breath of cosmopolitan culture can never circulate, then I would not be surprised if all right-thinking men would conclude that the emigration movement will be of considerably more significance to our nation than to any other on Earth.

Einar H. Kvaran, author, poet and previously Canadian immigrant and journalist at *Heimskringla*, from a lecture delivered in Reykjavík, November 2, 1895.

FOREWORD

When a large percentage of the population of Iceland decided to emigrate to North America in the last quarter of the nineteenth century, their departure left a huge rent in the fabric of Icelandic life. On the one hand, there were grounds for optimism: the Icelanders felt that they were well on the way to throwing off the yoke of Danish domination and carving a new space for their country in the community of nations. On the other, there was plenty of reason for despair. In many parts of the country, economic conditions were terrible. Dismal weather, natural disasters and a social system that gave the poor and landless little hope that their lives would be improved any time soon made Iceland a fertile ground for immigration agents from Canada and the United States, who gave promises of rich and fertile land, instant wealth and freedom.

Icelanders were not alone in this movement to the new world. In fact, they were near the middle of the great flood of emigration that was emptying Europe. Already, millions of English, Scottish and Irish settlers had departed. The movement from the Nordic countries was well on its way, and immigration agents were already plotting their assault on eastern Europe. Icelanders represented a tiny portion of the settlers in North America, a mere drop in the great tide that swept across the continent, but their departure left Iceland devastated. Some communities had so few people remaining that they were no longer functional. Abandoned farms and houses littered the landscape.

The Icelanders who remained, of course, felt a great resentment toward those who had abandoned the country. The fierce local pride of Icelanders meant that they did not react well to the notion that there were far better places to live than Iceland and that their neighbours had voted with their feet. There were few Icelanders left who hadn't themselves at least considered the possibility of leaving, and resentment was mixed with envy, especially when letters home extolled the virtues of the new place and seduced others to leave. Not all the letters were enthusiastic, however. Many settlers faced grim hardships, and they reported as much, but very few of those who left ever returned.

Iceland has been called the largest family in the world, and there is some truth to that. The country's historic isolation and the absence of immigration to Iceland has led to a narrowed gene pool and to a situation in which Icelanders can very quickly figure out how they are related to almost any other Icelander they meet. The rupture created by the great emigration was not just an historic event. It was also a family event. Everybody had relatives who had left, and so the resentment at their leaving was combined with a deep sense of loss. Most of the people who stayed saw people they loved get onto ships, knowing that they would never see them, or even hear from them, again.

Still, a ragged and patchy communication bound the two worlds together. Icelanders are nearly fanatical about genealogy, and they don't like to lose track of relatives. Those in what became known as New Iceland began to trace the links back home almost as soon as they arrived. Icelandic-Canadian books and magazines regularly reported on conditions in the home country, and Icelanders read those books and magazines as fervently as the New Icelanders did. Icelandic artists and intellectuals visited Canada and the United States, and Canadian and American artists, intellectuals and businessmen visited Iceland. The ties between the two Icelandic communities were sometimes thin and frayed, but they were never, even for a short time, completely broken.

Misconceptions flourished on both sides. Icelanders nursed a grievance at their betrayal by their North American cousins. New Icelanders told and retold the stories of the grim land from which they had fled, where poverty and disease were endemic and people lived in sod houses. Yet, on either side of the ocean, those who were enterprising enough to pay a visit returned with tales of the great generosity of their distant relatives and their amazing material success. And of course, it was all true. The Icelanders who come to North America have by and large been very successful, and those who stayed in Iceland have had equal success.

In recent years there has been a rebirth in interest on both sides. Icelandic choirs, orchestras and singers have visited Canada. Canadian galleries have exhibited Icelandic art, and Canadian publishers have translated and published Icelandic writing. At the same time, Canadian performers, writers and artists have toured Iceland, and Canadian writing has been translated into Icelandic and is even taught in Icelandic schools. The American experience is similar.

Lately there have been co-productions of films, and artists have collaborated on joint projects. The University of Iceland has signed an agreement with the University of Manitoba, which will lead to student and faculty exchanges and a series of joint conferences. Iceland has been particularly generous in its support of the Icelandic Department and Library at the University of Manitoba, and the Icelandic presence in Canadian life has recently received considerable publicity.

The publication of Gudjon Arngrimsson's *Nýa Ísland* in Icelandic marked a signal revival of interest in the Western Icelanders, as they are sometimes called in Iceland. The New Iceland novels of Bodvar Gudmundsson were Icelandic best-sellers, and they generated real interest in the western settlers. Arngrimsson's film *Fra Islandi*, along with *Nýa Ísland*, opened that history to many people who had only vague notions about the history of the Icelandic settlement in North America.

Canadian books about the settlement written and published during the twentieth century detail the founding and develop-ment of New Iceland from the perspective of the settlers and their descendants. Until now, there has been no book that pro-vides an Icelandic perspective. Arngrimsson's work looks at the conditions in Iceland itself and provides the details of the settlers' conditions at the time of leaving, the arrangements made for their passage and the effects of the out-migration on Iceland itself. It contains many photographs that have never been published before. It is an important and welcome addition to the literature about New Iceland, and it fills a gap in our understanding of that history.

—David Arnason

11

Eyes Across the Ocean

ON THE MOVE

For most Icelanders on their way west across the sea to what many of them perceived as the Promised Land, the first stop on the voyage was the Scottish port of Leith, from where they continued by train the same day to Glasgow.

For the majority, memories of this first day spent on foreign soil would remain with them for the rest of their lives, and colourful accounts of the strange and terrible wonders of the industrial revolution, in which they found themselves engulfed, can be found in countless letters sent to relatives and friends back home.

When the first bemused group of Icelanders arrived open-mouthed in Glasgow in 1873 and was pointed towards the soot-grimed warehouses and quaysides on the River Clyde, from where the great steamships packed with emigrants left for Canada, they suddenly realized for the first time that they were not alone. Every day of every year for over half a century, similar vessels would leave the great Scottish port, filled with passengers like themselves drawn from all over Europe, seeking a new life in the New World.

A vivid description of his last day spent on European soil appears in a letter by Björn Kristjánsson Skagfjörð, dated September 1, 1873:

> So much is happening here in this city. The streets are
> packed with people from morning to night, sometimes so
> tightly you can hardly move. There are wagons everywhere,
> some pulled by one horse, some by two. The horses are
> huge, some of them up to three yards round. Each is shod
> with iron, four nails in each shoe, otherwise they couldn't
> pull the wagons. We left Glasgow on Tuesday, August 12, at
> 2 p.m., and for a long time we sailed down the river on a
> steamer powered by two great paddles, one on each side.
> These turn continuously, with blades shaped like windmills,
> which churn up everything in their path, and are turned by
> a steam engine. When we reached the sea, the ship ploughed

on through a stiff breeze until we reached Liverpool, where we arrived at about the same time as we had left Glasgow the day before. There we were joined by people from many nations, Norwegians, Swedes, Danes, Germans, French and English.

The mass movement of people from Europe to the North American continent which took place between the end of the Napoleonic Wars in 1814 and the beginning of the Great Depression about 1930 is the greatest single migration in the history of mankind. All told, some 52 million Europeans bade farewell to their countries, homes, friends and relatives during this period and set off in search of a better life on the other side of the Atlantic. Icelandic immigrants, whose numbers totalled just under 20,000, accounted for only about 0.03% of this figure.

For most of these immigrants, regardless of their origin, it was a voyage into the unknown, as most had only a very vague notion of what awaited them. None of them knew if the long

Old meets new at the end of the 19th century. Double-decker trams like this one drawn by two massive Clydesdales were one of the first sights that greeted Icelanders on the first stage of their great voyage across the sea. From Glasgow, c. 1895.

The profound social and technological upheavals of the 19th century, which resulted in mass emigration from Europe, also produced some of the continent's first great cities. For Icelanders, one of the first experiences of urban life came among the seething mass of humanity which made up Glasgow's Argyle Street, seen here around 1895.

and arduous journey would really bring them a better life, and there was no way of knowing how things would have turned out had they stayed at home. Together, however, they laid the foundations of the economic, cultural, and political powers which the nations of North America would later become, and in their own way they contributed to the resultant prosperity later enjoyed by Europe.

Glasgow was only one of many European ports where immigrants gathered on their way west across the sea, and in midsummer, the docks and quaysides of what was fast becoming the second city of the British Empire thronged with a sea of humanity, providing several generations of the city's inhabitants with employment. Shipping lines, railway companies, hotels, guesthouses and a host of other service industries sprang up, their profits fuelled by the apparently endless stream of transient migrants.

What motivated these countless hordes of ordinary people to forsake the world they had always known for the uncertainties and dangers of a life beyond the sea? Why did some 15,000–20,000 Icelanders leave their native land for Canada? Why did Björn Kristjánsson Skagfjörð find himself far from home in a strange city wondering at the size of the horses while the recipient of his letter, Steinn Kristjánsson, a blacksmith from Akureyri, remained at home amid the familiar surroundings of Northern Iceland?

Answering these questions in general requires a close examination of a complex series of interacting social and economic factors, including population figures, cultural developments, employment, politics and religion. When considering Iceland in particular, a further range of considerations comes into play, such as climatic conditions and natural disasters.

But demographics tell us little when it comes to individuals. Their actions are dictated by more basic, personal factors. Frost damage to the crops of one, a shortage of land for another, while the death of a child may have been the catalyst which prompted yet another into seeking a new life far from home. Letters from friends and relatives beyond the sea encouraged some, silver-tongued agents persuaded others.

In short, there is no simple answer. A century later, we can only imagine the thoughts that must have passed through the mind of a 19th-century Icelander as he weighed the prospect of emigration. What kind of future will our children have? Will our parents come with us to America? What will become of the old and sick when their children and grandchildren have left them forever? Today, we can only guess at that strange mix of resignation and immense personal courage which moves people who believe themselves to have little opportunity within their own societies to risk everything on a dangerous voyage halfway across the world in the hope of a better life.

THE WINDS OF CHANGE

The 19th century saw a period of immense social, political and economic change in Europe, which made mass migration to the New World unavoidable. As the century wore on, what had

New means of transport, such as railways and steamships, allowed people to travel previously unheard-of distances in a relatively short time. This photograph shows Edinburgh's North Bridge and Waverley Station, from where Icelanders departed on their way from Leith to Glasgow.

begun as a trickle became a flood as unstoppable as the continent's major rivers.

Improvements in hygiene and medical science led to a general rise in life expectancy, and infant mortality, once viewed as an inescapable fact of life throughout the world, was also falling. As a result, populations rose dramatically, and in the years between 1800 and 1930, the population of Europe tripled from about 150 million to 450 million.

By mid-century, the continent could no longer produce the food required to feed this burgeoning population. Centuries-old farming methods and a shortage of arable land meant that those on the lower rungs of the land-owning ladder were forced to look elsewhere. As the pressure grew, increasing numbers of people began to drift towards the towns and cities in search of work, first to nearby towns and later to urban centres further afield. This, in turn, led to an explosion in the populations of major cities such as Berlin, London and Paris, and the creation of a new social class, the urban proletariat. For the first time in history, the majority of Europeans no longer lived in the country.

This dramatic growth in population was accompanied by the massive technological advances which came with the Industrial Revolution. New industries created new jobs, calling for new skills and altered working practices. As the cities grew, so too did the demand for skilled and unskilled labour to man the factories and industries on which they thrived. Labour was also required for construction, resulting in a massive expansion in the economies of almost all the countries of Western Europe.

Despite this, the cities could not keep up with the demands being made on them. Housing was in increasingly short supply, general living conditions were poor and lacking even the most basic services, and many new immigrants found themselves exchanging rural poverty for the urban variety.

Social attitudes were also changing. For centuries, when most people had been tied to the land, children were reared to follow in the footsteps of their fathers, but as the 19th century progressed and the cities grew, young people found themselves facing a new range of possibilities and choices. Expectations increased, and social ties, in place for generations, began to loosen. It was not only necessity that drove people to seek their fortune far across the sea. For some of Europe's youth, emigration was just one of a number of options in the quest for personal improvement.

Granton Harbour, about 1880, where many Icelanders disembarked after their voyage from Iceland. Now part of Edinburgh, Granton then hosted a mixture of sail and steamships.

At the same time, major developments in transportation which accompanied the Industrial Revolution made travel easier than ever before. Fast-moving steamships plied the oceans, while the railway fever that gripped much of the world during the latter half of the century enabled people to traverse countries, even continents, at speeds never before known. It is no accident that in several countries, many of the laws hindering travel were repealed during this period, providing the general populace with a freedom of movement previously unknown.

While the cities of Europe struggled to support their multi-plying populations, North America needed people. Much of the continent was unsettled, and vast, empty tracts of land, much of it ideal for agriculture, awaited those enterprising enough to claim it. Large numbers of people were also required to build up the continent's fledgling industries and to provide a solid foun-dation for the growing economies of Canada and the U.S. For North America, the displaced masses of Europe represented a precious human resource.

As formal and informal co-operation increased between governments, railway companies, and shipping lines on both sides of the Atlantic, the emigrant ships began to sail in large numbers. At the same time, European companies began invest-ing huge amounts of money in the New World, further fuelling the tide of emigration.

By the latter half of the 19th century, a whole generation of Europeans had grown up with the knowledge that the prospect of beginning a whole new life awaited them across the sea. Those born around 1840, when the first wave of emigration began, were adults by 1865 when the sea-lanes reopened at the end of the American Civil War.

A general rise in literacy also gave increasing numbers of Europeans access to the wealth of books, newspapers, and propa-ganda pamphlets proclaiming the virtues of emigration. Quick to spot the opportunity for profit, shipping lines and railway com-panies increased their services to meet increased demand. In the process, they found a range of creative new ways of advertising these services, some of them even hiring immigrants to return to their homelands and work as agents and salesmen.

Although these agents were as active in Iceland as elsewhere, the country's tiny population made personal and family ties

Smoke belches from the funnels of steamships as they cast off from Glasgow's Broomielaw about 1900. The 15,000–20,000 Icelanders who left for North America were a mere drop in the ocean of emigrants who boarded vessels here every day of the year for decades in search of a new life in the New World.

between those left behind and their emigrant relatives and friends more important, and letters like that of Björn Kristjánsson Skagfjörð, quoted earlier in this chapter, could often have more influence than the words of any company man.

THE EXODUS BEGINS

In reality, emigration from Europe across the Atlantic began in 1492 when Columbus discovered the New World, albeit as only a tiny trickle of what was to come. Among these early pioneers was the French explorer Jacques Cartier, believed to have been the first European to sail up the St. Lawrence River, in 1534. A century later, in 1635, only 85 Frenchmen are recorded as having lived in what was by then known as "New France." Most of these

The other side of prosperity. Industrialization brought with it the rise of slums and a new class of urban poor, although these children at least had access to fresh drinking water from public wells such as these. From Battersea, London, near the close of the 19th century.

early European settlements were clustered around the eastern seaboard of what is now Canada and the U.S., and for the next two centuries their growth would be steady rather than spectacular.

The first major wave of emigration from Europe is generally considered to have begun about 1830, led by Irish, English, and Scots emigrants. Of the 52 million emigrants who left Europe for North America during the years 1815-1930, 18.7 million came from the British Isles, 5.5 million of these from Ireland. Of the remainder, 9.9 were from Italy, 4.8 million from Germany, and 6.2 million from Spain and Portugal. The vast majority, some 33 million, settled in the U.S., 6.4 million in Argentina, 5 million in Canada, and 4 million in Brazil. A total of only 3.5 million settled in Australia.

Broadly speaking, the pattern of transatlantic emigration can be divided into four main periods, each occurring at about 20-year intervals, in 1850, 1870, 1890 and 1910, and for the most part they can be explained in terms of economic fluctuations taking place on both sides of the Atlantic at the time.

Transatlantic emigration began in earnest in 1845, in the wake of a series of disastrous harvests all over Europe resulting in widespread famine, notably in Ireland. Such was the scale of this wave of emigration that it is difficult to call it anything but a mass exodous.

A steamship of the type that plied the transatlantic emigrant routes. Built in 1871, this vessel, Spain, sailed mainly from Liverpool to New York until 1896. Each ship carried around 600 passengers, and the journey, using a mixture of steam and sail, took about a week.

In Ireland, the country worst affected of all and whose people were ravaged by the effects of several disastrous potato crops, an estimated 2-3% of the total population fled the country every year, setting a trend which would continue for several years, by which time the country's population would have been reduced to less than half its original size.

In the years that followed, the tide of emigration rose all over Europe, reaching its peak in 1853, by which time some 300,000-400,000 were leaving the continent each year, a rate of about 1,000 every day.

During the decade 1855-65, the flow of emigrants was stemmed, first by a marked improvement in harvests in Europe and a decline in those of North America, and later by the outbreak of the American Civil War. Peace, however, brought another wave of emigration, in this case peaking in 1870, by which time steam had replaced sail as the primary means of ocean transportation and the transport of emigrants had become a source of great profit to the railway operators and shipping lines. New markets arose, particularly in Sweden, Northern Italy, and Eastern and Northern Germany, and emigration to South America, notably Argentina, was considerable.

The year 1873 saw the onset of an economic depression on both sides of the Atlantic which would continue, with short respites, almost until the end of the century. This brought with it a corresponding drop in emigration, except from certain countries and regions, among them Iceland. U.K.-based shipping lines, who until then had claimed most of the market for themselves, found themselves facing increasingly stiff competition, particularly from Germany, resulting in a drop in fares.

By 1879, economic conditions in North America had improved, unlike those in Europe, and levels of emigration to the U.S. and Canada rose to an unprecedented level. During the 12-year period 1881-93, this rate reached an annual average of 700,000, with 2,000 people packing the emigrant ships every day of the year. The area from which they were drawn also grew and now included Finland, Southern Italy, Austria, Slovakia, Poland, Russia, and Ukraine.

The turn of the century brought with it a general decline in emigration, but 1903 saw the beginning of the final, most dramatic wave of emigration to North America, which would continue unabated until interrupted by the outbreak of the First World War more than a decade later. During these years, over 1.3 million men, women and children left Europe every year, almost 4,000 people each day. Drawn from all over the continent, they included for the first time significant numbers of

Food was included in the price of a ticket. The menu was often basic, the dining facilities poor, and seasickness was a common problem. This English sketch dating from about 1860-70 shows emigrants on their way to Australia.

Jews fleeing the pogroms which were becoming an increasing feature of life in the East.

By 1914, the greatest migration of people in European history was largely over. By then, some 100 million people of European descent were living in North America, but only about half had actually been born there. By the end of the Great War, the U.S. government had introduced a range of legislation designed to stem the tide of immigration, which still remains in force today. At the same time, general economic conditions throughout Europe had improved, although emigration persisted, albeit in greatly reduced numbers, until the onset of the Great Depression.

The 52 million men, women and children who made up this great human tide all came from countries and regions ravaged by hunger and poverty, Ireland being the most notable example. Emigrants also tended to come from the isolated and impoverished rural hinterland, rather than from the great industrial cities. As a result, close ties were often formed among people from these regions in their new home across the sea, providing them with a system of mutual support as well as a sense of the familiar, and the bonds between Iceland and Manitoba are a classic example of this tendency.

THE NORDIC FACTOR

Of the 50 million Europeans who emigrated to North America during the years 1815–1930, 2.5 million, or 5%, came from the Nordic countries. Given that the combined population of that region around 1800 was only 5.2 million, about 3% of the European total, this is in fact a larger figure than it might appear at first sight.

The first shipload of Scandinavian emigrants to sail for the New World was a group of 52 Quakers who left the Norwegian port of Stavanger in 1825, bound for New York. Accompanied by a few relatives and friends, they were not only the first group to set sail from the region, but the forerunners of a wave which by 1900 would have seen their country lose some 30% of its total population to transatlantic emigration, the highest proportion of all the countries in the region.

This was followed by Sweden, 21% of whose people sought new lives across the sea by the turn of the century. Only Ireland and the U.K. exported more of their populations. Between 1866 and 1870, no fewer than 150,000 Norwegian and Swedish immigrants landed in North America. Many small farmers, sometimes entire families, settled in the U.S., mainly on the plains of Minnesota and the Dakotas.

In his survey of Icelandic emigrants gleaned from sources on both sides of the Atlantic, Júníus H. Kristinsson estimated their number at 14,268, a figure now known to have been too low. Today, the total is generally believed to have been just under 20,000, some 20-25% of the total population. However, this is still a rough estimate.

During the same period, emigration from Finland was relatively low, only about 11%, while Denmark exported the least number of people to North America of all the Nordic countries.

The pleasures of the promenade deck were open only to the wealthiest passengers, who formed only a tiny proportion of emigrants. For most, the cramped conditions of steerage were the norm. From a German sketch of about 1890.

Why did they leave?

In an article which appeared in the publication *Austri* at the height of the transatlantic emigration in 1891, Guðmundur Hjaltason, a teacher, published a list of what he saw as ten possible motives for people to move from one country to another.

These included:

- Some move for riches.
- Others desire fame.
- The third group moves in search of freedom.
- The fourth group follows relatives or friends.
- The fifth group pursues pleasure.
- The sixth group moves in search of work.
- The seventh is looking for something new.
- The eighth group is lazy, and hoping for quick, easy profit.
- The ninth is restless.
- And many move for a combination of all these reasons.

As in the rest of Europe, the main reason for emigration from the region was a growing shortage of arable land among what was still a predominantly rural population, combined with the promise of a better life elsewhere.

LANDS ACROSS THE SEA

What awaited the first European immigrants to the U.S. and Canada were vast tracts of open prairie stretching as far as the eye could see, and untapped mineral wealth in the form of coal and iron.

At various times, whispers of gold were also heard in Europe, bringing with them corresponding surges in emigration. Following the horrors of the Civil War of 1861-65, the U.S. emerged as a major economic power, leading to an increased demand for people to fill what then appeared its inexhaustible open spaces, and to fill its cities where the prospect of work seemed equally limitless.

As was the case in Canada, Australia and New Zealand, immigrants from the British Isles were by far the most numerous, driven by a combination of necessity and a political belief that it was the duty of the rising British Empire to colonize as much of the world as possible.

Since the 17th century, Britain and France had competed for control of the North American continent. In the mid-18th century, the dispute erupted into open conflict, and defeat in the so-called Seven-Years' War, from which Britain emerged triumphant in 1763, cost the French control of their colonies in the region.

Despite this, when the great exodus began from Europe in the early 19th century, large numbers of French-speaking colonists remained in British North America, as Eastern Canada was then known, particularly in Quebec. To counteract this Gallic influence, immigrants from the British Isles were offered special privileges, including free passage, land, tools, seed, and food to help them through their first harvest. This had the intended consequences, and their numbers increased rapidly, thus laying the foundation for the large farming class of British descent which has played such a prominent role in the history of Canada.

The stream of emigrants from Europe flowed first to the eastern seaboard of North America, spreading gradually west across the Great Plains all the way to the Pacific. This process took some time, requiring as it did an organized transport infrastructure. The first Europeans to venture into these vast lands to stake their claims were usually not farmers but hunters, trappers who traded with the Native population, and a variety of adventurers.

They were followed by government surveyors, and finally those in search of land, either families intending to farm or speculators. The latter cleared the land, and sometimes even built on it, before selling out to settlers or other landbrokers. Real estate soon became a major industry, and the companies involved in it were often in the hands of the same money magnates back east as the railroads and shipping lines. Together, they formed a network of businesses whose mutual prosperity depended on the continued transportation of large numbers of people to the West.

THE MAKING OF CANADA

Formed from the former British North America, a loose union of Ontario, Quebec, New Brunswick and Nova Scotia, the four British colonies clustered around the eastern seaboard and the St. Lawrence, Canada achieved nationhood in 1867, just a few years before the arrival of the first Icelandic immigrants.

Apart from Quebec, whose population was mainly of French descent, they were composed mostly of immigrants from the Bristish Isles, although a few other nations were represented as well. In many ways, they were more closely tied to the mother country than to each other, and internal disputes were not uncommon. Their currencies varied, and customs barriers made trade between them difficult. Commercial links with the United States were strong, however, and by the end of the Civil War in 1865, the British government and local colonial leaders realized that the U.S. was now a military and economic force to be reckoned with. Faced by the potential threat posed by their more powerful neighbour, the colonies were persuaded to settle any internal differences and the result was the Dominion of Canada, based then, as now, on a federal union between the provinces.

Although legislative, executive, and judicial power lay with the parliament in Ottawa, the head of state was Queen Victoria, represented by the Governor General, and the ultimate court of appeal lay in London.

When Canada was created in 1867, the great expanse of land in the West known as the North West Territory was largely unsettled. Owned by the Hudson Bay Company, which had acquired it from the British government for the purpose of developing the fur trade and establishing a few trading posts, its only settlement of any real size was at Fort Garry, which lay at

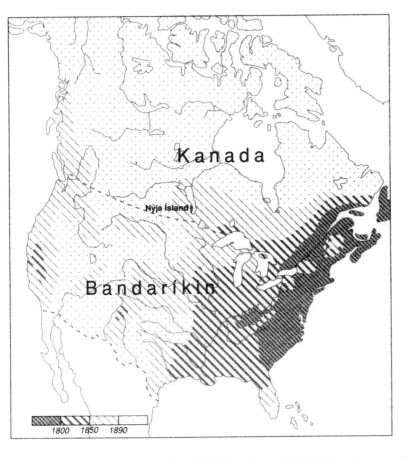

Around 1800, settlement in North America was confined exclusively to the eastern seaboard of the U.S. and Canada. By 1850-90, however, it had extended west across the continent to the Pacific coast, with the prairies of the midwest the last areas to be settled.

the confluence of the Red River and the Assiniboine River, the site of present-day Winnipeg. Colonized by Lord Selkirk's Scots in 1812 and a few French missionaries in 1818, half a century later its population consisted of a few hundred settlers of Scottish descent and people of mixed French–Native blood, known as Métis.

Although the government of the fledgling Canadian nation realized the rich agricultural potential of the region, access to it lay north along the Red River from Minnesota and North Dakota. Aware of the fact that the region would find itself part

The first settlement at Winnipeg was clustered around the walls of Fort Garry, at the junction of the Assiniboine and Red Rivers. This photograph dates from 1858, 17 years before the first Icelanders arrived in Manitoba. Only a small part of the fort can still be seen, hidden among the skyscrapers of the present-day city.

of the U.S. if nothing was done, Ottawa acted swiftly. In 1868, the region was purchased from the Hudson Bay Company, and government land surveyors and officials moved in. Fearful of the consequences to their independence, the Métis rebelled, and a short but bloody struggle ensued, which ended with their surrender and the flight of their leader, Louis Riel, deeper into the wilderness.

Two years later, in 1870, the province of Manitoba was formed from a small area of the former North West Territory, and it immediately became part of the Dominion of Canada. The land of the new province was good, if not perfect, covered in the south by plains of grass up to a metre high. Dense woods grew around its lakes and rivers and in the vast area to the north, and while long, cold winters made the growing season short, the land was well suited to agriculture. Distances from main markets were huge, however, and the only form of transportation was via the lakes and rivers, making the cost of getting produce to market extremely high.

Clearly, the only way to make Manitoba and much of the rest of Canada economically viable was improved transportation, and plans were laid in 1873 for the construction of a Trans-Canadian railway, stretching from the Atlantic to the Pacific.

In 1870, the Canadian government embarked on a policy of pointing immigrants not only to the unsettled areas of Ontario, the destination of the first Icelandic settlers, but also west to Manitoba. Although across the border, Dakota Territory, Nebraska, and Minnesota may have presented a more attractive proposition to immigrants, they had a much longer history of settlement, and large tracts of land were no longer plentiful, which was not a problem in Manitoba.

A combination of new agricultural machinery like this harvester and the massive size of their fields allowed North American farmers to produce large quantities of food at much lower costs than those of their European counterparts, resulting in the rise of a flourishing export trade.

In 1873, the Canadian government concluded an agreement with a group of German-speaking Mennonites living in Russia, offering them exclusive rights to an area of land in Manitoba, where they would be free to practise their religion and enjoy a limited degree of independence. Two years later, a similar agreement was made with Icelandic immigrants, and both groups would later play a prominent role in the history and development of the region.

By that time, immigration from Europe had become a major growth industry in Canada, bringing with it thousands of jobs and a rich source of income for several companies, the chief of which was the Allan Line.

Formed by a Scot, Alexander Allan, the company, which would play a key role in the story of Canadian immigration, rapidly rose to become one of the world's largest shipping lines.

Climatic Conditions

Harsh weather and volcanic eruptions are often cited as the main causes of emigration from Iceland to Canada and the U.S. But were they? The following is a weather annal from volume 9 of *Sagu Íslendinga*, *The History of the Icelanders*. Abridged and reworded in parts, it includes emigration figures for each year. As can be seen, there was not always a direct correlation between climatic conditions and levels of emigration. Indeed, it can hardly be seen by the end of the period, and the figures would suggest that the full effects of bad weather were probably not felt until a year or two after it occurred.

Although climate and natural disasters have always played a major role in the lives of Icelanders, it was probably a variety of social factors which tipped the balance when it came to emigration, backed up by the persuasive powers of the salesmen and agents. When Baldvin L. Baldvinsson was employed by the Canadian government as a full-time agent selling passages from Iceland in 1890, the level of emigration reached unprecedented heights. At the same time, it would have been somewhat strange if some Icelanders had not left the country at the same time as 50 million other Europeans were streaming across the Atlantic. It was hardly bad weather which drove 9.9 million Italians across the sea.

Although it had passed outside the control of the immediate family, the company was chaired by one of its founder's five sons, the Canadian-based Sir Hugh Allan.

By 1870, the Allan Line's network extended from five ports in the United Kingdom to 12 in the Americas, ranging from Quebec, Montreal, St. John's, Halifax, Portland, Boston, New York, Philadelphia, and Baltimore, to Montevideo, Buenos Aires, and Rosario.

For some years, the company, in conjunction with the Canadian authorities, had offered prospective immigrants cheap passages based upon a highly organized network consisting of agents and salesmen situated all over Europe. The Allan Line's principal agent for the Nordic countries, Mattson by name, was based in Sweden, and by 1872, Reykjavík merchant Guðmundur Lambertsen had become its Icelandic representative.

The emigrants were a product of the times in which they lived, and not mere victims of hard times or bad weather.

There is no doubt, however, that the main emigration years followed some unusually harsh conditions. Pack ice led to a general fall in temperatures all over the country, and the year 1859 ushered in a period of hardship. The year 1866 is considered one of the worst in the 19th century, with pack ice and storms resulting in a failure of the hay crop and a chronic shortage of fodder, and the years 1867-69 brought little improvement.

1870: slightly warmer than previous years, although there was pack ice in the spring.
 Emigrants: 6

1871: a lot of pack ice, but it did not last long. Weather generally fair.
 Emigrants: 12

1872: generally good, but ended with some heavy frosts.
 Emigrants: 22

1873: severe winter frosts and a cold spring. There was heavy pack ice, and the hay crop was poor. Snow fell early in the autumn.
 Emigrants: 323

1874: unusually cold winter, with over 20 degrees of frost and up to 30 in the north. The pack ice was heavy, and men were forced to cut

During these years, the population of Canada grew rapidly, rising from 3.6 million in 1871 to 5.4 million by 1900. In addition, a further 2 million, the same number as actually emigrated to Canada, are believed to have continued across the border into the U.S.

The story of the Icelanders who immigrated to Canada in the 19th century is in many ways typical of their counterparts from elsewhere in Europe. Their roots lay in isolated farms and small, rural communities. They were encouraged to emigrate, enjoyed assisted passages across the sea and knew where they wanted to go.

What made them different, however, were the unusually strong ties they felt to their homeland and its culture, and their dream of forming a new colony on the shores of Lake Winnipeg.

---

 fodder in February. The pack ice abated, but returned in June, delaying the growing season even further. The winter was remembered for its extreme cold, passing into popular folklore as "The Great Storm" or "The Big Freeze." The last months of the year were much better.

Emigrants: 391

1875: generally mild, particularly the winter. But when the ice melted, fire began, with massive eruptions in the northeast, first at Askja, then at the Sveinagjá in Mývatnsöræfi. Rare for the volcano, the Askja eruption was an ash episode, beginning in late March and destroying several farms in the Fljótsdalur region and damaging several others. The ash spread at amazing speed through the high atmosphere, reaching as far as Norway. In July, the Biskupstungur district of South Iceland was struck by fierce gales and hailstorms. Fishing was fair, and some of the hay crop in the East was cut before the autumn gales smothered it in volcanic ash.

Emigrants: 59

1876: heavy pack ice off the north coast affected the weather for the worse. However, it had passed by May, and conditions improved significantly. The hay crop was good, as was the fishing, except in Faxaflói, in the Southwest.

Emigrants: 1,190

THE LAND THEY LEFT BEHIND

When the first Icelandic emigrants set sail for North America, they left behind a country locked in the grip of a centuries-old tradition of subsistence farming. Better times may have lain just around the corner, but the winds of change were little more than a whisper among the scattered crofts and tiny communities that made up rural Iceland, and they would not make themselves felt until the turn of this century, by which time the majority of emigrants had already left.

In the meantime, the precarious life of the subsistence farmer remained very much the rule. For the vast majority of Icelanders, life was harsh, everything was home made, conditions were

1877: a hard winter and cold spring resulted in a poor hay crop. Fishing failed completely around Faxaflói, bringing famine to the local populace.
Emigrants: 59

1878: fair to begin with, but the late winter brought severe pack ice which remained until June. Hay crop generally sparse.
Emigrants: 473

1879: winter frosts in the north so severe that Eyjafjörður froze as far out as the island of Hrísey and people could walk out to Málmey in Skagafjörður, but an otherwise average year for the rest of the country.
Emigrants: 322

1880: a particularly good year all over the country, with a winter so mild it was hardly noticed. But following an excellent harvest, autumn brought worsening conditions, and harsh storms brought a cruel end to the year.
Emigrants: 94

1881: marked the beginning of two years of uninterrupted misery. The cold which began before New Year's continued, and January 9 saw the beginning of whiteout conditions and severe frosts which lasted for several days. In fact, it could be said that this weather persisted with a few ☞

primitive in the extreme, and there was a general ignorance of better agricultural methods.

One striking example of this lay in the complete lack of a transport infrastructure. No roads existed to connect the country's regions, a fact which prompted the English entrepreneur Coghill, who visited the country several times between 1875-90, to comment that, above all, Iceland needed three things: roads, roads, and roads.

In short, as far as Icelanders were concerned, the wheel might never have been discovered. The only modes of transport were on foot or on the ubiquitous Icelandic horse. When a regular postal service commenced in 1872, delivering mail a few times a year on horseback, it was hailed as a revolution. Ironically, the exodus to Canada and the U.S. led to a massive increase in this service, and the amount of correspondence delivered increased ten-fold in the years 1884-94, from 18,000 letters to 180,000.

Communications by sea were limited and mainly by means of small sailing vessels owned by merchants. In the years around 1870, the Danish government operated the mailboat *Diana*, which made six or seven trips each summer between Iceland and Denmark, carrying mail and a few other articles, mainly for government officials.

---

short breaks until April, with the final weeks bringing the worst cold of all, up to 37 degrees of frost in the North. Most of the country's major bays and fjords were locked in the grip of pack ice, Breiðafjörður as far as the islands. Polar bears came ashore, loose objects were blown away by the gales, and people remained indoors, preferably in bed. Whitsun, June 5, brought another terrible storm, in which an estimated 18,000 lambs perished. In many places, frost remained in the ground all summer.
Emigrants: 144

1882: a variable winter followed by a cold spring, with a belt of pack ice extending from the West Fjords all the way eastwards and down to Breiðamerkursandur in the far South. From June to September, the earth was covered in snow no fewer than 10 times, and, to add to the misery, an epidemic of measles swept the country that summer, claiming some 1,600 lives.
Emigrants: 347

Haukagil, in the Borgarfjörður region of West Iceland, seen here about 1890, is a typical example of a traditional Icelandic farm of the type which had survived for centuries. The women here are pictured wearing the distinctive tasseled headgear which caused much amusement across the sea.

1883: a much better year, with a fine hay crop, good fishing and good lambing season bringing a general recovery.

   Emigrants: 1,215

1884: an average winter, but variable summer, especially in the North. Heavy rain in the South, however, meant the hay crop could not be cut.

   Emigrants: 121

1885: a bad winter, with heavy snows. On January 15, a terrible avalanche in the East Fjords village of Seyðisfjörður swept 15 dwellings out to sea, killing 26 people and seriously injuring several others. The hay crop everywhere was poor, as was the fishing.

   Emigrants: 141

1886: another bad year, with a hard winter and much snow. Pack ice persisted well into the summer, and the fishing was poor everywhere.

   Emigrants: 506

In 1870, the population of Iceland was almost 70,000, about three-quarters of which earned a living from the land, 10% from the sea, and about 15% through commerce, handcrafts or employment as government officials.

Towns or other centres of population barely existed, consisting only of Reykjavík, with a population of about 2,000, and Akureyri, with a few hundred. Despite this, the population had grown, as elsewhere in Europe. No serious disease or epidemic had swept the country for some time, and land use had gradually spread to the marginal lands of stony mountain slopes and barren rocky promontories, where the life of the crofter was grim and the line between survival and starvation very thin indeed.

For Icelanders as a nation, the period also saw some of the greatest political upheavals in the country's history. An enforced constitutional law passed by the Danish parliament in 1871, declaring the country an inseparable part of Denmark, and the replacement the following year of the Danish minister in Copenhagen for Icelandic affairs with a resident Royal governor may have placed the ongoing struggle for independence temporarily on hold, but these changes also resulted in widespread unrest.

1887: a terrible winter, marred by severe frosts, storms and pack ice, which stretched all the way from the West Fjords as far south as Kúðafljótsós, some claimed the Westman Islands. Hay crop from last year was so poor that many were forced to take to the road and beg. Fishing good.

Emigrants: 1,947

1888: another hard winter, with pack ice gripping the country as far as the Westman Islands until the end of July. Although late, the hay crop was generally good, and the fishing excellent.

Emigrants: 1,109

1889: a good year for the most part, with large sales of sheep to Britain.

Emigrants: 702

1890: average weather, and average fishing. Sheep sales to Britain rose even more.

Emigrants: 217

This was alleviated only in part by the drafting of a special constitution for Iceland, presented personally by the Danish king, Christian IX, at the old parliament site at Þingvellir in 1874, on the occasion of the millennial celebrations of the country's settlement.

In 1870, as the attention of the authorities was occupied almost entirely by these disputes, the attention of much of Iceland's population was focused closer to home, on the problems created by the country's growing population, namely poverty and unemployment. Before 1870, fishing was largely a part-time occupation, viewed as little more than a supplementary means of income for farmers and farm labourers.

Iceland's primitive agricultural methods, however, were incapable of supporting a working population any larger than that of a century before. Clearly, fresh employment opportunities were desperately required, but oppressive social legislation made it impossible for young people to look for them.

For centuries, the landless classes which made up much of the population had been forced to tie themselves to local farms, a measure designed to spare parishes and other local authorities the burden of supporting indigent poor or itinerant beggars.

A native of the Kelduhverfi district, Northeastern Iceland, Kristján Ásgeir Benediktsson later emigrated to Canada where he became an author and journalist. As well as providing the best surviving account of life in Iceland as it was, he also wrote fiction under the pseudonym Snær Snæland.

1891: average weather and hay crop. Fishing varied, but the price of sheep fell, as did sales.

    Emigrants: 216

1892: bad winter of persistent blizzards and unusually severe frosts causing many major bays and fjords to freeze over. A fine spell in late summer saved the hay crop, except in the East Fjords, where it was very wet.

    Emigrants: 290

1893: a mild winter, with fair fishing.

    Emigrants: 725

1894: a fairly good year, with a hay crop to match. Fishing fair.

    Emigrants: 113

1895: a very mild winter, with hardly any snow. A fine spring resulted in a good hay crop. Fishing fine, except around Faxaflói.

    Emigrants: 9

Although in theory it was possible to buy freedom from these ties, few had the means to do so, and sporadic attempts to change the system had, not surprisingly, been successfully resisted by farmers and landowners.

In the 1860s, a young lad, Kristján Ásgeir Benediktsson, was growing up in Kelduhverfi, a district in the county of Norður-Þingeyjarsýsla, Northeastern Iceland. A strapping youth, he would later move to Canada, where he became an author, genealogist, and journalist in Winnipeg.

Writing in the newspaper *Heimskringla* in 1907, he recalled his youth in a series of lively articles, which, although based only on his own experiences, offer the most vivid of many contemporary descriptions of the Iceland of the time. A century later, Benediktsson's writings still provide the reader with a penetrating insight into life in Iceland which many of the early emigrants took with them to their graves.

His Iceland is the Old Iceland, handed down by these first settlers to their children and grandchildren in anecdote, poetry and song, its memory tinged, perhaps, with the touch of guilt felt by so many emigrants, regardless of their origins, for having left in the first place.

1896: a good winter, but hay cutting made difficult by heavy rains. An estimated 70 days of snow throughout the year were accompanied by 141 days of rain.
Emigrants: 10

1897: variable but difficult weather conditions. Another collapse in fishing around Faxaflói brought near-starvation to the local populace.
Emigrants: 55

1898: although the winter was extremely hard in the South and West, the year as a whole was not particularly harsh.
Emigrants: 87

1899: the blizzards which continued throughout the country well into spring gave way to a good summer, producing an excellent hay crop. Fishing good, except around Faxaflói.
Emigrants: 157

THE STRUGGLE FOR SURVIVAL

The writings of Kristján Ásgeir Benediktsson provide us with a vivid account of the monotonous struggle for survival which was the lot of so many Icelanders during the middle years of the last century.

As in all rural societies, life moved in tandem with the rhythm of the season. As the last snows of winter faded, the annual round of toil began, and before the lambing season turned work into a round-the-clock grind for all involved, there was manure to spread and stone walls to be mended. In June, the ewes were sheared and driven high up into the mountains which would provide their summer pasture.

Steeped in acidic stale urine, which cut through the lanolin and grime, their wool was then rinsed in fresh, running stream water. A highly valued commodity, it was the main trade item accepted by local merchants, who exchanged it for a variety of staples such as rye flour, peeled barley, beans, and rice. What was left paid for small luxuries like coffee, sugar, tobacco, or alcohol.

Haying also began in June and lasted well into September.

1900: an average year, for the most part. Fish finally returned to Faxaflói, as everywhere else.

Emigrants: 725

1901: a prosperous year on land and sea. Catches particularly good on decked vessels.

Emigrants: 358

1902: a hard winter, with pack ice persisting in the north and East Fjords until well into spring. A good summer, but average hay crop. Fishing fair.

Emigrants: 313

1903: an average year on land and sea.

Emigrants: 677

Cutting hay at Reykjahlíð, Mývatn, Northeast Iceland, in 1906 or 1907. Primitive tools meant that most of the summer was occupied by the backbreaking monotony of this task, which required every available pair of hands.

The work was back-breaking, and implements were scarce, as few farmers had the skills necessary to fashion a scythe.

> "You could say that men worked night and day during haying season," Benediktsson remembered. "By day, they turned or gathered the hay, at night, they cut it … In some places, they stood up to their waists in marshland from dawn to dusk. Elsewhere, they were half-blinded by flying sand and dust which filled their eyes, ears, and nose. Often they worked in driving rain and sleet, braving the elements as long as their scythes would cut. In some places, they faced a two-hour walk to and from the fields, a journey they made morning and night."

As soon as the last of the hay had been gathered in autumn, the painstaking business of rounding up the sheep began, a process so slow that five trips up the steep mountain slopes were sometimes required to recover one animal. Some were found dead at the bottom of cliffs or steep gullies, their demise ascribed by Benediktsson to the constant onslaught of flies and midges.

The turf farmhouses and crude steadings were also a hive of activity, with sheep to care for, hay to be stored, and last-minute repairs to be carried out before the onset of winter. To see themselves, their families and dependents through the long, dark months of winter, farmers slaughtered from 30 to 100 lambs per household.

For most Icelanders, the shortening days brought little respite from the relentless grind of daily life. Until weather conditions made it impossible, animals were kept outside. The first flurries of snow were the signal to bring cattle into the stables, where they remained for the next 26 weeks, at least. Horses were kept outside until well into the winter, by which time they were little more than skin and bone. According to Benediktsson, they were generally badly treated and fed on scraps of hay left by the cattle or sheep.

In addition to the daily round of chores such as gathering fuel, water, and other materials necessary to life, outside work in the winter centred on the sheep, which had to be fed, watered, and tended.

Indoors, life in the *baðstofa*, the communal living area which was the focus of daily life in Icelandic farmhouses, centred almost completely on wool. As the women spun, knitted, teased, stretched and cleaned it, the men combed, carded and knitted, one sock in an evening being considered the mark of a good knitter.

In the evening, when the men had finished work and had something to eat, they were handed knitting needles, carders,

Sheep being milked in a pen at Böggvisstaðir, Svarfaðardalur, Northern Iceland, about 1910.

or a book. The household sat quietly throughout the early evening, and some grabbed a short nap until the lamps were lit at 7 o'clock. This was a pleasure denied slow knitters, however, as they struggled to meet their production quota for the week. Failure to do so meant incurring the certain wrath of the farmer. Bedtime was not until sometime between 11 o'clock and midnight. From winter until Whitsun, the reading aloud of both secular and religious material was a common pastime in most households, and each evening closed with family prayers and worship. The main source of light in those days were lamps fuelled by whale, shark, seal, or other types of oil . . . These were often foul-smelling and painfully inadequate, giving off only a dim light. Some people burned candles as well. The most popular form of entertainment of an evening was the reciting of ancient rhymes, which the young folk found difficult to understand. Their roots often lay in the sagas and Eddas, and they were far from easy to understand for people who could barely read and who had absolutely no knowledge of grammar or language. But the older folk under-stood them well enough, and still quote from them. Sometimes, people dropped off to sleep during this communal recitation and had to be woken up for prayers and goodnight wishes.

THE ICELANDIC FARMHOUSE

In his writings, Kristján Ásgeir Benediktsson leaves us in no doubt that the general standard of housing in Iceland was very poor, whether for humans or animals. Squalid, old, and poorly ventilated, many buildings, such as they were, bore the mark of generations of neglect. Their construction was crude, with walls built of turf and stone, sometimes of turf alone. Roofs, construct-ed of driftwood, stone, and turf, leaked, and although the *baðstofa*, which was generally on the second storey, might have at least a partially timbered floor, the stable was often directly underneath.

> The cows stayed in all winter, along with any other beasts being kept there: rams, goats, orphaned lambs, and other animals requiring special care. The heat from the stable was

Old Icelandic turf houses required continual maintenance, meaning they were in a permanent state of reconstruction. This photograph dates from 1912, but people lived in such houses until well into this century.

considered very healthy, and if the *baðstofa* was directly above, close to stifling. Outside, there might be a blizzard and 20–30 degrees of frost, but those inside the *baðstofa* sat dripping in sweat. But in houses where the *baðstofa* was not above the stable, the cold was terrible. Besides, no one, young or old, showed the slightest reaction at all to the stench of manure which pervaded the house in the morning when the stable was being cleaned.

Beds were arranged under the sloping roof of the *baðstofa*. Box-shaped, they were two planks high. Food was stored in wooden eating bowls on shelves above the beds, and cleaning was a casual business, consisting mainly of an occasional sweep of the floor, apart from on holidays and other special occasions.

This was the age of tobacco, and men spat it all over the floor, making it difficult for the women to clean.

The pantry and kitchen were the workplaces of the women. Along the walls stood an assortment of wooden casks and barrels, containing *skyr* (yoghurt), buttermilk, and whey. Fuel and dried manure for burning were stored in the kitchen, along with basins, jugs, water, pots, pails, and tubs. An assortment of meat hung from the rafters above: smoked lamb, kidneys, hearts, sausages, and fish. Shoe leather might also be hung. Toilets and sanitation were non–existent.

The cramped, primitive conditions of the dingy farm kitchen were ill-suited to cleanliness. Working there was both difficult and tiring. This photograph dates from 1890-93.

No farmhouse had a toilet, but there were two mounds close to each house, sometimes more. These were known as the dirt mound and the ash mound, and in most places they were at the back of the house, although I also saw some directly opposite the front door. People used them as toilets. When the home fields had been hayed, they were used instead. Evidence of this practice could be seen everywhere with fields covered in excrement of all shapes and sizes. In storms and bad weather, the cowshed was used instead.

EDUCATION AND RELIGION

Before 1870, educational facilities for children barely existed in Iceland. During the years 1875-85, however, schools sprang up all over the country. Conditions, though, were primitive. Buildings were sparse and cold, and aids such as maps were available in only a few places. As a result, formal education for most people was patchy, as Kritján Ásgeir Benediktsson later remembered.

In those days, most men and women over the age of
confirmation could at least read their prayers. Many could
read very well, and loved books and learning of all kinds.
Generally speaking, most men could scribble their names, and
while some women couldn't spell, others could scrawl a little.
Children were taught to read and form their letters, but very
few were taught to write in the accepted sense of the word.

As a pastime, reading was widespread, especially on winter
evenings when one member of the household read aloud to
the others. The most popular works were *Njóla*, *Piltur og
Stúlka*, the Icelandic sagas, the sagas of the Norse Kings, folk-
tales and *A Thousand and One Nights*. Ballads were also
popular, and the poems of Þorlákur, Bjarni and Jónas were
read and learned by heart. The sermons of Bishop Jón Vídalín
and Mynster's reflections were held in high regard, and many
could recite the *Passion Psalms* of Hallgrímur Pétursson from
cover to cover. These were sung every day during Lent.

In 1870, the Icelanders still clung to the same religious beliefs
they had held for centuries, but while old worthies such as
Hallgrímur Pétursson, Jón Vídalín and Guðbrandur Þorláksson
might have remained the leading authorities in spritual affairs
among the general populace, the supernatural also played a
major role, as Benediktsson relates.

> Once people had gone to bed, the talk often turned to ghosts,
> apparitions, the hidden folk, outlaws, and dreams, as this was
> the main time of the day for conversation and discussion.
> Belief in ghosts was very strong, especially in apparitions and
> wraiths. I myself became so afraid of the dark that I was scared
> to go to sleep, even though there was someone below me and
> I was so tightly wrapped in my bedclothes I was almost
> smothered. But there were many worse than I. If some poor
> soul killed himself somewhere in the West of the country or
> east on the moors, he immediately appeared in the passageways
> of some of the farms in Kelduhverfi. It was considered a good
> precaution to make the sign of the cross when locking the
> front entrance of the house at night. Some older women did
> the same in the *baðstofa*, while many people crossed themselves
> three times around their bed at the close of evening prayers,
> accompanying the ritual with the words "May God give me a
> good night." As for me, I did all these things to protect myself
> from ghosts, and I have to say that it worked quite well.

When someone put out a lamp, he or she was supposed to utter the words: "God give me eternal light, which will never die." When setting off for church or on any other journey, you were supposed to read the "Traveller's Prayer" and the "Lord's Prayer," and make the sign of the cross. Day or night, you couldn't move for prayers or folk crossing themselves, in addition to family worship. Although people were generally sceptical of the church and its pastors, religion was an old habit whose roots lay very deep.

HEALTH AND NUTRITION

Apart from the country's chief medical officer, only seven doctors could be found working in Iceland around the year 1870. Badly paid, they all had other jobs from which they derived their main income, and in times of illness most people turned to a variety of quacks, homeopaths, and other men of similar learning closer to home, rather than going to a qualified doctor who might be a long way away.

Despite this, the doctors were to be thanked for the limited variety of preventive measures then in general use, including vaccination against smallpox. Although, according to Benediktsson, people washed fairly frequently, the general level of hygiene left much to be desired. Hydatids, a disease spread by worms found in sheep and dogs, was extremely common, while the population in 1870 included some 240 lepers. Although pay for midwives was even worse than that for doctors, midwives numbered 67 in 1874. Two hospitals, located in Reykjavík and Akureyri, served the whole country, offering a total of only 30 beds between them. One vet could be found in the whole of Iceland, much of whose time went into treating the "scab" then endemic among the country's sheep.

> Of course people didn't wash every day, but most of them at least washed their hands when they finished work if the job they'd been doing was dirty. If they were going somewhere special, they always gave their face, neck and hands a

Washing wool about 1920. When emigration began about 1870, wool was the main cash product for farmers. Washed in urine and rinsed in fresh water, it was then taken to market in large sacks or hand worked in the home.

thorough wash. . . . Women often washed their hair, first in steeped urine, then in soap and water. The heads of youngsters were often washed by the same method . . . Despite the efforts of their mothers, most children had a few head lice, but these were considered disgusting. As vagrants were usually crawling with lice, people were very reluctant to offer them shelter. Men had their hair cut short all the way round, and often wore it with a side parting. Most had full beards, but some shaved, leaving only a moustache or chin whiskers. The women combed their hair once or twice a day and wound it in pigtails, usually two or four, which they fastened under their caps with large hairpins.

Underwear was washed fairly often, usually about every fortnight. Homespun clothing was first washed in hot steeped urine, then rinsed in the nearest lake or stream and dried in the fresh air. The steeped urine was not heated in cooking pots, but along with dyed laundry or wool. Washing was stretched out to dry on the grass, often located near the farm yard. Bedding was washed more seldom than clothing. In the box beds was a layer of brushwood or woodshavings, covered by a goatskin, horsehide, or fleece. On top was a down quilt covered with a blanket, and so a pillow, overblanket and bedspread. These beds were very soft and comfortable, except when they were infested with fleas. These were worst in beds containing woodshavings and where the *baðstofa* was damp. They jumped all over the bed and up the walls when you were getting ready for bed, and their bites caused painful swellings.

According to Benediktsson's account, the daily diet was, at best, monotonous. When there was enough to eat, meals were taken three times a day.

Breakfast consisted of yoghurt and skimmed milk, which varied in consistency. These were mixed with porridge made from lichen, with a little rye meal and a few kernels of pearl barley added. Those working outside all day also got a little meat, but no one else. The mid-day meal was rye gruel, supplemented with two to four bits of meat. It was often stale or over-salted, and sometimes a big spoon of yoghurt was added. Some days there were beans, rice, and meat, on others black pudding, and bread. On others still there was dried fish, shark, bread, and drippings. Sheep's heads were served on Sundays until Christmas, when they were finished. On Saturdays there was usually milk porridge with either meat or black pudding. As flat bread was thought to last longer, it was preferred to pot bread. Supper was the same as breakfast.

Coffee was almost never seen in winter, except if there were guests, or on Sundays or holidays. At haying time, however, coffee was served every morning along with a lump of sugar, usually white, but sometimes brown. As there were no tongs and cube sugar was then unknown, the women often bit the sugar into lumps. The cups in which the coffee was served were usually dirty, as the women claimed they were too busy to wash them. Some women, however, licked them clean and wiped them on their aprons. Many farmers added *brennivín* (schnapps) to their coffee and served it to their guests either straight or with their coffee. When the workers returned home, exhausted in the evening after a hard day in the fields, the lady of the house gave them hot milk served with a lump of sugar and half a slice of bread which she buttered with her thumb. When the butter was hard, people wet their finger in their mouth to spread it more easily.

Guests were served coffee and a variety of home baking such as pancakes, doughnuts, waffles, and buttercakes. This picture dates from 1890-93, location unknown.

Although daily life was hard and there was little time left for recreation, the people of Kelduhverfi occasionally did find time to enjoy themselves.

Social gatherings in these days consisted mostly of weddings, christenings, birthdays, and funerals. The main holidays were Christmas, Easter, and Whitsun, followed by the First Day of Summer, New Year's and the First Day of Winter.

Special dishes consisted of rice pudding, roast meat, pot bread, and fresh butter. Holidays always saw the preparation of smoked lamb, flank mutton, rolled sausage, pickled or smoked sausage, brisket, pickled fish, and cured shark. In summer, sugared yoghurt with cream was added to the menu, while sweetened coffee was a perennial favourite at parties throughout the year. Home baking included Icelandic fritters, pancakes, *kleinur* (a type of doughnut), waffles, and buttercakes, along with a range of foreign dainties such as scones, sweet rolls, pastries, and cookies.

Strong drink consisted of Danish schnapps for the men, malt extract for the women, and hot rum punch for both. Beer was something they never tasted. A wedding feast at which there was not enough alcohol to quench everyone's thirst was considered ill-provided. Some staggered about, some fell asleep, and others just got sick. The priest drank most of all. Some got happy, some holy, and some got into fights which tended to be brief and were viewed more as entertainment. Sometimes there were accidents, when the odd guest drowned on the way home or fell off his horse and hurt himself. On the whole, though, most people simply had a good time, and the memories lingered for a long time afterwards.

This, then, was life in the Kelduhverfi district of Northeastern Iceland around 1870 as Kristján Ásgeir Benediktsson remembered it almost 40 years later. But this familiar pattern of rural life which had survived for centuries was about to be shattered forever by the news which was beginning to trickle in of opportunities for a fresh start in the New World. A few Icelanders had already left and prospered in their new home. The vast plains of North America offered the prospect of paid work, and there was no shortage of fertile land for an enterprising Icelandic farmer to cultivate and grow rich on. Times were changing.

Leaving Iceland

· ·

IN AMERICA ARE WONDERFUL FIELDS

When the first group of Icelanders left for North America around 1870, transatlantic emigration had been a feature of life in Europe for decades, and it is fair to assume that news of this development had already spread to Iceland, albeit slowly.

Almost fifty years earlier, in 1826, Magnús Stephensen, Chief Justice of the Supreme Court and a member of one of Iceland's most powerful families, published a long article about North America and emigration in *Klausturpósturinn*, in which he paints a glowing picture of the New World and its many attractions.

In 1826, the Supreme Court Judge Magnús Stephensen (above) wrote a flattering–and fanciful–account of the prosperity of "America, a great and powerful nation."

Soon after America was discovered in 1492, powerful, greedy Europeans were quick to put down roots, form settlements, cultivate its land and plunder its riches. They, in turn, attracted all manner of scholars and scientists, artists, craftsmen, artisans, merchants, farmers and labourers, and sold or granted them land. The result was a stream of immigrants from some of Europe's oldest-established and most respected nations, who, driven by a shortage of space or arable land, moved themselves and their families to America. Most, however, were fleeing unemployment or political persecution, especially during the period of war and unrest up to, and immediately following, the turn of the century. With their skills and science, they quickly planted America with wonderful fields, so much so that our continent will soon become their pupil. What that massive, half-empty continent required then, as it does now, however, was people to extract the gold, silver, and other precious metals from its mountains, where the rivers run with gold dust. From the mountain ranges of Mexico, Peru, Chile, Columbia, and other countries filled with gold, silver, and other precious metals, vast tracts of land are sprinkled far and wide with gold dust. Craftsmen, artisans, and labourers are also required to extract the riches of its soil and to cultivate

all manner of valuable plants and herbs useful to medical science and in the manufacture of dyes, confectionery, and all
types of valuable goods.

Later in his article, Stephensen provides an excellent account of
the reasons behind the growth of North America and the stream
of European immigrants, specifically in an Icelandic context.

> The way things look at present, the consequences for our
> own continent of a free and growing America will be sad in
> the extreme. Even countries as powerful as England are
> gripped by social unrest, rising unemployment, and
> increasing poverty, factors fuelled by the rapid increase in
> their populations every year. Vaccination has meant that
> smallpox and other diseases are no longer the major killers
> they once were, and at the same time the prolonged peace of
> recent years has reduced deaths from war. As a result, while
> the population of Northern Europe has increased, the
> amount of arable land available to feed it has remained the
> same, or even decreased in direct proportion to the rate that
> it has increased in the free colonies such as America—the
> rich and great.
>
> Thus, the old political adage that a rising population
> means increased national wealth has in most places been
> discredited, as has its application in the realm of national
> defence ... because the flight of people from the richest, best
> cultivated countries in the continent and the resulting
> shortages and rise in crime prove that nowhere in Europe
> have agricultural developments and employment
> opportunities kept pace with the needs of a rapidly growing
> population.
>
> What, then, of poor, barren Iceland, where there is no
> agriculture worth talking about, no industry of any
> significance, and the only means of survival is the hand-to-
> mouth existence available to a primitive race of poor
> shepherds and fishermen? So precarious has this way of life
> now become that it can barely support our present
> population of 50,000 souls, with every whim of nature
> bringing a fresh threat to survival, a truth most recently
> demonstrated by the hardship which followed the recent loss
> of animals, mainly sheep, through disease.

THE MORMON CONNECTION

Despite Stephensen's glowing—and somewhat fanciful—account of life in the New World, Icelanders remained oblivious to the attractions of North America during the early years of the 19th century. There were several reasons for this, the chief one being that the effects of the Industrial Revolution, with the accompanying increase in the flow of information and personal freedom, would not reach the country for several years.

In the Iceland of the early 19th century there was no free trade, communications with the outside world were highly limited, and navigation remained primitive. The economy was based on barter, while social constraints tied people to the locality of their birth. The only employment available lay in farming, and even fishing was only a part-time activity. Even if some group of enterprising Icelanders had entertained a notion of leaving their "harsh and barren land" for pastures greener somewhere across the sea, social and economic conditions would have made it virtually impossible for them to do so.

Ironically, perhaps, when it eventually did happen, it was not poverty or hunger that drove the first group of Icelanders to leave their native land, but a religion born far to the west in America—Mormonism.

The years immediately following their epic trek across the plains and subsequent settlement of Salt Lake City signalled a highly successful period of missionary activity by members of the Church of Jesus Christ of the Latter Day Saints throughout Europe. By mid-century, they had reached Denmark, where they won thousands of converts, among them a few Icelanders. Two of these returned to Iceland, and began preaching the new faith with a missionary zeal which quickly brought them a large number of converts, and not only among the country's poor.

In 1855, a group of five Icelanders set off for Utah, followed the next year by a further 11, mainly from the Westman Islands. A lull then ensued until after 1870, by which time the general stream of emigration had begun. From then on, a few Mormons could be found among the groups of Icelanders departing each year, until almost 200 had settled in the area in and around Spanish Fork and Salt Lake City itself.

Best known of the Icelandic Mormons was Eiríkur Ólafsson (above), a farmer and author from Brúnir. Over 50 when he emigrated to Utah in 1881, he returned home the following year as a missionary. Having met with little success, he soon went back to Utah, but returned to Iceland for good in 1891. There he served as the model for Nobel-prize winning novelist Halldór Laxness' character Steinar of Hlíðar in Paradísarheimt, (Paradise Regained).

Although these emigrants generally prospered in their new home, they had little contact with other Icelandic settlements in the U.S. or Canada, both due to the distances involved and to their religion, which was viewed with suspicion. Mormons still have a well-deserved reputation for industry and hard work, and their Icelandic brethren did well in business and public life. Although their ties with their homeland may have been weaker than was generally the case among other Icelandic emigrants, their descendants have celebrated their roots in several valuable ways, among them the microfilming of all Iceland's church registers, thus laying the foundation for the increasing interest in genealogy experienced in Iceland in recent years.

THE BRAZILIAN OPTION

One of the first Icelanders to consider emigration seriously as an option was Einar Ásmundsson (above). A farmer at Nes in Höfðahverfi, he could read several languages. He also taught navigation and was a great land improver.

For Icelanders, the winter of 1858-59 was extremely harsh, particularly in the North where severe food shortages would eventually lead, among other things, to the establishment of the country's first co-operative and the fresh employment opportunities it brought with it. But that was in the future. For the time being, conditions of near starvation forced local people to discuss emigration seriously as a real alternative. One of the options discussed was Greenland, but one farmer, Einar Ásmundsson of Nes, cast his eyes a little further south, pointing out the attractions of Brazil.

A society was formed to discuss the matter, which, as is often the case with unusual ideas, generated much controversy and some heated argument. In 1861, Kristján Ísfeld, a native of Mývatnssveit in the Northeast, became the first Icelander to set off for Brazil, reaching Rio de Janeiro two years later. The year he arrived, he was followed by four others from the Þingeyjarsýsla region, who left with the intention of finding land and forming a colony. They later wrote home, praising the virtues of their new home, but did not actively encourage others to follow. Despite this, many were enticed by the prospect, and by 1865 well over 100 had signed up for a trip that never took place.

Interest in Brazil revived in 1871 when the Brazilian government offered free passage to prospective settlers. Labourers were desperately required for the coffee plantations, and many Europeans had already settled there, mainly from Portugal, but also some from Germany, Denmark, and elsewhere. Those Icelanders already in Brazil kept in close touch with home by mail and informed those they left behind of this offer which aroused considerable interest. Although many registered for the trip, finding a ship to take these prospective emigrants to Copenhagen or Hamburg, from where the steamships left for Brazil, proved as difficult as it had six years earlier. By 1873, when it was clear that the scheme would come to nothing, just under 600 Icelanders had declared themselves ready to go. However, a combination of poor organization and dishonest foreign agents meant that only 34 made it to Copenhagen, eventually reaching Brazil after many difficulties. So ended Icelandic emigration to Brazil, just as passage to Canada was becoming more organized and readily available to the general public.

Of those who made it to Brazil, most settled in Southern Brazil, around the town of Curitiba, home of the pioneering Kristján Ísfeld. Although he died of jaundice before the next group arrived, they chose to settle in the same area and began farming or obtained work in the town. A few later returned home, while others headed north to Canada, but most stayed where they were, and their descendants remain there today.

THE ROAD TO AMERICA

No one knows for sure when or how ordinary Icelanders first became aware of the wealth of opportunities offered by North America. The roots of this development, however, have been traced to William Wickmann, a Danish merchant who emigrated to the United States in 1865 following ten years in Iceland.

A merchant from Eyrarbakki, South Iceland, Guðmundur Thorgrimsen (above) was one of the first proponents of emigration. His brother-in-law by marriage was Þorlákur G. Jónsson of Stórutjarnir, one of the earliest figures behind emigration from the North.

Eventually he settled in Wisconsin, from where he began corresponding with Guðmundur Thorgrimsen, his former employer and owner of the Lefolii store at Eyrarbakki, in southern Iceland.

Due to Thorgrimsen's influence, direct or indirect, a number of promising young men from the area left for Wickmann's ranch in Wisconsin, among them his son, Hans, and Páll Þorláksson, his nephew.

Their journey took them first to Reykjavík, and then via Copenhagen and Liverpool to Quebec City, from where they travelled by train to Milwaukee. After a brief rest, some continued, stopping for a short time on Washington Island on Lake Michigan, from where they wrote home. Among the group was Árni Guðmundsen, a young man of good family and the son of Þórður Guðmundsson, sheriff of Árnessýsla county, and his wife, Jóhanna Lárusdóttir.

Árni wrote his parents regularly, describing his life in intimate detail. These letters were then passed on to other family

The beginnings of Icelandic emigration to the New World are often traced to this building (right), the Lefolii store at Eyrarbakki, where the Dane Wickmann was assistant manager before emigrating to Wisconsin. News sent by him to Thorgrimsen and his former fellow-workers served as a catalyst which prompted others to follow.

The first group of Icelandic emigrants to set sail for North America. The photograph is taken in Leith, Scotland, in 1872, and appears in Thorstína Jackson's Saga Íslendinga í Norður-Dakóta. The accompanying text claims that although the author had not managed to contact anyone who knew the subjects personally, they were known to include the Rev. Hans Thorgrimsen, the Rev. Páll Þorláksson, Haraldur Þorláksson and his wife, María Sigurðardóttir, Árni Guðmundsen, Árni Björn Sveinbjörnsson and Jón Halldórsson.

members, and so gradually spread around the country. One such letter, dated August 22, 1872, was written just a few weeks after Árni and his friends arrived in their adopted country.

> I have to tell you that the last time I wrote, when we were at a sawmill in Muskegon, we were all half sick. As the heat was unbearable and the work unbelievably hard, we decided to move on to the island. After two weeks, Páll, Haraldur and his wife, Hans, Bjarni and Ólafur Hannesson decided to leave, but I wished to stay longer. With me were Ólafur from

Arnarbæli and Stefán, but Ólafur was very sick, and as we
were so weak that we could only work occasionally, we
decided to follow the others. We'd been there three weeks
and I'd earned $22, almost all of which was spent on food
and travel. Our possessions also cost us dearly as we had to
pay for transport, since it's almost impossible to carry much
luggage when you're moving about a lot. Páll, Haraldur and
María stayed behind in Milwaukee where they found work
easy to come by but badly paid. Páll, however, has been
promised a teaching position after September 1.

Wickmann and Jón Gíslason offered us a warm
welcome, and we're still here. Since arriving six days ago, we
have done little, although I've already obtained employment
with a Danish farmer on the next farm, a man by the name
of Koyen, from Jutland. I eat lunch with him, but take
breakfast and supper at Wickmann's. My job consists of
stripping bark from cedar trees, which are sold to the
government and made into telegraph poles. It's light work,
and I get paid 5 cents for each tree. As I've worked for three
days, I reckon I've already earned $1, plus food, which is
good enough to begin with. I'm thinking of becoming a
lumberjack, which would earn me 10 cents a day, but the
work's much harder, though more profitable. The other lads,
Hans, Bjarni and Stefán, are cutting firewood for Wickmann.
They're finding it hard going to begin with, but nobody's
pushing them hard. Ólafur Hannesson still has a fever, but it's
not too bad. The other Ólafur is not only half sick, but dying
of boredom and only wants to return home. One thing's
sure, he won't be fit for work for a while, at least not for
hard work. He has pains in his chest and back, just like he
had when he was at home. He sets the table and washes up
for the rest of us, as no woman has lived in the house since
Einar Bjarnason's daughter left. If Ólafur doesn't get better
this winter, we'll have to find some way of getting him
home next summer. But enough of that.

I'm enjoying life on this island and am in the best of
health. Nothing troubles me but earning some money. The
island is covered in thick, high forests, but it's not long since
it was settled, so things are still very primitive. The houses are
basic and the roads poor, but it's easy to live here as you can
get plenty of work chopping trees or fishing. Although I
wouldn't say it's the best place you could find in Wisconsin,

there's no point in wandering about. Anyway, I don't have the means to do so, and it's clear that we'll be staying here for the winter.

In Chicago, there's a lot of murders and robberies, and not a day passes without 1-4 men being killed. The police have a tough time, but can do little. I'm glad I'm not there.

Árni Guðmundsen was one of very few Icelanders who settled permanently on Washington Island, later becoming a highly successful farmer. In 1872, the same year he crossed the ocean, a group of Icelanders from the North was also heading in the same direction. Among them was Sigtryggur Jónasson, then a young magistrate's clerk from Möðruvellir in Hörgárdalur, who continued on to Canada alone. He later became one of the leading figures among the settlers, and his name would occupy a prominent place in the history of the Icelanders in Canada.

RITES OF PASSAGE

During the winter of 1872-73, a group in the North of Iceland interested in emigration began meeting with the purpose of forming an association dedicated to organizing passage to the U.S. and Canada. Their leaders were from the Þingeyjarsýsla and Eyjafjörður regions, and by the time they became active, the country was already well informed on the issue. Letters arriving from the West were passed from hand to hand, and the media of the time, newspapers and periodicals, published several of them. In Reykjavík, a local merchant, Guðmundur Lambertsen, had secured a position as agent for the Allan Line and had begun advertising for prospective emigrants in the newspapers.

Guðmundur Lambertsen (above) was a prosperous merchant in Reykjavík, who became an agent for the Allan Line in 1872, a position he did not hold for long.

In the late summer of 1873, the first large group of Icelanders set sail for North America, a journey which had been under preparation since the New Year. As a company

An innovator in several respects, Tryggvi Gunnarsson (above), managing director of the Gránufélag and later a member of the Althing and bank director, was in many ways responsible for developing the commerce which made emigration possible.

agent, Lambertsen was involved from the outset, as was Tryggvi Gunnarsson, a merchant with the Gránufélag company of Akureyri, who planned, among other things, to find buyers for the livestock of his departing countrymen. Several meetings were held, and the intrepid band of entrepreneurs from the North embarked on a difficult two-month journey around the country in the middle of winter to publicize the issue, the aim being to attract as many participants as possible to reduce costs. The group was led by Þorlákur G. Jónsson, a farmer from Stórutjarnir, whose son Páll had himself left the previous year.

Finally, just under 200 people registered for the trip, which was supposed to leave from Akureyri. In the interim, Gunnarsson had encountered a horse-trader named Walker, whose vessel was to transport the emigrants to Scotland on the first stage of their journey, but when the planned date of departure dawned in early July, the ship failed to appear, leaving the would-be emigrants to bide their time at Akureyri well into August.

The destination of this first group was Quebec City, but it did not plan to settle there. The idea of a New Iceland across the sea, where Icelanders could live together and prosper, may well have been born amid the general excitement on the quayside at Akureyri in that summer of 1873, but where exactly it would be was anybody's guess.

Until then, most of the group had intended to go to the United States, the traditional destination of European emigrants, where Páll Þorláksson planned to welcome them in Wisconsin. The story of their journey will be told later, but soon their letters began streaming home, some of which were published, particularly in *Norðanfari*, the local Akureyri newspaper. This correspondence did not come from the U.S., but from Canada, where the majority of them had stayed. Thus, Canada became the principal destination for Icelandic emigrants to North America, and it was to Canada that subsequent groups were directed.

As has been mentioned before, the Allan Line soon became a leader in this lucrative market, and the cheap sea passage and rail travel which resulted from the company's close co-operation with the Canadian government meant that Iceland was the only

Publicizing Emigration

The first advertisement for emigration appeared in the Akureyri newspaper *Norðanfari* around the same time as people in Northern Iceland were discussing the issue seriously for the first time.

The Emigration Association

This summer, Allan Brothers & Co plan to send a large steamship here if sufficient subscribers are obtained who wish to sail with it to Quebec or Portland, the best destinations for those intending to travel to Wisconsin. I hereby advise all those interested to furnish me with written confirmation of their intentions as soon as possible, or in association with others, so that the name and age of each individual appears clearly, in order that I may inform the company. At present, it is unable to name a price until after the association's meeting this winter, although the rate, of course, will be cheaper than elsewhere ...

Each year, the company operates 22 steamships on the route, the smallest of which is about 1,200 tons. Each is divided into watertight compartments so that should a hole appear in one, the rest of the vessel remains unaffected and can continue on its way. Each ship carries one or two doctors, and each passenger may carry ten square feet of luggage free of charge, but can otherwise take as much as he wishes at a fair price. Children from one to twelve years pay half fare ..., children under four years travel free of charge on the railway in North America ...

Further information and conditions of passage will be advertised later if the level of interest in sufficient.

Reykjavík, December 7, 1872

G. Lambertsen
(company agent)

Vopnafjörður, Eastern Iceland, 1881. The three sailing ships lying offshore are probably cargo ships, but the steamship is a vessel sent by Sigfús Eymundsson and the Allan Line to pick up emigrants. Along with Seyðisfjörður, Vopnafjörður was the main port of departure for those leaving Eastern Iceland for North America.

country in Europe which exported more emigrants to Canada than to the U.S.

The following year, 1874, brought with it not only the celebration of the 1,000th anniversary of Iceland's settlement, but also some particularly harsh weather conditions. Increasing numbers of Icelanders found themselves forced to consider emigration, including some who had backed out the year before. By now, Lambertsen could offer them assisted passages, along with 200 acres of land at journey's end. As a result, by mid-July a large group had assembled on the quayside at the Northern port of Sauðárkrókur, where they were forced to wait until the beginning of September.

Eventually, 375 set sail, most of them from the North. Páll Magnússon, one of the original founders of the Akureyri

Emigration Society, as it was now known, and Icelandic agent for the Norwegian-based shipping company Den Norsk-Amerikanske Dampskips-Line, had begun advertising in *Norðanfari* in the spring of 1874, but had problems securing a vessel. As a result, he was forced to conclude a last-minute agreement with Lambertsen and the Allan Line, hence the long delay.

THE RISING TIDE

For several reasons, the following summer, 1875, brought a temporary lull in emigration from Iceland, the principal one being a letter received from Sigtryggur Jónasson advising his fellow countrymen to stay put, as work was hard to come by and the search for a site for the proposed colony had, as yet, yielded no results.

At the same time, there were also other reasons much closer to home. Due to the long delays of the previous two years, the emigration issue had come to the attention of the Icelandic authorities. While many European countries had already enacted legislation protecting the rights of emigrants, Iceland had yet to follow suit, and although Denmark had passed a series of laws as early as 1868 relating to conditions on board emigrant ships and the responsibilities of agents with regard to insurance, these did not apply in Iceland.

At the beginning of 1876, the Althing passed legislation bringing the country into line with Denmark and Norway. Salesmen and agents now had to be licenced, and they had to deposit sufficient funds to insure their clients against delays and damages. Passenger contracts, validated by local police chiefs, became a legal requirement.

Among the agents who succeeded in raising funds sufficient to meet these requirements was Guðmundur Lambertsen, and in the autumn of 1875, news reached Iceland that a site for the colony had finally been found on the shores of Lake Winnipeg. The following summer, 1,200 emigrants left the

One of many emigrant contracts. This one bears the signature af Petrína Arngrímsdóttir, a 17-year-old servant girl who sailed with the Beaver Line in 1893 for 123 krónur, witnessed by Thorgrímur Gudmundsen, agent, and Einar Thorlacius, chief of police in Akureyri.

country in three groups. The destination of the majority was New Iceland, as the fledgling colony was now known.

For Lambertsen, 1876 was also a significant year. Following repeated complaints from passengers about conditions on passages organized by him, he was removed from his position as agent for the Allan Line. His replacement was Sigfús Eymundsson, a Reykjavík merchant and photographer, who, through a combination of hard work and astute business sense, gradually became the leading emigration agent in Iceland.

Eymundsson developed his own network of agents around the country, consisting mainly of merchants, postmen and richer farmers and, in 1879, the last piece of his transatlantic network fell into place when he concluded an agreement with a Scottish businessman by the name of Slimon, who gave him the use of his vessel, the *Camoens*, to transport emigrants to Scotland on the first stage of their journey to Canada.

The Allan Line, however, did not have a complete monopoly of the market. In 1876, one of its main competitors, the Anchor Line, began offering cheap passages, followed in 1891 by the Dominion Line, and in 1893 by the Beaver Line.

For many years, the emigrants remained closely associated with the lucrative livestock trade first launched by the Gránufélag trading company in 1873. While many Icelandic farmers could enjoy the feel of real money in their pockets for the first time as a result, one of the men to profit most from the venture was the Gránufélag chairman Tryggvi Gunnarsson. Bridge builder, bank chairman, and all-round entrepreneur, he was later responsible for many of the improvements which took place in northern Iceland during the years 1870–80, and it is no coincidence that he, along with a number of his associates, should have been one of the main proponents of emigration.

Initial news from New Iceland was not good, and interest in emigration dropped off in 1877, only to revive again the following year when 400 Icelanders left, most of them for the colony. By that time, however, the dream of New Iceland had already begun to lose some of its lustre. Many in the know claimed it was better for Icelanders to make their way in the New World as individuals rather than as a group, and the colony on the shores

A well-known photographer and merchant, Sigfús Eymundsson was the largest seller of passages to North America in Iceland.

of Lake Winnipeg would never again be the automatic destination of Icelanders leaving for Canada.

At the same time, improved weather conditions had led to a general fall in emigration until 1881, when a series of bad winters became a catalyst whose effects would last uninterrupted until 1894.

In 1883, economic conditions in New Iceland took a marked turn for the better, as did those in Winnipeg itself, by now the destination of choice for many Icelandic emigrants. Emigration reached its peak in the summer of 1887, when almost 2,000 men, women and children took passage for Canada in groups of 200-300. The following year, they were followed by a further 1,200.

By then, a new figure had taken to the stage. A native of Eyjafjörður, North Iceland, Baldvin L. Baldvinsson had spent more than a decade in Canada. Now, he had been appointed official agent of the Canadian government in Iceland, where he spent the winter of 1886-87 organizing further groups of emigrants. On February 20, 1887, he sent the following letter back to Canada for publication in the newspaper, *Heimskringla*:

The Miaca, *one of the main emigrant ships, seen here at Seyðisfjöður on August 13, 1887. That year was one of the worst for pack ice in Icelandic history, with ice eaching as far as the Westman Islands, according to some sources. The other vessel, either the* Grána *or* Rósa, *was owned by the* Gránufélag.

It should be noted that during my travels around the country this winter, I have been very well received everywhere and found considerable interest among the people in taking passage to Canada as soon as they can sell their livestock and other possession. I fear, however, that this will not be possible this year, as general conditions are very

Baldvin L. Baldvinsson

Few figures were as well known among the early Canadian Icelanders as Baldvin L. Baldvinsson. A native of Akureyri, he was employed for several years by the Canadian government to guide the emigrants, and no other individual played such a leading role in encouraging emigration.

Born in 1856 to Baldvin Jónsson and Helga Egilsdóttir, a midwife, he was brought up by his mother in Akureyri until the age of ten, but spent the next two years in Reykjavík until his grandmother, Guðný Kráksdóttir, took him back north, where she reared him as a foster child with her husband, Steinn Kristjánsson, a blacksmith.

In 1873, aged only 17, Baldvinsson emigrated to Canada, and during the voyage west was supervised by Kristjánsson's brother, Björn Kristjánsson Skagfjörð. Considered an intelligent youth by his contemporaries back home in Iceland, he spent some years in Toronto with Árni Friðriksson, where he became a shoemaker, while studying English at night school.

When the Icelanders moved to Manitoba, however, the temptation proved too much, and he headed west to Lake Winnipeg where his first cousin Sigtryggur Jónasson employed him aboard his boat, the *Victoria*, in the spring of 1882. His friend Árni Friðriksson employed him in a shop the following winter. Although Baldvinsson himself quickly set up his own shoemaking business in Winnipeg, he bad. Despite this, given a fair spring, I expect that 700 people will leave Iceland this summer.

What particularly attracts Icelanders to emigrate is not the fact that they do not have a clear idea of the difference between their own country and America, although many of them would confess they do not, but the poverty they face at

---

spent the next ten years travelling to and from Iceland on behalf of the Canadian government. All in all, he made six such trips, acting for the authorities in their dealings with the emigrants, and he is estimated to have helped over 7,000 Icelanders on their way to the West.

Baldvinsson turned his attentions back to his shoemaking business in 1894, and after a few successful years during which he diversified into real estate, he purchased the newspaper *Heimskringla* and became its editor in 1898, probably as part of a plan to establish himself in politics. By then, he had already unsccessfully run twice as a Conservative candidate for the Manitoba Legislature, losing the second time to his friend and cousin, Sigtryggur Jónasson, a Liberal. In the election held a year after his purchase of *Heimskringla*, however, Baldvinsson reversed this result, and was re-elected for a second term in 1903. During these years, he and Jónasson, then editor of *Lögberg*, argued fiercely through the pages of their newspapers, with no quarter asked and none given.

During his years in politics, Baldvinsson served as Deputy Secretary of the Manitoba Legislature. At the same time, he involved himself actively in the affairs of his fellow Icelanders in the province, and was one of the driving forces behind the fund-raising efforts of 1914 which eventually led to the formation of Eimskip, the Icelandic Steamship Company, back in Iceland.

Baldvinsson married Helga Sigurðardóttir from Skagafjörður in 1886, and they had six children. Sober in his habits and never afraid of hard work, he became wealthy. Easy-going and popular among almost everyone who knew him, he was a natural pragmatist in politics and social affairs.

Baldvin L. Baldvinsson died in 1936 in California, where he had spent his final years with one of his daughters.

Seyðisfjörður, about 1885. Iceland's ports were minuscule compared with the places seen by the emigrants on their way across the Atlantic. At best, they were fishing villages of a few hundred inhabitants, where the emigrants had to depend on local hospitailty for shelter as they waited for their transport across the sea.

home, combined with general dissatisfaction with a political system they are powerless to change. For many good farmers, it is the oppressive power of the local authorities that is forcing them to leave, which should come as no surprise, as this power is increasing almost daily. The present system, it could be said, rewards laziness and sloth, while suppressing industry and thrift.

I would also like to point out the fact that in Iceland, opposition to emigration is now almost non-existent, with the exception of a few conservative, old bureaucrats of the worst kind, and the odd independent or so-called state farmer who lives on his rents rather than by his own efforts.

Having said that, what hinders many from emigrating is the fact that they have received no news from relatives or friends who have already done so, and it must be said that this is a serious omission on the part of Icelanders in the West, who either cannot be bothered to write or are too mean to pay the cost of posting a letter, even though the average letter costs only 5 cents, about the same price as half a glass of beer in Winnipeg. I do not want to believe that Icelanders are so miserly that they don't want to let their friends and relatives back home know where they are in America, unless, perhaps, they have borrowed money from them for the journey.

By the time of Baldvinsson's visit, emigration was a well-known fact of Icelandic life, especially in the North and East, where almost everyone had friends or relatives somewhere in North America. Although the news they sent back varied and not everyone prospered equally, it cannot have escaped the notice of young Icelanders that here was a land of opportunity.

Despite Baldvinsson's assertions to the contrary, controversy over emigration was growing in Iceland, and a series of lively, sometimes bitter, debates began on the pages of the country's newspapers. The most powerful of these, *Ísafold*, strongly opposed emigration and employed the poet Benedikt Gröndal to speak against it. In his pamphlet "On Emigration," published by the Ísafold Press in 1888, Gröndal pointed to the potential

The sheep and horse trade with the British Isles was a basic requirement for emigration. For the first time, it provided farmers with a source of hard cash, and also the vessels that carried the emigrants on the first stage of their journey. On the first trip to Scotland, there were more horses than people. The vessel seen here loading sheep at Seyðisfjörður around the turn of the century is the Fridthjof.

harm to the nation which could result from mass emigration, while claiming at the same time that it was mostly useless, feckless individuals who had left anyway.

The general tone of the pamphlet reflected Gröndal's caustic wit and was considered rather cold. Another of the country's leading writers, Jón Ólafsson, who himself had just returned from an incident-packed stay in America, answered Gröndal in a pamphlet bearing the impressive title, "A Word of Sense on Emigrants and Emigration: An Answer and Address to Editor Bjarni Jónasson on the Unsubstantiated Lies, Slander and Ill-Advised Rubbish Disseminated and Published by *Ísafold*. Benedikt Gröndal Stripped, Chastised and Set in the Stocks."

Gröndal replied with a smaller booklet, and the result was a libel suit. But *Ísafold* was a powerful newspaper, and opposition to emigration increased as conditions in Iceland improved.

On March 8, 1893, Baldvinsson and Sigurður Kristófersson held a public meeting in Reykjavík after travelling the country on a lecture tour which had been generally well received. Reporting on the meeting, *Ísafold* made its position clear.

A well-known figure among the Manitoba Icelanders, Sigurður Kristófersson was one of the members of the first Icelandic expediton to the province. In 1877 he married Caroline Taylor, John Taylor's niece, and he later became a prosperous farmer in the Argyle Settlement in Southern Manitoba.

Long before the lecture began, the mob had crowded into the building, and only half of those who wished to could get in. At the appointed hour, the agent Sigurður Kristófersson took to the platform, but when he was about to begin his address he was drowned out by the piercing blast of whistles, accompanied by loud jeering. Unable to make himself heard, he began ringing the bell for order, but to no avail. Baldvin then took over, but the result was no better. If anything, the whistling became louder, while the audience booed, hissed, jeered and stamped its feet. Baldvin quickly returned to his seat, and Sigurður tried again, but with the same result. As he rang the bell repeatedly, shouts erupted from the crowd: "Down with the agents! Away with them! Throw them out!"

This reaction is . . . nothing more than an expression of public disgust of a type heard all over the world against individuals to whom, for one reason or another, the public does not wish to listen. This only goes to show that here in Iceland the preaching of the agents is not seen as "evangelical," here there is no support for "American" exaggeration, and here people have the intiative and good sense to express their opposition to these "apostles."

Little by little, the numbers of emigrants declined from year to year, with a few exceptions such as in 1893, when the cut-price fares offered by the Beaver Line proved tempting to many. Baldvinsson, Kristófersson and others also toured Iceland that year, as did Sigtryggur Jónasson.

Emigration increased again for a few years at the beginning of the 20th century, only to fall away again, and by the time the outbreak of the First World War closed the North Atlantic sea lanes in 1914, what had once been a stream had been reduced to a trickle. After the war, limited emigration began again, but in a different form, as attitudes in Canada and the U.S. towards mass emigration from Europe had changed, and most of the land had been settled.

Some two-thirds of all Icelandic emigrants came from the North and East. Mainly young, about four-fifths of them were under 40. Distribution between the sexes was about equal, both among families and individuals. The emigrants were not only drawn from the poor or those the parish councils wished to get

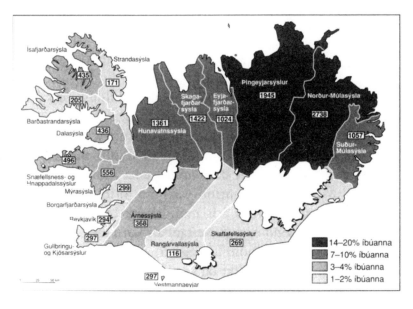

Icelandic emigration by region. As the map shows, most of the emigrants came from the North and East, led by the county of Norður-Múlasýsla with 2,738. The map is taken from Vesturfaraskrá, which lists 482 as being of "no fixed abode."

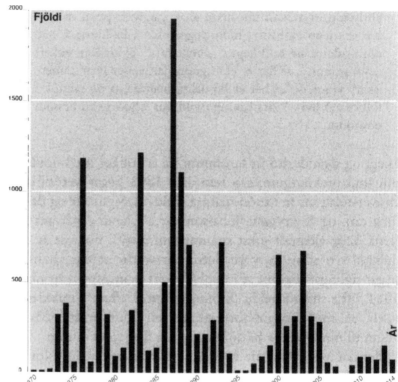

Emigration from 1870–1914, as documented in Vesturfaraskrá. The chart shows the marked variations between the years, peaking in 1887 but with over 1,000 people leaving in 1876, 1883 and 1888.

off the poor rolls. Many were prosperous young farmers and sons of farmers who emigrated by choice, not necessity.

In the later years of emigration, those who left were much better prepared than their predecessors. While the first emigrants set off into the unknown, those who followed were very well informed on what awaited them, and were often received in their new homeland by friends or relatives. The cultural world that they entered was, for a time, almost the same as the one they had just left. Icelandic newspapers were sent to North America, and vice versa. The same journalists and authors wrote in both, and books published on both sides of the Atlantic travelled in the same way as correspondence between the emigrants and their native land.

THE ROAD TO THE WEST

When we last left the 200 or so Icelanders who comprised the first large group of immigrants to North America, they were stranded on the quayside at Akureyri in July, 1873, awaiting a ship which would not appear for several weeks.

We can only guess at the thoughts and fears that must have passed through their minds during the long wait, as they scanned the horizon anxiously for signs of the vessel that would carry them to Scotland on the first stage of their long journey across the sea.

Although some could seek shelter in the homes of relatives or friends, they had to feed and clothe themselves in the meantime, and the long delay must have put an added strain on their already meagre resources.

Akureyri, "capital" of Northern Iceland, seen between 1880 and 1890. The steamship lying offshore is probably the Camoens.

The mailboat Thyra (right), seen here lying off Sauðárkrókur at the end of the last century, was sometimes used to ship emigrants, particularly in 1892–93. As can be seen, there was little space on board for many passengers.

The emigrant ship Camoens (above) lies trapped in pack ice at Trékyllisvík, North Iceland, in the summer of 1887.

Finally, at the beginning of August, the *Queen*, soon re-christened "Drottningin" by the Icelanders, slipped into port unannounced. On board was the trio of the agent Guðmundur Lambertsen, Grænufélagið chairman Tryggvi Gunnarsson, and the Scottish horse trader Walker, accompanied by 230 prize equine specimens he had collected on the voyage north.

The arrival of the vessel caused some consternation. After weeks of inactivity, everything now had to be done on the double, and any last-minute affairs taken care of immediately. Some of the passengers had been reluctant to sell their horses, riding tack and other possessions before it was sure that the ship would come. As things turned out, this was a wise precaution, since it soon became obvious that there was not room on board for everyone who wished to travel. A committee was hastily formed to solve the problem, and when it had concluded its deliberations, 40-50 prospective emigrants faced the bitter disappointment of being left behind.

For those who did get on board, however, their problems were just beginning. With their luggage, they were herded through a hatchway into a dark passageway below deck, just above the horses which were stored in the lower hold. Shocked and offended by such dreadful conditions, many of them left the ship immediately, not caring whether they ever saw their few possessions again.

The emigrants embarked on the evening of August 4, and shortly after midnight the *Queen* set sail. As a result, it is August 5, 1873, which has gone down in history as the date on which the first organized group of emigrants left Iceland for the New World.

In this group was Björn Kristjánsson Skagfjörð, a native of Skagafjörður, in the North, whose impressions of life in Leith and Glasgow appeared in the previous chapter. Almost 40 years old, he was accompanied by his wife Guðlaug and two children, aged eight and one. A literate man, he later sent a letter to *Norðanfari*, offering a description of his experiences as seen through the keenly observant eye of a peasant famer.

A sight such as this would have greeted the emigrants waiting ashore when the Queen *docked at Akureyri in the summer of 1873. Among the passengers in the photograph, taken a few years later aboard an unknown vessel, is Tryggvi Gunnarsson (third from right), one of the key figures in the early years of emigration.*

Björn Kristjánsson Skagfjörð (above) seen here in later life with his wife, Guðlaug Pállsdóttir. The couple settled in Dakota in 1880, after a few years in New Iceland.

As you know, 135 of us boarded the steamship *Queen* on the evening of the 4th of August. About an hour and a half after midnight, we weighed anchor, set sail, and had reached the mouth of the fjord before the last of us had taken to our berths. About 6 o'clock the next morning, we lay off Flateyjardalur, and many awoke with the nightmare that they had become seasick. The vessel ploughed on slowly into the teeth of a stiff easterly gale, and by mid-day we were north of Langanesröst. By then, most of the women were sick, as were many of the men, and the weather worsened as we turned south.

The wind persisted throughout the next day, by which time everybody, apart from the most experienced seamen, was seasick. Our course now lay in a straight line to the

The Farewell of Stebbi from Sel

Among the passengers aboard the *Queen* was an 18-year-old youth of poetic ability, Stefán Guðmundsson from Víðimýrarsel, who was on his way west with his parents and 11-year-old sister. During the long wait for the ship, he passed the time by composing verse, and on August 9, 1873, only four days after their departure, a poem appeared in the newspaper *Norðanfari*. Titled "Farewell," it appeared under the name of his father, accompanied by the comment: "The following poem was composed by Stefán, son of Guðmundur, when the *SS Queen* left Akureyri on August 4, 1873, with over 150 passengers on board, all heading for North America." What follows are four of its seven verses.

The hour quickly passes, for the last time
I bid farewell to the land of my birth
Which will remain etched in my memory forever
Though I never see it again

The hour quickly passes, and I must bid
Farewell to the loved ones I will see no more
Until the Lord calls us all together
In that happy place where adversity dies

east, and the sail was hoisted and we proceeded at great speed.

August 7. The same wind, though more from the south. About mid-day, we sighted the Faroe Islands 6 miles to the west. Women and children all without nourishment.

August 8. Around mid-day we reached Lerwick in the Shetland Islands, where we stopped for four hours and sold 30 horses. Some Icelanders went ashore to a dispensary and purchased medicine for those who were seasick and a few other necessities. The apothecary showed them round the town and was extremely kind.

August 12. We arrived in Aberdeen, which in Iceland would be considered a big place, with houses scattered around, separated by fields, some green, others cultivated.

The hour quickly passes, to low, peaceful graves
I bid farewell, as I speed away
From where the bones of my ancestors sleep
And the innocent memory of youth heals

Farewell to old Iceland
And my beloved friends from whom I must depart
The purity of your memory is enshrined in my tears
I have nothing else—but bid you farewell

Guðmundsson's first published work, "Farewell" was certainly not his last. He later Americanized his name to Stephan G. Stephansson, and spent his first years in the West in the Lake Shawano settlement in Wisconsin. In 1880, he took his wife and child and moved to the new Icelandic settlement in North Dakota where he and his family remained until 1889, when they moved along with several other Icelanders to Markerville, Alberta, close to the Rocky Mountains. Despite the distance involved, he kept in close touch with his fellow-countrymen in Manitoba, and excercised considerable influence through his prolific writings in their publications.

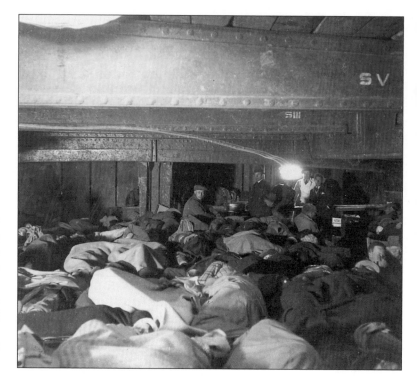

Rest and be thankful: conditions aboard the emigrant ships were far from luxurious, especially on the way to Scotland. Here, a group of travellers prepares for sleep aboard an unknown vessel, sometime between 1910 and 1915.

There, we saw steamships being built, and it was amazing to see them on dry land. There, we also saw steam-powered coaches, horse-drawn wagons and many other sights I don't have time to describe. The remaining horses, now about 220 in total, 5-7 having died on the voyage, were unloaded in Aberdeen, and you can imagine how much the air improved for us, crammed as we were into Walker's floating stables where men were packed up above and horses died down below from lack of air, neglect and overcrowding. Walker left us with a few songs, the last one being to the tune of "Eldgamla Ísafold" ["God Save the Queen"], which was supposed to wish us good luck, although few of my companions joined in wishing him the same as we were still disgusted by his treatment of us.

About 5 o'clock the next morning, the emigrants arrived at Granton, now part of Edinburgh, where customs officials searched the *Queen* but found nothing. Skagfjörð continues:

Undína's Farewell

No fewer than four poets are said to have left aboard the *Queen* in the summer of 1873—Sigurður Jón Jóhannesson (b. 1841), Stephan G. Stephansson (b. 1853), Kristinn Stefánsson (b. 1856) and Helga Steinvör Baldvinsdóttir, who was only 14 when she left for the New World with her parents and five brothers and sisters. Using the pseudonymn "Undína," Helga published several works in newspapers and magazines in her adopted homeland, one of which was "On Leaving Iceland, 1873":

The trusty ship may carry
A fragile maiden across the foam
From the cold isle of ice
To the wide, blue ocean

Now into the briny waves
The bright sun sets
Like a warm tear flowing
From pained eyes

Mountains fade, farms fade
Valleys fade so quickly
Springs of crystal clearness fade
Joy fades, far and near

Farewell woman and sable cover
Farewell blooming trees
Farewell fields to me so dear
Farewell passing moment

Undína settled in four places in North America: first in Ontario, then Dakota, then Manitoba, and finally with her daughter in Washington State. Twice married, she was a highly gifted seamstress and later became a vociferous campaigner for women's rights with the Suffragettes. Her first book of poetry was published ten years after her death in 1942.

A short time after we landed, an agent from the Allan Line came to talk to us, followed soon after by a steam-powered wagon which we boarded. Our luggage we carried about 60 fathoms up the quayside, where we loaded it onto an open cart. The steam wagon we boarded was like a little square house on wheels, with cross benches, doors and large windows on both sides. We then boarded, 29–30 to a car, and the doors were locked, although we could open the windows. At mid-day on Sunday, our convoy set off on a journey so incredible that I barely can find words to describe it. We travelled so fast that it was like going downhill on skis. Half an hour later we arrived in Edinburgh, where we spent the 4–5-hour-long wait looking at the city. G. Lambertsen took us for such a long walk that many of us were exhausted by the time we got back to the train. Our sightseeing was done at great speed, but one sight which stunned us all was the monument to Sir Walter Scott, whose statue, carved in marble and bigger than any man, sits on a chair between the feet of a massive tower. We left for Glasgow between 4 and 6 o'clock. The scenery on this route varies between fertile fields and leafy woods, although in some places there are wide open spaces. The farmhouses are all made of stone, and the famers are clearly better off

On board a large steamship en route from the British Isles to America, 1893.

Only two photographs of Icelandic emigrants on board ship are known to exist. This one was taken by Sigfús Eymundsson aboard the Camoens, *probably about 1887, and he seems to have managed to get most of the passengers to pose in the stern. Photography at the time was considered no laughing matter, and smiles are rare on the faces of the subjects. For these people, there was the added gravity of an uncertain future far from home.*

than we Icelanders. As far as I remember, we went through about six tunnels on the way, and all of us enjoyed the journey very much. It seemed the sick improved by the minute except when the train went underground, where the air and smoke were unpleasant.

When we arrived in Glasgow, we had to walk a long way through the city, and the weaker among us and the children got very tired. Two agents accompanied us all the way to the Allan Line warehouses, where we were given a free meal as we had been promised. This consisted of coffee, plenty of bread and an egg per person, and we then retired to comfortable beds. I think we were all relieved to get some

Conditions below deck on a large emigrant ship in the early years of emigration were cramped and extremely unpleasant. Fleas, lice, and even rats were common, adding to the daily problems. This drawing was done aboard the English vessel Dreadnought, *and the height of the hold is greatly exaggerated.*

rest, and we were given breakfast the next morning, August 11, followed by a lunch of fine broth with potatoes and meat, with the same for supper.

Skagfjörð's account of Glasgow appears at the beginning of Chapter 1 and describes the party's departure just after midnight on August 11. Their route took them down the Clyde, towed for a time by a paddle-driven tug. The following night they reached Liverpool, where they were joined by other passengers from various nations: Norwegians, Swedes, Danes, Germans, French and English.

We left Liverpool on August 14, trusting God to protect us on our long voyage across the wide Atlantic.
August 15. A stiff sidewind from the south caused sea-sickness among some of the passengers.

August 16. A north wind and choppy sea. Our food on board consisted of coffee and bread for breakfast, a fortifying meal of cabbage soup with potatoes or beans for lunch, and an evening meal of tea, one slice of bread and a little biscuit and butter. Some didn't care for the morning or evening meal, but no one in his senses would have complained of hunger. A Danish interpreter on board made sure everything went smoothly, and there was also a Danish doctor to tend to the sick. The hold was swept every day and the benches washed, and if this was not done properly the culprits were made to do it again.

On Sunday, the 17th, the weather took a turn for the worse, and many of the women became seasick. We Icelanders read together at three places on board. The vessel carried almost 600 passengers, 500 of them travelling third class. The rest were English gentlemen who could afford to pay more. That day, we passed two sailing ships heading in the same direction as we were. There was one man on board who had spent 40 years in America, in the province of Ontario and the town of Ottawa, of which he spoke well. He told us that winter lasted from 3-5 months, usually beginning in December and ending in March. The main occupations there are farming, forestry, various types of fishing, and the wages between $1^1/_2$ and 2 dollars per day. There was also a poor Norwegian farmer on the ship who was aged over 60 and had 7 children. Two of his daughters had worked as maids in Iowa in America for the past four years and had now saved enough to send their father a ticket costing 350 dollars and a little spending money to enable him to join them in the West.

August 18. Slightly calmer, and everyone is feeling a bit better, but so foggy we could see nothing.

August 19. A stiff northerly breeze, with brilliantly clear skies.

August 20. Fine, sunny weather. Most of us spent the day up on deck.

August 21. We maintained our course through a northerly wind ... a few icebergs were sighted around the ship. Sunset, 8 p.m.

August 22. Bright, sunny weather. We still saw icebergs, wind from the south. At 8 p.m., we sighted the Fair Island [Belle Isle], as it is called, to starboard, and at the same time, saw Newfoundland to port, along with the southeastern tip of Labrador. As we moved closer to shore, we saw forests on the east coast which looked like shadows in the sunshine. This morning, an English child died, and the body was cast overboard after the ship's chaplain had held a short service.

August 23. Bright weather to the south, but no sign of land. Those who had been sick were gradually improving.

The second Eymundsson photograph of departing emigrants. Taken amidships aboard the Camoens, it shows more of the women and children than its counterpart. Many of the women are covered in woollen blankets, while the men wear dark jackets, some with white shirts. The heads of almost all are covered, the men's with hats and the women's with the distinctive, long-tailed skotthúfa. Persuading the children to stay still presumably presented the photographer with something of a problem.

My wife and four other women spent the entire voyage in bed, but neither of the children was sick from the time we left England. Benzen, the Danish interpreter, has helped us greatly, and the medical care we received would have been a great deal less had he not been with us.

August 24. Today, an infant less than one year old, belonging to Sigurður Jakobsson from Dalasýsla, passed away. The chaplain, who is English, held a service few of us understood. After the body had been committed to the sea, he continued for a short time with his eyes closed and right hand raised. Those involved thanked him with a handshake.

At 6 p.m we sighted land on both sides, far away to starboard but closer to port. This was the part of Canada which lies northwest of New Brunswick, and consists of rolling mountains covered in huge forests. On the coast were settlements as far as the eye could see, although the visibility was poor. The bay we were sailing through looked very broad to the southwest and was dotted with small islands, some inhabited but all covered with woods. By now, dusk had fallen, and that night we sailed up the St. Lawrence River, where I was disappointed not to see the shore, as it is said to be a beautiful sight.

We arrived in Quebec City on Monday, August 25, 20 days and $5^{1}/_{2}$ hours after leaving Akureyri. Here we were well received and could buy anything we needed. We were pursued by men and women offering us fresh milk, but necessities are all very expensive here. Páll Þorláksson had been waiting for us for 5 days, and we would probably all have headed for Milwaukee had Lambertsen not made arrangements for us in Ontario. Finally, 112 of us went there, and the rest went with Páll. At 2 p.m. that day, the Icelanders all boarded a train, along with many of the foreigners. The same day ... we reached Richmond, where some of us purchased food. That night, we left for Montreal, where we arrived at 2 p.m. and stopped for a short time and some bought tea and bread to quench our hunger and thirst.

On August 26, we left for Kingston. Most of the route passes through forests, with settlements along the railway tracks, and would be considered a pretty sight back home. We left Kingston that evening intending to proceed, but about 10 o'clock, Kristinn Ólafsson's wife gave birth to a baby, forcing us to stop to let them off the train. The train then carried on until it met another one which it couldn't pass, as the line is only single track. We then stopped until dawn, to allow the other train to reverse in safety back up the track to where the line doubled, all of which passed without mishap. The rule is to send a telegraphed message in advance to monitor the train's position.

We reached Toronto at 8 o'clock on August 27, having taken 42 hours to travel from Quebec, a distance of about 500 English miles. Toronto is the capital of Ontario, and we were fed free of charge for the two days we had to wait there.

We left Toronto on August 29, travelling first on a train until 2 p.m. Then, we transferred to horse-drawn wagons which carried us to a reception area in the town of Gravenhurst, where we spent the night.

We left Gravenhurst on the 30th on a steamship across Lake Muskoka to Rosseau, where we are today. We will stay here in the reception building until Tuesday, and will be given free food. Tomorrow, some of us are going to look at land, which those who can afford will probably purchase as it is said to be very good.

The little advice I can give you, my fellow countrymen who may be thinking of emigrating across the sea, is to make arrangements in advance and register with a company like the Allan Line which has treated us very well. The other most important thing for those travelling in a group is to choose your members well. Make sure they are healthy people of good character, and not drunks or slatterns. When passing through cities, such as in England, stick together, and walk with purpose. Never walk alone, especially not youngsters. If you heed this advice, then you need not fear pickpockets in England or anywhere else. I would also advise you to have the same interpreter as we had, and am sending you his address ... Mr Peter Benzen, office, Liverpool.

In many respects, Skagfjörð and his companions were typical of those first groups of Icelandic emigrants, but valuable lessons were quickly learned from these first voyages. Never again would humans and livestock share the same quarters, even when carried on the same vessel. Legislation of 1876 ensured much higher levels of organization, schedules were more precise, and the rights of passengers protected. As emigration became more common, those who followed learned and benefited from the experiences of those early pioneers.

A HARD ROAD, AND LONG

The emigrant ships usually left Iceland at the height of summer when the pack ice had melted. The voyage to Granton averaged 4-6 days, with the wait in Glasgow lasting anything from a few hours to two weeks in a few cases. The voyage across the Atlantic to Quebec City usually took 10 days. From Quebec City most Icelanders usually had tickets all the way to Winnipeg, a further 2-3 days away. When they arrived, the majority spent their first few days with relatives or friends, or in the variety of boarding houses which were springing up in the city.

The voyage of 1874 was an exception, however, in that the Allan Line vessel the *St. Patrick* sailed directly from Iceland to Quebec, and although departure was delayed by several weeks, it was said to have gone well.

No organized group left in 1875, but the following year, another Allan Line ship, the *Verona*, carried several large groups to Scotland, from which point they crossed the Atlantic. The first left the northern port of Sauðárkrókur on Friday, June 30, and after a short stop at Akureyri, left the country with 752 emigrants on board. Among them was Jóhann Ó. Briem, a native of Eyjafjörður who would later become an influential figure in New Iceland. Later, he published an account of his experiences in *Framfari*.

Jóhann Briem (above), one of the leaders of the New Iceland colonists.

> We reached Granton on Thursday, July 6, and left immediately for Glasgow, from where we set sail on Tuesday the 11th aboard the Allan Line vessel *Austria*, arriving safely at Quebec City on Saturday, July 22. Almost half the group

Despite their size, the emigrant ships pitched considerably in bad weather, and the cramped, airless conditions below decks were a breeding ground for diseases. As a result, many chose to stay on deck, even in the worst storms. From a late 19th-century English sketch.

had decided to carry on to New Iceland, despite the fact that we had been warned by the authorities, first in Iceland and again in Glasgow, that the settlement there was capable of receiving only a very few families.

But as we sailed up the St. Lawrence, an agent from Nova Scotia came aboard and advised us not to go there for the same reasons. Along with him was an Icelander, Ólafur Brynjólfsson from Bólstaðarhlíð, who had lived for a time in Nova Scotia.

The *Verona* returned immediately from Granton to Iceland, where she collected another group of emigrants at

Seyðisfjörður. Among them was Þorleifur Jóakimsson, who later published a three-booklet history of the New Iceland settlement, which includes an account of his voyage, written several years later.

> On the evening of Wednesday, July 12, almost 400 emigrants left Seyðisfjörður aboard the steamship *Verona*. Our interpreter was Mr. Halldór Briem, son of Eggert Briem, sheriff of Skagafjarðarsýsla. We arrived at Granton the following Sunday, the 16th, and left for Glasgow by train the same day.
>
> One day, while we were still in Glasgow, Queen Victoria visited the city with much pomp. She was then just beginning to appear in public again 15 years after the death of her husband, Prince Albert, in 1861.
>
> We left Glasgow for America about 12 o'clock on Thursday, July 20. The voyage across the Atlantic went well, and people tried to find various ways to pass the time. On Sundays, we read and sang, and some days there was dancing and wrestling. The best wrestlers were Árni Sveinsson and Þórður Þorsteinsson from Breiðdalur, Sigurgeir Björnsson of Hagi in Vopnafjörður, and Sigurjón Jónsson from Hjarðarhagi in Jökuldalur.
>
> We reached Quebec around noon on Monday, July 31. Just before we landed, an Icelandic woman died. Her name was Gróa, and she was the wife of Jón Ásmundsson from Fáskrúðsfjörður.

Later a farmer in North Dakota, Þorleifur Jóakimsson Jackson (above) was the author of three booklets Landnámssaga Nýja Íslands, Frá Austri til Vesturs *and* Framhald á Landnámssögu Nýja Íslands, *a valuable history of New Iceland.*

The last group to leave that summer was by far the smallest, about 20 passengers, most of them from Southern Iceland.

For most of the emigrants, the long journey was an ordeal. For some, it proved too much. The vessels which took them to Scotland were not passenger ships, but ordinary cargo ships, and the emigrants were crammed into holds usually used to transport livestock, fish, wool and other goods. In these cramped, dark conditions they ate, slept and spent most of their time. Weather conditions were often rough, forcing crews to close the hatches, and the only source of sustenance for most of the passengers was often the meagre supplies they had brought with them.

Conditions en route across the Atlantic were sometimes little better, even though the emigrant ships were larger vessels

At the height of the emigration years, thousands of Europeans left for the shores of North America every single day. This sketch, dating from about 1870, depicts one such group as it takes its farewell on the dockside at Hamburg. The insets show conditions in third class, and the first sighting of land.

Pictured here in Winnipeg, Gestur Pálsson (left) was a 38-year-old journalist with the Reykjavík papers Þjóðólfur and Suðri until he crossed the sea to become editor of Heimskringla. He never saw Iceland again, dying the year after he landed in Canada.

intended for passengers. Of course, the atmosphere on board was filled with anticipation, new friends were made, some fell in love, and children experienced the thrill of life at sea. Life at sea no doubt did have its lighter moments as the passengers sat up on deck in heat they had never experienced before, and marvelled at the strange dishes which comprised their daily fare. The vast majority, however, travelled third class, often up to 500 at a time, and given the poor health of many of the emigrants to begin with, deaths were sometimes a feature of life on board.

In 1890, the author and poet Gestur Pálsson sailed to Canada to take up a new appointment as editor of *Heimskringla*. His account of the journey contains several complaints about his countrymen, in particular their poor personal hygiene.

Pálsson sailed second class, while the other 180 Icelanders, two of whom died on the way, travelled steerage.

The Icelandic emigrants were in poor health to begin with. Although fewer were seasick as the voyage wore on, influenza and its consequences proved harmful to many. The ship had a well-equipped, comfortable hospital in which the sick were confined, and the treatment they received from the doctor was of the best.

One of our group, Sigurður Jónsson from Víðidalsá, a fine young man but very sickly, fell ill with pneumonia the night after we left Scotland and died on our fifth day at sea. It was strange how deeply his death affected us all. When people are packed together on the open sea hundreds of

As the 19th century wore on, conditions aboard the emigrant ships gradually improved. Passengers aboard the SS Circassia, *seen here playing deck quoits in 1896.*

miles from land, the loss of one of their companions is felt very keenly. The English passengers in second class discussed his death with me as if he had been a close relative, and the expression on the face of Captain Carruthers was so grave when he spoke of the matter that you would have thought he had lost a close family member he had known for years.

Bodies are not kept for long at sea, and making the coffin takes little time. Sigurður died at night and was buried at sea the following day. I doubt whether Carruthers could have known that I was a "lapsed" theologian and I don't think I looked much like a man of the cloth, but it was I he requested say a short sermon, or at least to read a

The route taken by the Icelanders to North America lay from their country's main ports via Scotland on board mailboats or special emigrant vessels. When these ships reached Granton or Leith, they immediately sailed again for Iceland to pick up more passengers or cargo. The emigrants themselves travelled by train to Glasgow, where they joined hundreds of others from all over Europe for the transatlantic voyage to Quebec City, from where they left by train for points elsewhere on the continent, most often Manitoba.

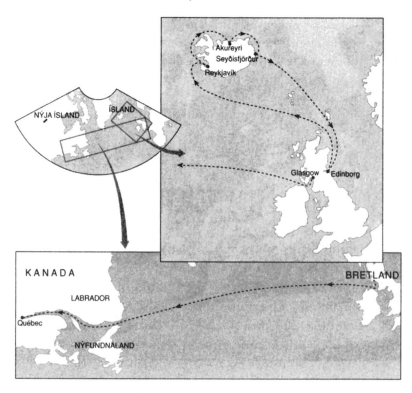

few words from the Scriptures. I had to decline, however, as I was afraid the role would not suit me. As things turned out, the situation was saved by the ship's doctor who decreed that as the weather was chilly and many of the passengers in poor health, the ceremony should be as short as possible. As a result, it was decided that Carruthers would read the funeral service from the English seamen's hymnal, which can be found on board every ship. And so the ship stopped, the English flag was lowered to half mast, and everyone on board, English and Icelandic, was ordered up on deck and lined up on one side. A small section of the rail was removed, and the body, sewn into sailcloth and wound in the English flag, was placed in the gap. We Icelanders sang a few verses from "Allt eins og blómstrið eina," Carruthers read a chapter from the hymnal, we sang a few more verses, and the body was lowered over the side. A small hole appeared in the waves which closed immediately, and this strange burial was over.

There was no procession of well-dressed mourners, no ornate church and no wreaths to cover the coffin, but for me it was the most moving funeral I have ever witnessed, an abject lesson in the awesome magnitude of death and the smallness of life.

UNDER A PRAIRIE SKY

When the emigrants stepped ashore in Canada, their journey was far from over. What awaited them now was a life of uncertainty and difficult decisions as to what to do next. Each group was always accompanied by a leader or interpreter, and most were met by someone who knew the area. Ignorant of local customs and surrounded by a language few of them could understand, some of the Icelanders soon fell victim to the assortment of confidence tricksters, salesmen and swindlers who patrolled the wharves and piers in search of a likely immigrant to relieve of money or possessions.

Not all, however, were so easily conned. In July 1887, a vessel carrying close to 900 Icelanders docked at Quebec City and was immediately surrounded by a cluster of would-be sales-men. Well-versed from their homeland in the art of buying now, smiling sweetly, and paying never, some of the Icelanders were quick to accept the apparent munificence of their Canadian "hosts," while failing to understand demands for payment. One of the group, having drunk several glasses of milk, declared that as he had asked the seller to give him the drink, he was under no obligation to pay for it. A scuffle ensued, which was eventu-ally broken up by an interpreter who had great difficulty in persuading the Icelander that the vendor had not, in fact, been offering free samples of his wares.

For the most part, these new immigrants were looked down upon by their older-established counterparts. They were often poor, spoke little English, and had few means of protecting themselves. As the trains filled, they found themselves at the back of the queue, and were left behind altogether or packed into carriages never intended to accommodate such large num-bers. They paid vastly inflated prices for bad food and high rents for sub-standard accommodation.

A group of newly arrived immigrants awaits landing permission at Quebec City, first port of call for the vast majority of Icelanders, about 1912.

The length of the journey faced by the Icelanders from Quebec City to Manitoba can be appreciated from the inset map of Iceland, shown here on the same scale. After arriving in Toronto, they continued by Great Lakes' steamship to Duluth, where they boarded a train for the Red River. After 1883, the entire journey was made by train.

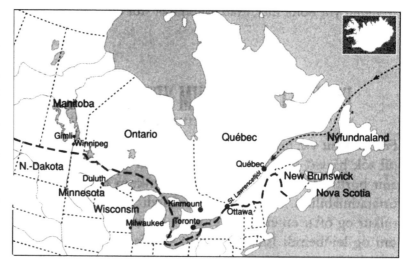

The journey by train across the vast country was monotonous, broken only by stops made at isolated stations every few hours or so. This photograph was taken by Sigfús Eymundsson during a visit in 1893. Probably from Dakota, it shows a typical small prairie town built around the tracks.

The guides were not always up to their job, and the Icelanders knew nothing of the railway companies and had only a hazy knowledge of the geography of the vast land in which they now found themselves. Unable to speak English, few of them were able to ask questions, and they could only blindly follow the instructions they were given by means of hand signals and gestures.

Some lost their tickets or food, others got lost themselves and never reached their destination. There are even stories of emigrants who left their train somewhere along the route in search of food or refreshment in the naïve belief that it would await their return, only to watch as it disappeared into the distance carrying their luggage, families, and travelling companions. Now alone, they found themselves strangers in a strange land surrounded by a language they could neither speak nor understand.

Sometimes they found plans laid at home altered when they arrived in Canada, and they were sent to destinations they had not asked for, although it is doubtful whether they realized this themselves until it was too late. Engaged couples who had travelled with different groups the same year intending to reunite in the New World might find themselves separated. At the other end of the romantic spectrum, some deserted spouses in Iceland and remarried across the sea without ever bothering with the inconvenience of divorce.

Although Icelanders were generally considered quick to learn English and become self-sufficient, there were glaring exceptions to this rule. Shortly after 1880, an Icelandic farmer set sail for Canada, but decided to leave his housekeeper behind. Devoted to her erstwhile master, however, she smuggled herself aboard ship, but was discovered a short time after it set sail. Pitying her plight, her fellow passengers clubbed together to buy her a ticket, and she arrived in Quebec empty-handed and utterly penniless. Undeterred, she smuggled herself aboard a train for Winnipeg, but this time her luck had run out and she was quickly caught and thrown off at the next station by the unsympathetic conductor. Alone in the world, she was found by a local farmer who took pity on her, and she lived with him for a year without his ever discovering where she was from as she never learned a word of English. Finally, the farmer advertised in a newspaper for someone who could speak her language, and it occurred to an Icelander in Toronto where she might be from. Collecting the girl himself, he sent her on to Winnipeg, where she discovered that her former master was now living on a farm 150 kilometres away. She was then placed alone on a train, but, forgetting the name of the town, carried on a further 150 kilometres to a destination where, once again, no one understood her or she them. Luckily for her, however, the locals had some knowledge of Icelanders, and, suspecting where she might be from, sent her back. Finally, she was reunited with the farmer she loved so much, and they settled down together after her marathon adventure.

Þorleifur Jóakimsson, who emigrated to Canada in 1876 and is quoted earlier in this chapter, later described his experiences on the journey from Quebec City to Winnipeg. The journey of the "Large Group," as the emigrants of that year became known at home, took its members west, as was the common experience of millions of other European immigrants of the time. Although some of these treks were well organized, fiascos

The Canadian Pacific Railway served as a source both of transport and employment for countless thousands of immigrants. When immigration stood at its height, passengers were packed into third-class carriages like this one, known as "colonist cars." This illustration was probably part of a CPR advertisement.

were also common. The same afternoon as Jóakimsson and his companions landed at Quebec City, they were loaded on board a train. Two days later, they arrived in Toronto after a brief halt in Montreal. He later remembered:

The Icelandic Millennium Festival in Milwaukee, 1874

The American city of Milwaukee was the scene of an historic occasion at the beginning of August, 1874, when the first-ever formal gathering of Icelanders in the New World was held there to celebrate the 1,000th anniversary of their country's settlement by the Norse, and a sermon was preached in Icelandic. The excitement of the day is recaptured in a letter from Páll Þorláksson to the editor of the Akureyri newspaper *Norðanfari*, which appeared on October 14 that same year.

"On August 2, we Icelanders, between 60 and 70 in number, celebrated the thousandth anniversary of our dear native land. We had assembled in Milwaukee a few days previously, elected a three-man committee to prepare and organize the celebrations, and requested the Rev. Jón Bjarnason, who has spent July and August in Milwaukee during his summer vacation from his employment as a teacher of Latin and Greek at the Latin School in Decorah, Iowa, to preach for us from the 90th Psalm, or whatever other text would symbolize Iceland. On August 2, we assembled at 2 p.m. in the church of Geelmuyden, a Norwegian parish in Milwaukee, to listen to the first Icelandic sermon ever, as far as is known, to be preached on this side of the Atlantic. Several Norwegians joined us in the church, and enjoyed hearing the Word 'as their ancient forefathers would have said it,' although they claimed to understand very little. The Rev. Jón held such a brilliant sermon on the merciful protection of God of the Icelandic people, and his wife, Lára, daughter of our great Icelandic organist Pétur Guðjohnsen, sang

There were a few Icelanders in Toronto who had emigrated in 1873 and 1874, and everyone thought it a pleasure to talk to them ...

On the evening of Thursday, August 3, we left Toronto

so beautifully that the Norwegians heaped them with praise. When the service was over, we formed a procession in the street outside the church, led by two flag bearers dressed in traditional Icelandic costume, one carrying an Icelandic flag we had designed ourselves, blue with a white falcon, the other the Stars and Stripes. Behind them we lined up in pairs, first the men, then the women, some in traditional costume, and proceeded through the city to a public park which the committee had rented for 5 dollars and had already decked with food and drink. Then the entertainment began, with speeches and song. Jón Ólafsson made a long, colourful speech dedicated to Iceland, and Ólafur Ólafsson proposed a toast to all Icelanders in America. We also toasted Vínland and all the Norwegians here, several of whom were present, and thanked them for their fraternal reception of us, their Nordic cousins, now re-united in the same land visited by Leifur Eiriksson 1,000 years ago. Then we toasted the Icelandic language, and the many Americans who raised funds to send books to Iceland this summer, especially Professor Fiske of Cornell University, and Professor R. B. Anderson of Madison University, Wisconsin. Professor Anderson has just published a book entitled *America Not Discovered by Columbus*, which I have unfortunately not yet been able to read. Both these excellent men were invited to attend our celebrations, but neither was able to attend. Everything went well at this, our first national festival, and everyone returned home happy and enriched by a day they will long remember, the day when a few Icelanders gathered in Milwaukee (Vínland) to celebrate the mil-lennial anniversary of the settlement of Iceland, their native land, but the man who deserves the real praise is he who first discovered this rich, vast country."

Halldór Briem led the "Large Group" on its journey across the prairie. Later editor of Framfari, *he subsequently returned home to Iceland, where he became first a teacher at Möðruvallaskóli in Hörgárdalur in the North, and later head librarian of the National Library of Iceland.*

for Collingwood, where we immediately boarded a ship which carried us to Duluth, which we reached on the evening of Monday, August 7. Conditions on board were extremely crowded. There were pigs and sheep on board, and some of the single men had to sleep on bales of hay intended as fodder. Supplies of drinking water were running low, and several of us became sick in our stomachs …

We stayed in Duluth until the morning of Saturday, August 12, when we boarded a train which took us west across the Minnesota prairie to Fisher's Landing, a village on the banks of the Red River. Some liked the look of the rich, grassy prairie and said it would have been good to settle there.

Late that evening, the train stopped. We had reached the end of the line, but the driver failed to inform the interpreter, so everyone remained in the carriages all night, not knowing what we were to do the next morning.

At first light, we saw a line of trees up ahead from which a young boy soon emerged. Halldór Briem asked where on Earth we were, and was informed that on the other side of the bush was Fisher's Landing, where a steamship was expected from Winnipeg later that day to pick us up. We then left the train, and some of us went to explore the surrounding countryside.

Even though it was Sunday, the saloons were all open, and one of our party was tempted to stay in one of them the whole day, where he drank until dark with another Icelander, an old man. When he eventually sobered up, he realized he had been robbed of almost his entire savings of 25 pounds sterling. Both drinkers later died of smallpox a short time after reaching New Iceland.

Around mid-day the next day, Monday, August 14, we set off from Fisher's Landing for Winnipeg. On the way,

many of us became sick from drinking stale water,
particularly the children.

We arrived in Winnipeg, then a small town only six years
old, on the morning of August 17. The first Icelander we
met was Friðjón Friðriksson, who spoke for a short time
with Halldór Briem before the rest of us disembarked.

The rest of the week we spent in Winnipeg, using the
time to purchase a variety of necessities. Late on Saturday, we
set off down the Red River and it could be said that the rest
of the journey to Gimli went well. Some did not travel all
the way, but settled in the south of the colony.

Generally, most of those immigrants who were not headed
straight for family or friends went to the Immigration Hall in
Winnipeg, where they were met by other Icelanders eager for
news from home, who offered to show them around.
Government officials helped in the search for work, which most
were keen to find as soon as possible, as they were often
seriously short of money. The jobs they got were usually
temporary, providing them with an opportunity to learn the
language, earn some money, learn new skills, and prepare for a
future in their adopted homeland.

A PLACE TO CALL HOME

As the number of Icelanders in Canada and the U.S. increased
following the years 1873-74, pressure mounted to find somewhere permanent to settle, and countless letters and other written sources of the time make it clear that this was viewed as a
basic condition for further emigration from Iceland.

Until such a place could be found, however, the immigrants
remained in a state of limbo, unlike those of other nationalities
such as Norwegians, who had been there longer and could
choose from several regions, districts, and settlements already
claimed by their compatriots and where their language was
freely spoken.

 107

For a few years after 1870, when William Wickmann had encouraged the first southerners to emigrate, Milwaukee had been a focal point for Icelandic immigration to the New World. The city also served the same function for immigrants from Germany.

As the number of Icelandic immigrants increased, some of them began to leave Milwaukee in search of employment. Some headed north, settling initially on Washington Island in Lake Michigan, while others settled in Shawano County, where they established a settlement they called Ljósavatnsbyggð. By 1874, some 70 Icelanders attended a ceremony in Milwaukee to celebrate the millennial anniversary of the settlement of their country.

The first Icelander to settle in Canada, however, was Sigtryggur Jónasson, who emigrated to Ontario in 1872.

In 1873, the first large group of Icelanders left for North America, intending to settle in Milwaukee from where Páll Þorláksson travelled to welcome them in Quebec. However, only between 40 and 50 returned with him, while more than 100 chose to continue on to Toronto and north to the Muskoka district, where land was plentiful and work could be found around the town of Rosseau.

Writing home later that winter, one of the group, Vigfús Sigurðsson, a bookbinder, described how he and his companions passed their first days in their new homeland. The first three days they spent at a government reception centre, existing

Sigtryggur Jónasson, seen here in 1876.

The first group of Icelanders who left with Páll Þorláksson from Quebec City for Milwaukee in 1873 fell victim to a train crash, when another train hit the back of theirs. Although several passengers were killed, the Icelanders all escaped with minor injuries. Among those hurt was the poet and author Stephan G. Stephansson. Þorláksson pursued the rights of his countrymen vigorously and forced the railway company to pay them damages. The photograph, taken in Manitoba, shows a similar accident from about the same time.

on a diet of bread, tea, and syrup, with which they were provided free of charge.

Now we could no longer be idle, and some began to consider accepting grants of land, which was plentiful. Some settled claims up near the forests about 4 miles away, others moved further on. I took no land, as I had no money and thought only of finding work. After a week, I found a job I was told would last 6 weeks for a promised wage of 16 dollars a month. It was building a road northeast through the forest, and to get there I had to walk a distance of 20 English miles.

However, Sigurðsson lost his new job after only 16 days, and began wandering the district in search of land or work, before finally returning to Rosseau:

> I'd now had an opportunity to see the country and form a few impressions. For the most part, it is flat with a few rolling hills but no mountains, and covered everywhere with thick forests through which you can see nothing. In some places, you can't even see the sky, except from the grassy plains.
>
> When I got back to Rosseau, some had already left, including Ólafur from Espihóll and three other families. Some had returned to Toronto. Others had great difficulty finding work, epecially the women, who tended not to last long as maids, complaining they were worked too hard. Baldvin Helgason and Davíð from Bakkasel rented a house five miles into the forest close to land they have since purchased, along with the uncultivated land on which it stands, for 150 dollars. No one built a house in the autumn, but two single men from Húnavatnssýsla erected a cabin this winter. At the last count, only eight families remained in the Immigrants' House.

People did what they could to find work, but in the winter of 1873-74 it was hard to come by and poorly paid. The problems which arose among the settlers can mainly be traced to ignorance of local customs, working methods, and language. In the spring of 1874, shortly after the letter above had been written, Sigtryggur Jónasson, who had then lived in Ontario for two years, began acting as an interpreter and advisor to the settlers. As a result, he became an agent for the Ontario government, and when another group of Icelanders announced their impending arrival that summer, he was sent to meet them.

By then, serious discussions had begun on the establishment of an Icelandic settlement in Nova Scotia or New Brunswick, where the government had offered emigrants various privileges. Many of the Icelanders who arrived in 1874 intended to settle there, but by then it was an open secret throughout Canada that the best land in both provinces had been claimed long ago. So the majority of the 375 Icelanders who arrived aboard the *St.*

Patrick late that summer headed for Ontario, and the town of Kinmount, where they were to be employed building a railway. At the same time, others began exploring the neighbouring countryside in search of suitable land.

TRAGEDY IN KINMOUNT

A concise account of life among the Icelandic settlers in Canada before the discovery of a site for New Iceland appears in two letters written by Sigtryggur Jónasson and published in the newspaper *Norðanfari* in the winter of 1874-75.

The tone of one of them, dated October 13, 1874, and composed just before the party reached Kinmount, is cautiously optimistic.

Laying the railway: Icelandic men in Kinmount could feed their wives and families on wages earned as labourers on the CPR. This photograph from British Columbia probably dates from before 1880.

You may perhaps be interested to hear some news of how the Icelanders who came here to Ontario this summer are now faring. Had they arrived in time for the harvest, the plan initially was to find employment for them on local farms and so give them an opportunity to get to know the country before they began farming for themselves. But because they arrived so late, we could do no better than find work for all the single women and move the menfolk and their dependents to Kinmount, where they can spend the winter working on the railway for a good wage, 1 dollar and 12½ cents per day. Should they choose, they can also work here next summer. While houses were being built for them here, they were fed in Toronto free for two weeks. They have all just arrived, many of them have already begun to work, and Icelanders generally are considered good employees. Conditions, however, remain tough while they are settling in, but the majority are in good spirits and unafraid of the future, as they know that everything possible will be done to help them on their way. Parcels of land are freely available along and near the tracks, and I will soon be going with them to look at these more closely. They can then choose their own plots and send the government the claim number to allow them to be cleared and houses built so they can commence farming in the spring. Although the authorities have not yet provided a written guarantee to do this, I believe they will do so on condition that the cost of such improvements will be repaid in full later. I have no more news at present. Although the weather has been a little chilly recently, we still expect another six weeks of good weather.

When Jónasson wrote his next letter only four months later, however, the tone was much gloomier. In it, he mentions several things which, for reasons known only to him, he had omitted from his earlier missive. At the very beginning of winter, many of the infants had become sick, and in the depths of an Ontario winter, Sigtryggur Jónasson, still only 22 years old, composed his next communication home to Akureyri.

The government found work for all the Icelanders on the Victoria Railway, which is being built from the town of Lindsey, about 60 miles northeast of Toronto and 40 miles from Kinmount. It also had four log cabins built as temporary accommodation for the workers. The two larger ones are 70 feet long and 20 feet wide, but the others are only 35 feet long and 20 feet wide. They are built in the local settler style, with walls made of piled-up logs chinked with moss and clay. When the Icelanders arrived, this housing proved both insufficient and too low, so another two were constructed, each 35 feet long and 20 feet broad, one of them with a loft. Lofts were also added to the two larger cabins, and ten temporary stoves were distributed among all of them. The intention was to sell them to the Icelanders, and most of them were sold, although the government paid the cost of transporting them.

Life was hard for many of the Icelanders after they arrived at Kinmount, mainly due to sickness. When they landed at Quebec, many had stomach problems causing vomiting and diarrhoea, and more fell ill in Toronto. Few seemed to get better, even though a doctor tended the sick every day and gave them medicine.

The Icelanders were moved here from Toronto in two groups, the first on October 9 and the second on the 12th,

An ox-drawn wagon train crossing the Manitoba prairie in the summer of 1873. The transport used by the Kinmount Icelanders was horse-drawn.

a distance of 102 English miles. Their route lay 88 miles northeast of Toronto on the Nippising Railway to the town of Cobakonk. The 14 miles from there to Kinmount were completed in horse-drawn wagons. To reach Kinmount the same day, we had to leave Toronto at 8 a.m., reaching Cobakonk just after mid-day. After lunch, the women and children were transferred to the wagons, which had been ordered in advance. Up till now, everything had gone well, apart from the sick, but then things began to go wrong. The healthy among the men were supposed to walk the 14 miles and the sicklier ones were to be driven, but it was the healthy who boarded first. As a result, much time was wasted sorting this out and reloading the wagons, and much of the journey was made in the dark, a very unpleasant experience on a rough road and in heavy rain. When the first group reached Kinmount, the weather had been fine, but it later deteriorated into the coldest day that October. This was one reason why so many of the infants died soon after our arrival.

Two infants had died in Toronto and one on the way to Cobakonk, where another sick child was left in the care of its mother. At Kinmount, however, 12 children died, along with a girl in her 17th year. There was a doctor here, but we desparately needed another, as this one was nearly

Labourers in their camp somewhere in Canada at the close of the 19th century. The accommodations of Icelanders working for the railway or logging operations has been similar.

dead from drinking whiskey. It took some time for the railway company to find a replacement, but when he arrived, things gradually began to improve, although some still have stomach sickness. He believes that most of the sickness was due to the changes in climate, food and water. In his report, the first doctor from Lindsey claimed that people had become infected from a single individual during the sea crossing. Whatever the reason, it has caused us a lot of harm in a variety of ways.

In addition, the Kinmount Icelanders had to contend with broken promises regarding work, and the extreme cold, as Jónasson describes in his letter.

As work is so hard to come by in America and wages low, the railway company was able to use this to cut pay by 90 cents an hour at the beginning of last month. This can't go on for long, though, as there will be plenty of work again come the spring. The winter has been most unsuited to railway construction, due to heavy frosts and snow. The snow has averaged up to 3 feet deep, and if the company had not been obliged to employ the Icelanders, it would have paid them off for one or two months. It's been impossible to do anything except tunnel through hills, fill ditches, blast rocks and fell trees, and the Icelanders are not very good at the last two due to lack of experience. Notwithstanding, a few of them are helping the blasters, and I'm going to get a few of the younger ones fixed up with work cutting trees, as they have to learn sometime.

Jónasson goes on to say that a few Icelanders have been to look at land in the vicinity, but he criticizes their lack of activity and initiative in this respect. He then goes on to emphasize the urgency of finding a permanent settlement for the Icelanders.

Life for the railway labourer was tough and uncompromising. First, the track bed had to be levelled, and the sleepers and tracks laid. As can be seen from this photograph, taken during the construction of the CPR through Manitoba about 1882, primitive cranes were used to lift the track into position.

It's enough to say that there have been some sharp differences of opinion among the Icelanders in America as to where it would be best for us to settle. Opinion can be divided into two groups: those who believe Wisconsin to be the best option, and those who prefer Nebraska. Last summer, a third school of thought appeared, advocating Alaska, the former possession of Russia in America. They have already looked at land there and are strongly in favour, particularly due to the rich fishing. Without knowing too much about it myself, I am of the opinion that Alaska is too far north to be much more fertile than old Iceland, and I can't help thinking that we would soon be as isolated from the civilized world on Kodiak Island as we were in the country we just left. Opinion among the Icelanders in Canada is now divided into two main groups: supporters of Nova Scotia, where the authorities are offering much better terms than here in Ontario and we would be closer to Iceland, and those who prefer to stay here in Ontario and see what happens. At one time, the government of Nova Scotia offered us free transportation, but it has since withdrawn this offer.

While this uncertainty persists, I find it unadvisable to encourage anyone to move to a place where they might not last long and which might ruin them financially in the process if, that is, they have any money to lose to begin with. And even if the authorities are promising great things, I still believe it's better for men to rely on their own devices. Personally, I'm still of the opinion that Ontario has many advantages over all other options as a site for an Icelandic colony, as, when all is said and done, the Icelanders here have prospered more than anywhere else in America, no matter what anyone else might say.

In consequence, I believe it's better for us to stay put, while those in America are learning from experience. I'll let you know later how things are progressing.

Despite Jónasson's advice, some of his fellow emigrants persisted in their interest in Nova Scotia, and 80 of them fled the dreadful conditions of Kinmount for the province, where they met some other Icelanders in the Mooseland district, near Halifax. There, they established the colony of Markland in the winter of 1874–75, led by Jóhannes Arngrímsson of Bægisá, who also served as their liaison with the authorities. Two years later, they were joined by some more Icelanders from Wisconsin, Ontario and Iceland itself, but as had been predicted, the colony proved a failure, and in 1882–83 almost all 35 families who had settled there packed up and headed west.

THE SEARCH WIDENS

About the same time as the Markland colony was being established, another Icelandic settlement was taking shape in Shawano County, Wisconsin, on the shores of Lake Shawano. Known to the Icelanders as Ljósavatnsbyggð (Bright Water Settlment), it had been founded by Páll Þorláksson, then just 20, and his father, Þorlákur G. Jónsson of Stórutjarnir, who settled here along with other family members and friends. The Ljósavatn settlement, however, would be short-lived, and the settlers dispersed to Minnesota and Dakota.

In a letter home to Iceland dated October 14, 1874, Páll Þorláksson described the settlement as follows:

> Encouraged by some Icelanders in Wisconsin, all farmers from Bárðardalur, Eyjafjörður and East Iceland, my brother Haraldur and I set off with our father in search of land in Northern Wisconsin. The place we chose to settle was in Shawano County, which would be called in Icelandic *Ljósavatnssýsla*. The land here is mostly forest, dotted with several lakes and rivers, the biggest of which is Lake Shawano (*Ljósavatn*), which covers an area of about 20 or 30 English miles. Just east of the lake, close to the road northwest of Green Bay, 10–12 other Icelanders settled land a few weeks ago, and intend spending the winter working

Páll Þorláksson, founder of the Lake Shawano settlement in Wisconsin, and later a pastor in Dakota.

Many of those who moved to New Iceland had lived for a time in the East, where they had become accustomed to Canadian and American life and customs, and some of them later acquired teams of oxen which they used to travel by wagon and sleigh.

as woodcutters close to their holdings. In the weeks since they made their claims, each of which is 80 acres, they have spent their time building cabins for themselves, and they certainly don't have far to go to look for wood.

The first Icelandic settlement in Minnesota, dating from May 1875, was in Lincoln County. Its founder was Gunnlaugur

Pétursson of Hákonarstaðir in Jökuldalur, East Iceland, who had lived for a time in Wisconsin where he had worked for Norwegians. Other Wisconsin Icelanders followed the next year and were joined by more from Ontario and Iceland itself the year after that. Farming prospered in the region, and apart from the Mormon community at Spanish Fork, Utah, this was one of the first Icelandic settlements to take root in the New World.

In the spring of 1875, a small band of Icelanders settled near the town of Firth, Nebraska, about the same time as Jón Ólafsson, Ólafur Ólafsson and Páll Björnsson were setting off on their expedition to Alaska, but the Nebraska settlement remained very small, and the Alaska scheme came to nothing.

At the beginning of 1875, the majority of the Icelandic immigrants, probably around 300–400 souls, remained scattered through Ontario, in the areas around Rosseau and Kinmount. As they found work, they gained some experience in the farming techniques of their new homeland, and occasionally they met to discuss their future. Few of them were content with their lot, and talk turned to Manitoba, to which settlers were now streaming from Ontario, as land was both freely available and promising.

Around this time, a local evangelist named John Taylor befriended the Icelanders in Ontario and took it upon himself to encourage the Canadian government to help them move west to Manitoba.

Jón Ólafsson, dressed in the uniform of an American seaman. The photograph was taken during his expedition to Alaska.

WEST TO MANITOBA

On May 30, 1875, at a meeting held at Kinmount, Taylor informed the Icelanders of the results of his negotiations with the authorities, and a committee was immediately formed to travel west in search of a site suitable for settlement. Selected to travel with Taylor were Sigtryggur Jónasson and Einar Jónasson, who were joined by three other young men. And so it was that the expedition to find a site for an Icelandic colony in the West

Einar Jónasson

came to consist of an English gentleman in his sixties and five Icelanders in their early twenties.

Taylor and the two Jónassons set off on their momentous journey on July 2, 1875, just over a month after the Kinmount meeting. Shortly afterwards, one of their fellow scouts, Skafti Arason, wrote:

> We took the train to St. Paul, from there to Duluth, and so west across Minnesota to Moorhead, where we met Taylor, Sigtryggur and Einar. From there, we took a steamboat down

John Taylor

Born in Bridgetown, Barbados, in 1812, John Taylor was 63 when he led the Icelanders from Kinmount to New Iceland. His father had served as a quarter-master in the British fleet for several years, and Taylor had an excellent education, first at home, and then at school in Bridgetown. Details of his university education are uncertain, but he probably attended the University of Nova Scotia before proceeding to Oxford, where he graduated in theology but never took orders. One of his contemporaries at Oxford was reputed to have later become Minister of the Interior in Canada at the time of the formation of the New Iceland settlement, which would go a long way in explaining his great success in negotiating with the government.

In 1848 Taylor's father left Barbados for Ontario, accompanied by John, who began teaching in the Latin School. About the same time, he married his wife Elizabeth, 13 years his junior, who had emigrated from Birmingham, England, with her father and was the Red River to Winnipeg, which we reached on Friday, July 16. At the time, things looked bad in Manitoba, which had been plagued by grasshoppers, as I recall, for seven years. By now, they had consumed all the crops in the neighbourhood of Winnipeg which had been sown that spring, as well as the grass on the prairie. However, a few miles west of the town, the harvest was quite good.

It's safe to say that we were the first Icelanders to set foot in Manitoba. Two or three years earlier, Winnipeg had only been a small village, but it had since grown considerably.

Skafti Arason

as deeply religious as her husband. For some years, Taylor ran a business in Peterborough, Ontario, but in 1865 he joined the Canadian Bible Society and supervised missionary activity among the lumberjacks in the region north of Kinmount.

Taylor was introduced to the Icelanders by his niece, Caroline, or Carrie, who met them in Kinmount while on her way to visit him. Intrigued by these people, she asked Taylor to help them.

Taylor granted her request and embarked on what would become a grand adventure, accompanying Sigtryggur Jónasson and the others on their expedition to Manitoba and becoming the leader of the Icelanders on their journey to New Iceland. He remained as leader when the group arrived at Gimli, but his influence seems to have gradually dwindled. He never learned Icelandic, which, of course, hindered communications with his fellow settlers, and he died in 1884.

As well as his wife, Taylor was accompanied on his journey by his brother William and his three nieces: Carrie, who later married Sigurður Kristófersson, Susie, who married Halldór Briem, and Jane, who later went to Toronto. Taylor was also accompanied by a hired man, Everett Parsonage, who later settled near Pilot Mound and played a role in founding the Argyle Settlement along with William Taylor and was followed by several New Icelanders.

There was no railway in the province then, but the Canadian-Pacific Railroad is now under construction between the Great Lakes and Selkirk.

Upon arriving in Winnipeg, we began searching for a likely place for our people to settle. We thought it advisable to go further west, but there was insufficient land nearby on which to form a colony for Icelanders, who are so poor that they could afford neither draught animals nor the implements necessary for farming. With this in mind, we decided to look at the western shore of Lake Winnipeg, as we had been told that the lake's waters were filled with many species of fish and the land was good.

Setting off in an open boat with three guides, we sailed down the Red River and north along the lake's western shore as far as the White Mud River, now known as the Icelandic River. The land was covered in forests, with wide tracts of grass in between and along the shoreline. The trees, however, were small, and looked easier to clear than those of

Using a combination of oar and sail, the New Iceland expedition travelled down the Red River and Lake Winnipeg to the mouth of the Icelandic River on board a York boat like these, accompanied by Métis guides.

Ontario. The soil seemed fertile, and the land flat and low-lying, but dry. Under the circumstances, it appeared to us that a better place could not be found, and so we returned to Winnipeg secure in the knowledge that we were doing the right thing in advising our people to move there.

As soon as the party returned to Winnipeg, Taylor telegraphed the government in Ottawa, which responded immediately with a formal reply, confirmed on October 9, stating that the land in question was now reserved for the Icelanders. Meanwhile, the Icelandic delegation sat down in Winnipeg on August 5 and composed a detailed report on its travels and findings. The report, signed by all six expedition members, was intended for the Canadian government as well as the Icelanders back in Kinmount, and was later published as a small book, entitled *New Iceland in Canada: a reliable description of the location and state of the land which the Canadian government has set aside for the establishment of an Icelandic colony, with a full report on the conditions under which it is given free of charge, and how much it costs to get there.*

The work contains a list compiled by John Taylor of the attractions of the New Iceland site:

1. No grasshoppers.
2. Easy to reach.
3. Large fields well suited for hay.
4. Rich fishing.
5. Nowhere better in Canada for growing wheat.
6. Plenty of timber for housing, fencing, and cooking.
7. A natural harbour between the mainland and Mikley (Big Island).
8. Water-based transportation from the settlement in all directions.
9. The Canadian Pacific Railroad passes the southern end of the colony.

As is clear from their report, the Icelanders were in complete agreement with Taylor.

The land is better than anything we could have had anywhere else. It skirts a lake filled with fish and can be reached by train and steamer from both Ontario and Quebec City. Things can be moved on shore in summer and on the ice in winter. At the southern end of the colony, less than 25 miles from the lake, the Canadian Pacific Railway crosses the Red River and may reach as far as Lake Superior within the next two years.

Although there is plenty of timber for houses and fuel, clearing the land is not difficult, as the poplars are soft and their roots shallow. The soil can be ploughed two years after the trees have been cut, and the area is also better than any other in Manitoba in that it is free of grasshoppers, as they avoid forests and marshes. When we ask people here what the land is like in Manitoba, they reply it would be excellent were it not for the grasshoppers. Everyone we've spoken to who has moved from Ontario prefers Manitoba and, by acquiring land for the Icelanders which is free of grasshoppers, we have spared them the region's greatest drawback. Two types of insect do live in the area, however, mosquitoes and horseflies. Black flies, a plague in Ontario, do not live here, and there are no dangerous animals apart from bears and wolves, which present little threat to humans.

When discussing fishing, we mentioned the Indians who live around Lake Winnipeg. It should be added that a few of them live in tents and cabins near Sandy Bar, but

Kristján Jónsson.

they present no threat as not only are they Christian and civilized, but belong to the most peaceful of the tribes. As far as Indians go, there is no safer place in the West, and when the Icelanders arrive, the Indians will be moved elsewhere.

To the best of our knowledge, the land we have acquired for our colony is the best available in the West, and better than anything else we have been offered until now.

The report is signed by Sigtryggur Jónasson and Einar Jónasson, and witnessed by the other members of the group: Skafti Arason from Hringver, Sigurður Kristófersson from Ytri Neslönd, and Kristján Jónsson from Héðinshöfði.

Just three months later, on the eve of winter, the realities of settling in the Canadian wilderness would confront these same men (with the exception of Sigtryggur Jónasson, who sailed for Iceland), along with some 200 other Icelandic pioneers who ventured to New Iceland that fall.

THE PROMISED LAND

Following their trip to Manitoba, Taylor and the Jónassons returned to Kinmount to meet the Icelanders, who had been awaiting their return with keen anticipation. When the intital excitement wore off, however, the problem of how to get the penniless Icelanders to their new home on the shores of Lake Winnipeg remained. Somehow, financial and material assistance had to be obtained from somewhere.

To get it, John Taylor and Sigtryggur Jónasson set off once again for Ottawa to apply for government funding to take the Icelanders to their new home. The intital response was discouraging. No existing laws or customs made provisions for such grants, but eventually it was the Prime Minister himself, Alexander MacKenzie, who gave the go-ahead, acting on the advice of Lord Dufferin, the Canadian Governor-General,

Lord Dufferin,
Governor-General of
Canada 1872–78.

Alexander MacKenzie,
Prime Minister of Canada
1873–78.

who had visited Iceland as a young man in 1856 and had developed a liking for the country and its people.

When it was clear that the necessary funding would be forthcoming, Taylor and Jónasson set off on another journey through Ontario to seek out Icelanders throughout the province, most of whom accepted the offer. During their travels, both men remained in close touch with Ottawa. In the fall of 1875, Jónasson was employed to go to Iceland to help organize and assist prospective emigrants from the ash-sticken districts in Eastern Iceland. For his part, Taylor was appointed leader of the Icelandic trek to the West, with Friðjón Friðriksson as his interpreter.

The Icelanders assembled in Toronto, in the same reception centre where they had arrived the previous year, and on September 25, close to 300 boarded the train that would take them on the first stage of their journey to New Iceland. The same afternoon, they arrived at the town of Sarnia, on the shores of Lake Huron, where an artist from the magazine *Canadian Illustrated News* drew a series of sketches of the group, which appeared in the publication a few weeks later, on November 13.

After spending the night in Sarnia, the party boarded the steamship *Ontario*, which proved much too small for its cargo of humans, cattle, horses, pigs, sheep, and poultry. As a result, the Icelanders were forced to cram their possessions underneath them as best they could, and in these cramped conditions spent the next four days sailing into the teeth of a stomach-churning headwind north across Lake Huron and west along the length

The first group of Icelanders reaches Sarnia, Ontario, on September 25, 1875, as depicted in an engraving in the Canadian Illustrated News. *After leaving the train on the quayside, they boarded the steamship* Ontario, *seen here making steam for its journey to Duluth. The artist takes particular notice of the tasseled headgear of the women.*

of Lake Superior. All in all, the voyage took almost as long as that from Scotland to Canada.

On September 30 landfall was finally made at Duluth, then a small town of only 300 inhabitants, where the party met another group of Icelanders who had travelled hundreds of kilometres from Milwaukee to meet the vessel. After a night spent celebrating, the group set off on the recently completed railway west across the Minnesota prairie. The weekend was spent in the town of Glydon, where the Icelanders were housed in a large factory in conditions that did not impress them. On the Sunday, John Taylor, assisted by Friðjón Friðriksson, preached a sermon in which he stated that he had been chosen to lead the group into the great unknown, a claim which moved some of the

Ólafur Ólafsson, who gave Gimli its name.

Icelanders to rechristen him Moses, their wit no doubt sharpened by the spirits that flowed freely at the dance following the church service.

The next day, the party boarded a train that took it to the hamlet of Fisher's Landing, on the banks of the Red River on the Minnesota–Dakota border. There, Taylor and the Icelanders boarded the *International*, a paddlewheeler. The vessel towed two large flat-bottomed barges, filled to the brim with the immigrants and their luggage, but the week-long voyage downriver to Winnipeg was fraught with frequent delays as the *International* ran repeatedly aground in the shallows.

It was during this voyage that Ólafur Ólafsson of Espihóll suggested that the name of the new settlement should be Gimli. A well-off farmer when he decided to leave his holding in Eyjafjörður, Northern Iceland, Ólafsson had emigrated in 1873 and spent his first year in Canada, later moving to Wisconsin. From there he had left with Jón Ólafsson and Páll Björnsson in search of a settlement site in Alaska. There he spent the winter of 1875-76, and he had just returned to Wisconsin when the Icelanders set off for Manitoba. His travels, however, were far from over, as he would later make three more moves, first to North Dakota, then to Alberta, and in the end back to Winnipeg, where he lived out his life.

A small group of children perches precariously atop a pile of matresses and a rocking chair en route to the "Promised Land." Although the photograph shows British immigrants on the Saskatchewan River, it typifies the experience of the first Canadian Icelanders.

On the afternoon of October 11, the party reached Winnipeg, a big moment in the life of what was then a primitive pioneer town of 3,000 people. Crowds of people, many of whom expected the Icelanders to be Eskimos, packed the quayside to take a first look at them. Their expectations were corrected next day by the *Manitoba Free Press*:

> They are smart looking, intelligent and excellent people, and are a most valuable acquisition to the population of our Province.

Despite these warm words, their arrival in Winnipeg was not the happy event many of the Icelanders had expected. No hay had been put up in the settlement, in preparation for cattle which were to accompany the settlers, the result, apparently, of some misunderstanding which would have telling consequences. A sufficient supply of fodder was vital to see the settlers through their first winter, and the arriving Icelanders were under the impression that the trio already in Winnipeg,

The riverboat International, *pictured here outside the Immigrant Shed in Winnipeg, probably in 1875, the same year as it carried 200 Icelanders on their way down the Red River.*

129

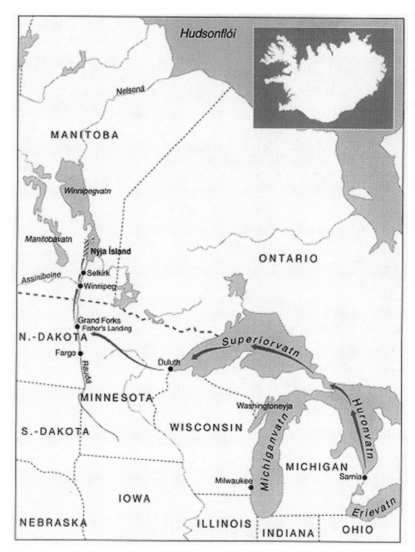

The route taken by the first immigrants to New Iceland lay through the Great Lakes to Duluth. From there, they traversed Minnesota by train to the Red River, where they embarked on a riverboat for Winnipeg, before completing the final stage of their journey up Lake Winnipeg to New Iceland. The map of Iceland is on the same scale.

Skafti Arason, Kristján Jónsson and Sigurður Kristófersson, would have made the necessary arrangements. Instead, the three had obtained work with the CPR.

Faced with the prospect of a winter in the wilderness with no milk, some tried to find work in Winnipeg, and Taylor appears to have encouraged them to do so. At the same time, immigration authorities in the town advised them to leave the women and children behind, at least until the menfolk had built some shelter. However, facilities in Winnipeg were inadequate for a group of this size, and the 60 families themselves did not wish to be split up. The upshot was that only 50-80 Icelanders stayed behind, among them Björn Kristjánsson Skagfjörð and his wife and family, whose description of Glasgow appears at the beginning of this book.

For the rest, there was little else to do but carry on, despite the risks involved. Taylor had received funds from the government sufficient to cover basic necessities and food supplies which would supposedly last until Christmas, when it would be possible to return to Winnipeg by sleigh.

Meanwhile, the Icelanders somehow had to reach their destination more than 150 kilometres away at the mouth of the Icelandic River. The major means of transport on Lake Winnipeg was the steamship *Coleville*, operated by the Hudson Bay Company, but the Icelanders dismissed the fare as too high. The alternative lay in a fleet of huge, flat-bottomed panniers up to 10 metres long and one metre high, used to transport goods and timber up and down the Red River, and towed either by steamships or allowed to drift with the current. With few options to choose from, the Icelanders purchased six of these vessels along with a single York boat, and, with all their worldly goods and possessions safely aboard, they set off on their journey into the unknown.

One of those on board was Stefán Eyjólfsson, who later wrote this account of the voyage in his memoirs, in the style of the old Icelandic sagas.

> The day dawned when everything was ready, and the
> boats lay tied up east of Notre Dame Street in Winnipeg.
> As we boarded, the weather was fine, with clear skies.
> Later that day, I stood with John Taylor on the banks of
> the Red River, and we watched our people busy with
> their preparations. As I gazed to the north where we
> were heading, I turned to Taylor and said, "Now it's
> cloudy in the north." Taylor looked at me, thought for a
> moment, and replied, "The sky is clear, and I can't see
> the clouds of which you speak. If you are losing your

The Dakota was a typical Red River paddle steamer, seen here sometime between 1870 and 1880. The flat-bottomed pannier in the foreground is typical of the craft used to take the Icelanders downriver to New Iceland.

courage, however, this is your last chance to stay behind, as I've tried to advise you and others to do." "I will not stay behind," I replied. The sky was indeed clear, but the goddesses of the future had clouded my vision.

The fleet cast off on Saturday, October 16. Although the weather was sunny and warm and the spirits of the Icelanders high, the journey took a long time. The large, heavy craft proved difficult to steer, especially when travelling in a convoy of six. Each boat carried 40 people, and many wanted to act as skipper and race the others. The barges ran aground on rocks and had to be pulled off, and downstream where the current was sluggish, the barges were pulled along with ropes by men who had waded ashore.

Weather conditions, however, remained highly favourable, and as the party reached the mouth of the Red River at its

*Stefán Eyjólfsson
and his wife, Guðrún
Þorláksdóttir.*

entrance to Lake Winnipeg, the current gradually dropped until the boats stopped moving entirely. At this point, they were taken in tow by the *Coleville* as previously arranged, and in this way the tiny convoy of just over 200 Icelanders and their baggage slowly made its way up the vast expanse of Lake Winnipeg.

To begin with, everything went well, but as the afternoon of Thursday, October 21, the penultimate day of summer, wore on, the wind began to rise and the weather took a turn for the worse. The flat-bottomed craft were no match for the rising waves, and shortly after 4 p.m., in the shelter of Willow Point, the *Coleville*'s skipper dropped anchor about a kilometre and a half offshore. The convoy had barely reached the halfway point of its journey to the mouth of the Icelandic River, and a 40-kilometre voyage through storm-tossed waters remained.

The *Coleville*'s skipper considered it too risky to continue and decided to turn back to the Red River. As a result, there was nothing else for the Icelanders to do but go ashore, and the crew of the York boat set off in search of a suitable place at which to land. The rest of the boats were then towed to shore, and the first landfall of the Icelanders in New Iceland was a narrow peninsula, two kilometres long, known as Willow Point, which the Icelanders immmediately renamed *Víðines*, or *Víðirnes*. There they spent the night, content at having come this far after their long, uncertain journey, but filled with anxiety as to what the future might hold. As things turned out, they would have no time for reflection.

The Founding of New Iceland

FIRST STEPS

The morning after their arrival at Willow Point, which they quickly re-named *Víðirnes*, the Icelanders began exploring their new surroundings. To the north, a broad bay lined with heavy stands of poplar offered not only the prospect of building materials and shelter in plenty, but also a fine natural harbour. Such were its attractions, in fact, that it was chosen as the site for a town the Icelanders decided to name *Gimli*.

For the colonists, those first days in their new home were a period of intense activity. There were possessions and supplies to be brought by the York boat the three kilometres from Willow Point, land to be cleared, and log cabins to be built before the onset of winter. The first of these was intended to house the supplies they had bought in Winnipeg, but the work went badly to begin with as most of the Icelanders had yet to be initiated into the mysteries of wielding an axe.

John Taylor's hired man, Everett Parsonage, however, proved an expert in the art, as did one of the Icelanders, Flóvent Jónsson from Skriðuland, and the pair set about teaching the others.

Considered a master in the art of tree felling by his countrymen, Flóvent Jónsson was one of the first Icelanders to settle on the banks of the Icelandic River.

The next cabin to be built was that of Friðjón Friðriksson, who had assisted Taylor in his dealings with the Canadian government. Divided by a partition wall, one side housed Friðriksson and the other a store which became a focal point for the distribution of food and utensils.

One of the settlers, Skafti Arason, described these first days as follows:

> The race was on to finish the cabins before winter. We didn't
> have to worry about housing any animals, because the only
> one we had between the lot of us was a puppy I was given
> in Winnipeg. When everyone had finished, Friðjón
> Friðriksson had built his little shop, and the government
> agent John Taylor had raised a good-sized dwelling for

himself and his family, made of double logs filled with earth. We thought our new settlement quite substantial. We then elected a five-man council, and named the place Gimli.

Many of the colonists had to wait weeks for a roof over their heads, and some sought temporary shelter in the boats that had brought them from Winnipeg. A layer of ice already covered the surface of Lake Winnipeg, and these crude shelters proved cold and uninviting. When the boats were eventually emptied, they were taken apart and the wood used to make roofs, floor, and doors.

In the meantime, the settlers took shelter in buffalo hide tents obtained on loan from the Hudson Bay Company by John Taylor. The tents were of poor quality and badly sewn.

The Cree tepees pictured here date from around the turn of the century, while the crude shelters erected by many of the first arrivals in New Iceland in October 1875 were buffalo hide tents.

On the eve of winter, they offered little in the way of shelter, but it was in one of them that a baby boy entered the world on a bitterly cold day, November 9, 1875. As a biting wind blew flurries of snow through the holes in their flimsy tent, Sigríður Ólafsdóttir, wife of Jóhann Vilhjálmur Jónsson from Torfufell in Eyjafjörður, Northern Iceland, went into labour and gave birth to a son whom the couple named Jón Ólafur. Despite the conditions, the mother recovered well, and Jón Ólafur Jóhannsson lived to a ripe old age.

Not all of the colonists were as fortunate, however. Many were already weak after their previous winter in Kinmount and exposure to the elements on the long journey from Toronto, and several became sick, although most of them not seriously.

Born on November 9, 1875, Jón Ólafur Jóhannsson was the first locally born Icelandic child to survive in New Iceland.

Despite the fact that it had been housed first, the food bought in Winnipeg with loaned goverment money quickly became damaged. Only the foul-tasting buffalo pemmican proved a match for the conditions, while the beans, wheat and other supplies sold to the Icelanders turned out to have been of poor quality to begin with. Initial attempts at fishing ended mostly in failure, as the mesh of the nets proved too wide. In a bid to boost flagging morale, John Taylor offered a reward of five dollars to the first Icelander to land a fish from Lake Winnipeg, the prize eventually going to Kristmundur Benjamínsson from Ægissíða on Vatnsnes for a goldeye, the sight of which caused a considerable stir among his fellow colonists, who had never seen one before. Perhaps it was the name of his former home in Iceland that brought him luck, *Ægir* being the Old Norse god of the sea.

The Icelanders, however, had little time to hone their fishing skills. Ice came unusually early to Lake Winnipeg that winter, and although it had hardened sufficiently by the end of November to take the weight of a man, ice-fishing was an art the colonists knew of only from hearsay, and there was no one to show them how to do it. At the same time, the cold, biting winds blowing across the exposed surface of the lake were starting to make life difficult, but this was only the beginning. By the time it was over, the winter of 1875-76 would be one of the worst on record since the region was settled, with temperatures plunging to a body-numbing -40°C for days on end.

Said to be the oldest log cabin in Gimli, this cottage, built in 1876 by Friðjón Friðriksson, was moved in 1909 and inhabited for a time after that. Standing in front are Árni Þórðarson, Jóhanna Björnsdóttir, and her husband, Henry Cooney.

Northern Voices

No complete register exists of the first settlers in New Iceland, as some of the original group who arrived in the autumn of 1875 soon returned to Winnipeg, while others left the following summer.

An essay on the subject by Guðlaugur Magnússon appeared in the Almanak of Ólafur S. Thorgeirsson for 1899, in which he compiled a list of farmers said to be "among" the first settlers, although it is clear that several names are missing, including those of all the women and children.

Magnússon's list, however, gives an idea of the names of some of the first colonists and their place of origin in Iceland.

The colonists were badly equipped to face such conditions. Most of them still wore the thin boots and shoes they had purchased in Ontario, and the only clothes they had on their backs were what they had brought with them from Iceland or bought the previous year in Kinmount. Despite this, the Icelanders were said to tolerate the cold very well, some of them not even wearing gloves while working in the forest.

What stood between them and the elements were the cabins they had built. Generally small, one-roomed structures about 15-20 square metres, they were as low and lacking in windows as possible. In all, they totalled 30 in number, a figure dictated by the number of stoves they had bought with the government loan. Sometimes two or three families were crammed into the same rough dwelling, but overcrowding was better than cold.

Since his arrival in Rosseau two years before, Sigtryggur Jónasson had been the undisputed leader of the Canadian-Icelanders, but he was not with them that first winter in New Iceland. Instead, he was at home in Iceland on behalf of the

Múlasýslur (east):
> Jón Guttormsson from Arnheiðarstaðir, Fljótsdalur
> Guðmundur Sveinsson from Fljótsdalur

From Þingeyjarsýslur:
> Friðjón Friðriksson from Harðbakur, Melrakkaslétta
> Árni Friðriksson, his brother
> Sigurður Sigurbjörnsson from Sjóarland, Þistilfjörður
> Kristján Jónsson from Héðinshöfði, Tjörnes
> Skafti Arason from Hringver, Þingeyjarsýsla
> Benedikt Arason, his brother
> Jón Hjálmarsson from Hvarf, Ljósavatnsskarð
> Benedikt Jónasson from Mjóidalur, Bárðardalur
> Sigurður Kristófersson from Neslönd, Mývatn
> Páll Jóhannsson from Víkingavatn, Þingeyjarsýsla

Canadian government searching for likely emigrants, and it is clear from the correspondence of some of the colonists that his leadership was sorely missed.

WINTER COMES

By the beginning of December, the cabins had been completed, and three men, Stefán Eyjólfsson, Páll Jóhannsson from Víkingavatn, and Everett Parsonage were sent out to hunt for food. Armed with guns, they headed north where the found tracks, but the Cree had been there before them, and they returned home empty-handed on December 24 after two weeks spent outside in the bitter frost.

By the end of December, just over two months after their arrival in New Iceland, most of the settlers had chosen land for

 Indriði Indriðason from Laxamýri, Þingeyjarsýsla
Sigurbjörn Jóhannsson from Laxamýri, Þingeyjarsýsla
Eyjafjarðarsýsla (north):
Ólafur Ólafsson from Espihóll, Eyjafjörður
Sigurbjörn Hallgrímsson from Lögmannshlíð, Akureyri
Magnús Hallgrímsson, his brother
Jakob Jónsson from Munkaþverá, Eyjafjörður
Jón Jónsson, his brother
Jóhann V. Jónsson from Torfufell, Eyjafjörður
Þorlákur Björnsson from Fornhagi, Hörgárdalur
Friðbjörn Björnsson, his brother
Jónas Jónasson from Akureyri, brother of Sigtryggur Jónasson
Flóvent Jónsson from Skriðuland, Eyjafjörður
Jón Hallgrímsson from Eyjafjörður

farming, but only four had as yet built on their claims, the majority being still busy felling logs. Competition was keenest for the land lying closest to Gimli and along the lake shore. At the end of December 1875, Skafti Arason wrote in his diary:

> Most have already claimed land, but only four of us have as yet built on ours. The price of staples is as follows: a sack of wheat flour (96 pd.) $3.75; potatoes, when they can be found, 90 cents a bushel; salt pork 60 cents a pound, smoked pork (bacon) 18 cents; flat beans 7 cents pd., salt 3 cents pd, vinegar 40 cents a jar, paraffin 60 cents a gallon. There is little else left, and even if there were, few have money to buy it as most have already received supplies from the government loan.

About a month later, another entry reads as follows:

> Most men are now building on their land all along the lake. Provisions are low, mainly tea, coffee and a little pork and pemmican. A little wheat flour has reached us from Winnipeg, sold at 4½ cents a pound, along with peas at 4

After an unpromising start as one of the three members of the ill-fated hunting party of December 1875, Páll Jóhannsson, seen here the same year with his wife, Guðleif Jónsdóttir, rose to become one of the most prominent citizens of New Iceland.

Guðmundur Sigurðsson, a native of Eyjafjörður
Vigfús Sigurðsson, bookbinder, Eyjafjörður
Helgi Sigurðsson from Vatnsendi, Eyjafjörður
Sigurður Jónsson from Arnarstaðir, Eyjafjörður
Jakob Eyfjörð from Kristnes, Eyjafjörður
Jóhannes Sigurðsson from Árskógsströnd, Eyjafjörður
Skagafjarðarsýsla (north):
Jónas Stefánsson from Þverá, Skagafjörður
Jón Gottvil Pálmason from Efra Nes, Skagi
Jakob Espolín from Frostastaðir, Skagafjörður
Árni Jónsson from Úlfsstaðakot, Skagafjörður
Bjarni Jónasson from Heiðarsel, Skagafjörður
Jósef Schram from Skagafjörður

cents a pound, and wheatmeal at 4 cents a pound. The meal is ground up in large coffee grinders and made into bread.

When the Icelanders arrived in 1875, Canadian government surveyors had not yet mapped New Iceland, apart from a small section at its southern end. When the lake froze, the Icelanders began doing this themselves as best they could, beginning from the south. Each homestead was half a mile, about 800 metres, on each side, and although these crude measurements were not considered absolute, they provided some guidelines for the settlers until an official survey was conducted the following winter, and in keeping with age-old Icelandic custom, each now gave his farm an Icelandic name.

The Icelanders had made their journey into the wilderness without the benefit of clergy, but on weekends John Taylor conducted services which were well attended by his adopted flock. Taylor preached in English, with Friðjón Friðriksson providing a simultaneous translation. As a means of entertainment, a handwritten newsletter was produced and passed from hand to hand,

Húnavatnssýsla (northwest):
Samson Bjarnason from Vatnsnes, Húnavatnssýsla
Friðrik Bjarnason, his brother
Gísli Jóhannsson from Vatnsnes, Húnavatnssýsla
Bjarni Sigurðsson from Vatnsnes, Húnavatnssýsla
Jónatan Halldórsson from Miðfjörður, Húnavatnssýsla
Rafn Jónsson from Kirkjuhvammur, Húnavatnssýsla
Kristmundur Benjamínsson from Ægissíða, Vatnsnes
Benedikt Ólafsson from Eiðsstaðir, Blöndudalur
Jósef Guðmundsson from Húnavatnssýsla
Guðmundur Ólafsson from Ósar, Vatnsnes
Dalasýsla (west):
Einar Jónasson from Harastaðir, Dalasýsla
Jón Gíslason from Hundadalur, Dalasýsla
Björn Jósúa Björnsson from Bær, Dalasýsla
Sigurður Jósúa Björnsson from the same place

but this first attempt at publication proved short-lived. Entitled *Nýi Þjóðólfur* and edited by Jón Guðmundsson from Hjalthús in Þingeyjarsýsla, it appeared only three times. Education, though, fared better, and a school at Gimli opened its doors for the first time early that winter, with teaching conducted by Taylor's niece, Caroline Taylor, and emphasis placed on teaching English to children and adults alike.

The biggest social event came on New Year's Eve. At the stroke of midnight, all who were able gathered round a large bonfire which had been built on the frozen lake to celebrate the dawn of 1876. Following a speech, the old year disappeared in the guise of an old white-bearded man who limped off to the west, and the new year appeared in the form of a youth accompanied by 12 acolytes representing the months, six dressed in green robes, and six in white. The end of their speech signalled a general round of song and dance around the fire, followed by a party at the home of John Taylor, where the fare consisted of a giant pike richly seasoned with a variety of spices.

Sigurður Jakobsson from Dalasýsla
Jósef Miðdal from Miðdalur, Dalasýsla
Strandasýsla (West Fjords):
Oddleifur Sigurðsson from Bær in Hrútafjörður, Strandasýsla
Snæfellsnes (west):
Jóhannes Magnússon from Stykkishólmur
Guðlaugur Magnússon, his brother

As can be seen, several names are missing from this list in addition to those of the women and children, including those of Stefán Eyjólfsson, Magnús Stefánsson, Jónas Guðmundsson, and Jón Guðmundsson. It is also known that Árni Friðriksson, whose name does appear, did not arrive in New Iceland until 1876. Despite its obvious deficiencies, however, Magnússon's list shows that the vast majority of the New Iceland colonists originated in North and Northeast Iceland. Undoubtedly, many of them knew each other well, some of them were related, and the forests and prairies of Manitoba would have rung with the throaty tones of a northern accent.

An Icelandic fisherman's shelter on the shores of Lake Winnipeg. Although dating from the early years of this century, the photograph shows the conditions under which some of the early settlers lived for several months of the year. Dog sleds, never common in New Iceland, were a later development.

Celebrations complete, it was back to the more serious business of life in the new colony. On January 4, a meeting was held and a five-man council was elected, consisting of John Taylor,

Friðjón Friðriksson

Friðjón Friðriksson was born in the Þingeyjarsýsla region of Northern Iceland in 1849. The son of Friðrik Jónsson and Þórhildur Friðriksdóttir, he lived with his parents to the age of 18, when he began working at a variety of jobs. In 1873, having just married his 16-year-old cousin, Guðný Sesselja Sigurðardóttir, he left for North America with the first group of emigrants.

The newlyweds accompanied the group to the Muskoka region of Ontario, but then carried on to Milwaukee where the couple obtained work with a doctor, Friðjón acting as his assistant while his wife kept house. As well as tending cattle and other domestic chores, Friðjón proved useful to his new employer, his fluent knowledge of Danish and English acquired during a spell with a merchant in Iceland proving particularly helpful when accompanying him on visits.

In the autumn of 1874 the couple left for Toronto, where Friðriksson worked for a short time in a shoemaker's shop owned by his brother Árni and Baldvin L. Baldvinsson, but that same winter, they

Ólafur Ólafsson from Espihóll, Friðjón Friðriksson from Harðbakur, Jakob Jónsson from Munkaþverá and Jóhannes Magnússon from Stykkishólmur. Entrusted with safeguarding the interests of the colonists and their welfare, the first task facing it was the care and distribution of the government supplies on which the Icelanders relied for their first two winters in New Iceland.

For many of the colonists, that first winter proved a stern test, and brought real hardship to some, as Stefán Eyjólfsson later recorded in his memoirs.

> Communications with the outside world were almost
> impossible due to heavy snow and the lack of roads. To get
> us through the hardest times, it had been intended to obtain
> frozen milk and fresh meat from other settlements, but this
> proved impossible. After New Year's, supplies were running
> low, and although it was attempted to bring food to the
> most needy, it proved so difficult that they could not even be

moved north to Kinmount, where Friðjón worked in a store owned by Sigtryggur Jónasson.

On the journey to New Iceland, Friðriksson acted as interpreter and special assistant to John Taylor, sent by the Canadian government as an agent, and as the latter was competely unversed in the ways and customs of Icelanders, he often had to excercise considerable tact in his role as go-between. At the same time, he became custodian of the government loan given to the Icelanders, and assigned it as necessary.

In the spring of 1876, Friðriksson opened his own store in Gimli, and although almost destitute, he managed to obtain thousands of dollars worth of goods from Winnipeg on credit. For a time his business flourished, boosted by the arrival of the Large Group the same autumn, but the smallpox epidemic of the following winter, coupled with increased competition from Winnipeg and Selkirk, destroyed it completely, and only his post as postmaster saved Friðriksson from total ruin.

It was in his capacity as postmaster that Friðriksson first ☞

This cluster of log cabins in a forest clearing served as a base for woodcutters from New Iceland.

provided with the most basic necessities. On one occasion, I brought a few pike to Gimli, about 30-40 fish I had caught at the mouth of the Red River. Taylor said I would have to give it to the people there, as some of them had almost completely run out of food. He paid me from his own

displayed the keen business acumen and sense of diplomacy which would serve him so well throughout his life. In the summer of 1877, while the colony was still under strict quarantine, he succeeded in slipping out to the outside world to purchase potatoes and other necessities, an "escape" effected by using a mixture of threats and persuasion. When news of his escapade got out, however, the police were sent to arrest him, but he managed to convince them that there were two men of the same name in New Iceland. His namesake, he claimed, had disappeared, and a respectable figure such as the postmaster could not possibly be the perpetrator of such a criminal act!

When the first administration of New Iceland was formed, Friðriksson was elected vice-governor, so becoming the most powerful figure in the colony apart from the governor himself, Sigtryggur

The total lack of cows during their first winter had grave consequences for the settlers, especially those with children. The cattle seen in this picture were the descendants of the beasts bought with government loan money. Gimli can be seen in the background.

pocket, and told me where the need was greatest. We caught a lot of rabbits, which helped some, but fishing in the Red River was more than the men could stand as there was neither refuge nor shelter from the elements.

As spring approached, people began to fall ill from scurvy and other complaints. One man alone lost 7 of his 9 children, three of them dying in the home of Ólafur Ólafsson, where I myself lived most often. Altogether, I think 35 or 36 people died that winter, spring, or later on of the same causes . . . That winter was the greatest tragedy in the

Jónasson, with whom he later founded and ran the Jónasson-Friðriksson sawmill, which served as a source of life in the colony during its hardest years.

Friðjón Friðriksson and his wife, Guðný, first lived in Gimli, but later moved north to Icelandic River. When the sawmill began to decline, they moved to Winnipeg, and two years later they finally settled at Glenboro in the Argyle district, where Friðjón ran a store for 20 years with great success. In 1906 the couple returned to Winnipeg, where Friðriksson died in 1913. They had five children, three of whom survived, and one of their daughters, Áróra, married Tómas H. Jónsson, who later became Minister of Justice for Manitoba. Three of Friðriksson's brothers, Árni, Olgeir and Friðbjörn, also moved west and became farmers and businessmen in Winnipeg and Glenboro.

history of New Iceland, and worse than the smallpox winter that followed, although that was bad enough.

THE MOSQUITO PLAGUE

Little was done in New Iceland in the spring of 1876 to prepare the ground for sowing. There were two main reasons for this: inexperience among the Icelanders regarding the ways of crop growing, and a chronic shortage of labour to carry out the necessary work. Some of the settlers and those who had no land left the colony and headed south into Manitoba in search of work. Stefán Eyjólfsson made a brave attempt to sow seven acres of wheat in a field about two miles west of Gimli, but his crop

Over 120 years later, it is difficult to imagine the immense physical effort required in settling the vast prairie wilderness. This photograph, one of very few surviving on the subject, shows a team of men attempting to free a York boat stranded in shallows.

failed completely due to lack of proper preparation. Others were forced to eat their crop seed, and at the end of April, Skafti Arason wrote in his diary:

> Very little has been brought in this month, as the roads are still blocked. We are now living on fish, a few beans, and wheat grain intended for sowing.

A month later, he added:

> About May 20, the ice on the lake melted and a steamboat arrived at Víðirnes (Willow Point) harbour carrying supplies of potatoes and flour. By then, most of the people had become ill from scurvy, and many had died. Many others did not recover until they had got milk.

The arrival that summer of the cows expected the previous autumn, and the milk they provided, brought a general improvement in conditions, especially for the children. Migrating birds also provided a ready source of food, with wild berries and herbs adding variety. No healthy man needed fear hunger in New Iceland that summer, as Arason describes in his journal:

> In late May, Guðmundur Ólafsson and Jón Guttormsson bought two cows ... Around mid-June, 20 cows with their calves came to the colony. Three belonged to John Taylor, four to me and my brother and sister, and one to Sigurður Kristófersson. The other 12 were alloted to the families who owned no cows, one to every two or three families. Fish were plentiful from April 20 and right through the summer.

Fish or not, heavy rains made the summer of 1876 unfavourable to agriculture, and the hay crop difficult to cut. Labour was in short supply, and although there were few animals to feed, those there suffered badly from the swarms of mosquitoes which infested the woods, a plague which rendered them almost useless. Despite this, the first oxen were imported to New Iceland that summer.

As communications by land were difficult, the colonists depended entirely on Lake Winnipeg for their contact with the outside world, travelling on small boats and barges which had brought them down the Red River the previous year. That

The first year of a settler family's life is the subject of this illustration by an unknown Canadian artist about 1882. The home consists of a simple log cabin with a single window, and a rough shelter for their "herd"—a pair of oxen and a single cow. A sizeable clearing has been made in the forest, and a fence erected round a ploughed field of grain and vegetables. The only form of transport is the sleigh which stands in the steading awaiting the coming of winter, and the farmer's wife and child stand in the doorway as he and a helper, possibly his son, wrestle with a heavy tree trunk, helped by the oxen.

summer, a few of the settlers made their first trip north to the Whitemud River, which had been christened the Icelandic River, their original destination the previous autumn, when weather conditions had made it impossible to continue. Following a dispute with the Natives, three families settled there.

THE SMALLPOX WINTER

In the autumn of 1876, around a thousand members of the "Large Group" arrived in New Iceland after a difficult journey from Iceland, which for some of them had taken seven weeks. On their arrival, they received little help from the existing colonists, as many had left in search of work and those remaining behind were generally in poor health.

The summer and autumn of 1876 brought much sickness among the colonists, as the crude conditions in which they lived made even the most basic forms of hygiene difficult to practise. Parents had little idea of how best to protect their children from the searing heat, much of the food they ate was strange, and drinking water often poor. As a result, they were ill prepared to face the biting northerly gales and blizzard conditions which signalled the onset of winter.

By the autumn of 1876, the coastline of New Iceland, a strip of land some 50 km long, had been fully settled. As few of the new arrivals could obtain land anywhere south of Árnes, that area was also quickly settled north as far as the banks of the Icelandic River. Many of the colonists chose to row themselves, their families and possessions north on Lake Winnipeg from Gimli to Big Island, first known as Mikley and later re-christened Hecla Island, where they claimed land. When the Icelanders arrived on the island, they found a sawmill, but it had ceased operation and been left in the care of a watchman.

For the new arrivals and older colonists alike, the race was now on to beat the first snows of winter. There was wood to be cut for fuel, shelter to be built for themselves and their families, stables to be constructed for the cows (which were often shared among three or four households), and hay to be cut and carried home for fodder. Usually, however, the first task facing the would-be homesteader was to find land, make his own crude survey, and claim it.

We are told little of the role of women and children in the early years of New Iceland. The division of labour was doubtless the same as it had been at home, with the womenfolk taking care of the children and performing the endless round of cooking, cleaning, and other domestic chores. No less than the men, they had to adapt to new ways in their new home, as they learned to cope with housing conditions and food very different from anything they had ever known. In addition, it was usually to them that the harrowing task of tending to sick and dying children fell.

In the winter of 1876-77, the Canadian government

conducted an official survey of the New Iceland colony, which proved to be a strip of land 58 km long, running from Boundary Creek in the south to the Icelandic River in the north. Averaging 14.5 km in breadth, it varied from 18 km at its widest to 13 km at its narrowest, and covered a total area of 850 km². In all, it included 1,296 parcels of land, each 800 m x 800 m in size, with straight lines cut around every square-mile section to show how each should be divided into four farms.

About the same time, three sites were surveyed as potential towns: Gimli to the south, Sandvík to the north, and Lundur on the banks of the Icelandic River, but of the three, only Gimli and Lundur (Riverton) would stand the test of time.

A Medical Man Writes Home

One of the most graphic—and harrowing—accounts of the smallpox epidemic of 1876–77 can be found in a letter written by a young medical student, Augustus Baldwin, to his sister Phoebe on March 13, 1877. In it, he describes his experiences from November 26, 1876, when he and his companion, Dr. Lynch, arrived at Gimli to vaccinate and treat the colonists. Despite its idiosyncratic spelling and syntax, it provides a telling account not only of the dreadful effects of the disease itself, but also of the pitiful conditions in which the Icelanders lived.

Next morning, I went over with Dr. Lynch—to visit the Hospital. It was full of patients, of course all with smallpox. They were to be seen in every stage, some dieng—and some convalescent. The next day, I went to visit several houses and such a sight you never saw—Every house had somebody down with the disease—The settlement extends about forty five Miles. And the houses were of the worst discription. I had to stoop to go into nearly every house—There were some doors so low, that I had to go on my hands and knees to get in—And such filth, I cannot describe it—And fancy, I had to sleep in these wretched houses. I always slept with my clothes on, so that I would not get lice on me. I wore a

Shortly after the arrival of the "Large Group" in the autumn of 1876, work began on the construction of an 8-metre-broad road running the length of the colony along the shore of Lake Winnipeg, and when tree felling and land clearing began they provided a source of labour for many of the Icelanders.

However, that same autumn also saw the outbreak of a mysterious illness among the colonists which no one at first was able to identify. Characterized by general malaise, fever and a rash, the first cases were identified at Icelandic River, where it remained confined for about six weeks. The possiblility that it might be smallpox did occur to some, but no one worried unduly, as most of the victims appeared to be recovering. By

leather coat. The houses are all one room. And in some there would be 18 or 19 in them. They would all be huddled together like so many pigs —And then those houses that had room, they would have their cows in them—I had to sleep several times in the same house in which they had their cows at the other end of the room—in which I was sleeping—You can imagin that it would not smell very sweet—And one of the cows were neigh hir accouchement—And the way she would grunt and groan. She would not let me sleep very much—

Delicate sensitivities put aside, Baldwin spent the winter in the colony, tending the sick and treating them as best he could. His guide, whom he does not name, contracted the disease and had to be replaced. He faced terrible weather and freezing conditions, and at one point became sick himself, although not of smallpox. Through it all, he practised his calling wherever he found a need, at one point being forced to amputate three legs from two men, but most of the time he struggled through the winter cold from farm to farm, doing his best to alleviate the terrible sufferings of the Icelanders.

mid-November, however, the situation had become much more serious, and when at least three Icelanders and four Cree had died, John Taylor wrote to Winnipeg requesting medical help. The response was swift, and later that month, three doctors, Young, Lynch and Baldwin, arrived at the scene.

Immediately, they identified the disease as smallpox, and an emergency hospital was set up in the warehouse in Gimli, a rough log construction less than 50 m² in size. Despite the cramped conditions, only one of the first 64 patients died, but as news of the epidemic spread, panic gripped the colonists, most of whom were forced to stay indoors due to the extreme cold, their fear increasing in tandem with their isolation.

When news of the epidemic reached Winnipeg, panic broke out in the town, and New Iceland was placed in quarantine. A quarantine station was hastily established south of the colony at Netley Creek, where travellers were bathed, dressed in government-issue clothing, and detained for 15 days before being allowed to continue on their way if they proved symptom free.

According to one source, some of the Icelanders, quick to spot a good opportunity when they saw one, turned up at the

For three months I did nothing but treat for small pox—so you can imagin that I have seen enough of it—when I went to some of the houses, I would find perhaps some six or eight sick, some that had only a few hours to live—You would see Old Men and women, Young men and girls, and poor little infants that would make the hardest heart ache for them, and to see them at their Mother's breast and perhaps the next time I came around their little bodies would be put out side till they had time to make a rough box to bury them in. On my second trip I hear that there was a family on Big Black Island. So I went to see them. And such a sight. The Mother had just got over the small pox and her infant on her brest, dieing and they had not a thing to cover the poor thing—The house was so small that I could not stand up in it. I was compeled to sit down. I brought my tea and pamacan, and me and my Indian guide had station dressed in their worst rags and left with a new set of clothing, but if they did, it was small compensation for the terrible price they had to pay. In December alone, some 40 perished from smallpox, their deaths hastened, in the opinion of the doctors, by the extreme cold. As the period of quarantine wore on, hunger too became a problem, as no supplies were reaching the settlers, and the lethargy, hopelessness and general weakness which accompany starvation were added to the horrors of the disease itself.

By the turn of the year, the epidemic had spread through the entire colony, with only 11 homesteads of some 200 escaping its devastating effects, although its effects varied, as most adult colonists had been vaccinated at home in Iceland.

If things were bad for the Icelanders, they were much worse for the Natives, as demonstrated by this curt account from the memoirs of Magnús Stefánsson from Fjöll in Kelduhverfi, who served as interpreter to the doctors.

> Once during the smallpox winter, I accompanied Dr.
> Baldwin east across the Lake to Sandy River. We rode on
> dog sleighs with the well-known Native, John Ramsay,

to have our dinner on that a lone—after a whole days travel—They had no flour infact, had nothing but fish.—I left what medicine and nurishment I had—which I brought for the sick—and to see their eyes brighten up, to hopes that it came in time to save their little one can never be forgoten—But alas, the little thing only nine months old, dies next day. And then they had to put the little thing on top of the house till they could get some boards to make a box for the little one—I had a pretty hard time myself, but when I looked at the poor Icelanders I faired like a King . . .

All in all, 102 Icelanders, mainly children and youths, are believed to have died in the smallpox epidemic of 1876-77.

acting as our guide. There was a large village at Sandy River consisting both of tepees and houses. It contained not a living soul. The entire population of 200 had been wiped out. We set fire to everything and burned it to ashes.

After the New Year, the epidemic began to die down in New Iceland, although in January, it claimed another 17 victims. By the end of February, there were no further cases at Gimli, and the colony recorded its last death from smallpox at the beginning of March. Although a variety of other diseases, notably scurvy, continued to plague the Icelanders, the epidemic was declared officially over at the begining of April.

When it was over, the outbreak had lasted six months, and claimed the lives of 102 Icelanders, mainly children and teenagers. No such figures exist to record the sufferings of the Native people.

Although the colony had been officially declared smallpox-free, the quarantine blockade at Netley Creek remained in place until well into the summer, cutting New Iceland off from the outside world for almost 10 months altogether. Even the colony's postal service ceased almost completely, as outgoing letters had to be treated in carbolic acid fumes. In addition, other colonists tended to avoid any unnecessary contact with the New Icelanders for some time after the outbreak was over, making it difficult for them to find work.

When the quarantine was eventually lifted, it was decided to disinfect the entire colony. This process was overseen by the recently elected governor, Sigtryggur Jónasson, under the supervision of a Dr. Beddome, who sent the following instructions to the chairmen of the councils of the four districts which comprised the New Iceland colony:

> The cleansing should be conducted by removing every article from every house. Wash all clothing and bedding in boiling, soapy water and dry it. Scrub every house and its furnishings with boiling, soapy water, and whitewash the houses inside and out. Remove the down from all quilts and pillows. Dry it in the wire baskets intended for the purpose, and place it above fires of smoking sulphur sticks. Quilt covers and pillowcases should be boiled in soapy water, or burned if they are in poor condition.

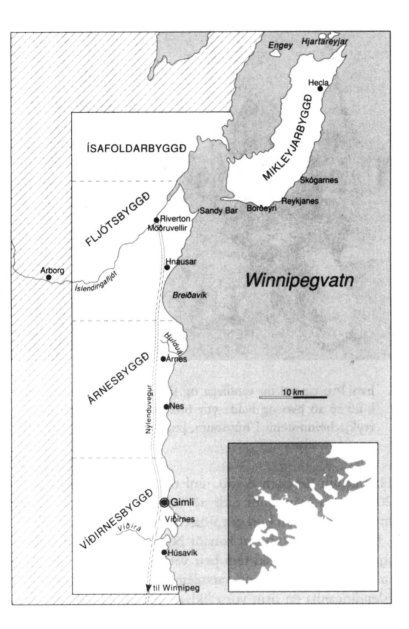

ÍSAFOLDARBYGGÐ

MIKLEYJARBYGGÐ

Engey Hjartareyjar

Hecla

Skógarnes

Reykjanes

FLJÓTSBYGGÐ

Sandy Bar Borðeyri

Riverton
Möðruvellir

Hnausar

Arborg

Íslendingafljót

Winnipegvatn

Breiðavík

ÁRNESBYGGÐ

Huldua

Árnes

Nýlenduvegur

Nes

10 km

VÍÐIRNESBYGGÐ

Gimli

Viðirnes

Víðirá

Húsavík

til Winnipeg

The New Iceland colony consisted of four districts; Víðirnesbyggð (Willow Point), Árnesbyggð (River Point), Fljótsbyggð (Icelandic River) and Mikleyjarbyggð (Big Island). Strictly speaking, the strip of land to the north known as Ísafoldarbyggð was not originally part of the colony, but its rich grass-land attracted a large number of settlers. The first colonists planned to reach the mouth of the Icelandic River, but got no further than Gimli, which, along with the Icelandic River settlement from which it was separated by a two-day journey, soon became the focal point of the colony. Árborg, now one of the main areas of population in the region, originally lay outside the colony, but grew rapidly after the arrival of the railway. The map shows only the chief farms, but the number of available homesteads totalled 1,296. By comparison, the inset shows a map of Reykjavík and the surrounding area on the same scale.

People should strip in the tents which will be provided, one for the men, another for the women, and discard the clothes in which they stand, which should then be washed by others. They should then scrub themselves thoroughly, and dress themselves in fresh clothing which has been washed and smoked in sulphur. Lastly, sulphur should be

The first two years in New Iceland were particularly difficult for the youngest colonists. Large numbers died from disease and exposure, while the survivors quickly had to learn to fend for themselves. This photograph was taken in the second decade of this century on an unknown farm in the colony.

burned in the houses when everything has been moved back inside.

The disinfection was carried out from June 8-30, and the quarantine centre at Netley Creek finally closed on July 20, ten months after the epidemic began, and four months after the last case had been identified.

The smallpox epidemic and its consequences paralyzed New Iceland. Due to the long isolation it brought, the colonists were forced to eke out a meagre existence on government loan supplies and any fish they could catch. Physically, its effects would remain etched on the faces of many of the Icelanders in the form of the pock marks they took with them to their graves, but the mental scars were probably much deeper.

Ironically, weather conditions in the spring and summer of 1877 proved very favourable for agriculture, producing a fine hay crop and good harvest for those who had managed to plant seed. The herd of government cows increased by 230, bringing a vast improvement to the daily life and diet of every household. The newspaper *Framfari* appeared for the first time, and the spiritual welfare of the colonists was improved by the arrival of two Icelandic Lutheran pastors. Few new immigrants arrived from Iceland that summer, however, as news of the epidemic had reached home.

Despite the terrible hardships the population of New Iceland had undergone, the end of the second year proved a turning point in the colony's history. The whole region had now been explored and its best land claimed. Its population, now about 1,100, had acquired valuable experience of life in the Canadian wilderness, and of the customs and working practices of neighbouring settlers from other nations. Outside the colony, many Icelanders had settled in Winnipeg and were beginning to make their way in their new home.

The problems of New Iceland were, however, far from over. Ahead lay many hard years, but eventually most of the colonists would reap the benefits of their efforts. Gradually, they adapted to conditions in their new home, learned how to plant and harvest crops, improved their fisheries, and educated their children. Others, however, chose to leave New Iceland and make a new life elsewhere.

Although based very much on native Icelandic customs and tradition, life for the colonists was much more varied than that which they had left behind. Until 1897, only a few non-Icelanders settled in New Iceland, and Icelandic was spoken in every home. Little by little, however, the old social mores of rural Iceland faded under the influence of the cosmopolitan culture of the New World, as parents encouraged their children to learn English and accepted intermarriage with those of other nations.

THE GOVERNOR-GENERAL PAYS A VISIT

On September 14, 1877, the citizens of New Iceland received the most important visitor in the settlement's short history when Lord Dufferin, the Governor-General of Canada, arrived in the fledgling village of Gimli.

By no means an unknown figure to the Icelanders, Dufferin had visited their country some 20 years before, and had personally intervened two years previously to secure the government loan that had made their colony possible.

As a result, he was welcomed enthusiastically, his reception made all the warmer by the brilliant sunshine reflecting off the surface of the lake. During a short tour of the settlement, which included a visit to every home in Gimli and several farms nearby, he greeted the settlers with a handshake and discussed their needs and priorities. The business of the day complete, there then followed an informal gathering attended by more than 100 Icelanders. After a speech by Friðjón Friðriksson, a written copy of which was presented to the Governor translated into English, Dufferin replied, praising the Icelanders for their hard work and enterprise. The rest of his address, later translated into Icelandic and published in *Framfari*, shows Her Majesty's representative's practical concern for the welfare of these new subjects.

> The three arts most necessary to a Canadian colonist are the felling of timber, the ploughing of land, and the construction of highways, but as in your own country no one of you had ever seen a tree, a cornfield, or a road, it is not to be expected that you should immediately exhibit any expertness in these accomplishments, but practice and experience will soon make you masters of all three, for you possess in a far greater degree than is probably imagined that which is the essence and foundation of all superiority —intelligence, education, and intellectual activity. In fact I have not entered a single hut or cottage in the settlement which did not contain, no matter how bare its walls or scanty its furniture, a library of 20-30 volumes; and I am informed that there is scarcely a child amongst you who cannot read and write.

Dufferin then proceeded to encourage the colonists in their efforts, while offering them a reminder of the true essence of Canada as seen at the time.

> And remember that in coming amongst us you will find yourselves associated with a race both kindly hearted and cognate to your own, nor in becoming Englishmen and subjects of Queen Victoria need you forget your own time-honoured customs or the picturesque annals of your forefathers. On the contrary, I trust you will continue to cherish for all time the heart-stirring literature of your nation, and that from generation to generation your little ones will continue to learn in your ancient Sagas that industry, energy, fortitude, perseverance, and stubborn endurance have ever been the characteristics of the noble Icelandic race.

New Land, New Life

STRANGE DAYS

Although life on the prairie needs no introduction to those who live there, to the Icelanders it was a world apart from anything they had ever known, beginning with the cornerstone of agrarian life, the seasons themselves.

Unlike Iceland, with its notoriously unpredictable weather and well-documented ability to produce four seasons in the space of a few hours irrespective of the time of the year, Manitoba enjoys a relatively stable continental climate of hot summers and cold winters, with significant variations in temperature between night and day.

Compared with the land they had left, the Icelanders found the seasons in their new home clearly defined and difficult to deal with, at least at first. Nothing they had ever experienced had prepared them for the sudden thaws of early April which can bring a sharp rise in temperatures from -15-30°C to 15-30°C in the space of just a few weeks, or for the long, hot springs and summers which follow.

But as we have already seen, it was the return of winter in October and the subsequent imprisonment of Lake Winnipeg in its icy grip for the next five months that affected the first settlers most of all. This strange sense of permanence, tied to a near absence of the ferocious gales that habitually lash their native land for several months of the year, meant the early settlers had to learn quickly to adapt to a whole new way of life.

At the same time, its position at 51°N places New Iceland on the same latitude as European cities such as Brussels or Dresden. As a result, daylight is much more evenly distributed than in old Iceland, with no short summer nights or short winter days to mark the time of year. Coupled with thunderstorms and the occasional tornado, weather phenomena almost unknown in their homeland, the Icelanders found the prairie climate very strange indeed.

The colony's rich variety of insect life was considered one of the major drawbacks of New Iceland. The reason can be readily seen from this photograph, probably about 1920.

This relative stability was not confined to climate alone. Far from the mountains of their native land, the early Icelandic settlers must have found the vastness of the wide prairie sky and the endless rolling plains and forests both exciting and vaguely threatening. But they were also quick to appreciate its natural beauty, particularly that of its great forests, whose autumn splendour was captured in a poem by Stephan G. Stephansson.

> Leaves fell from every branch
> In the gentle whisper of autumn
> Every one in its own soft breeze
> These shooting stars of the forest frieze
> The sky rained colour

If the climate and landscape were strange, the richness of prairie wildlife was positively astounding, with its variety of creatures of all shapes and sizes. Of the larger animals, moose were prized for their meat, their English name, which sounds the same as the Icelandic word for *mouse*, giving rise to a wealth of jokes and witty anecdotes among the Icelanders. On a smaller scale, the colonists quickly learned to trap rabbits and hares, and prairie chickens were so numerous that even children could easily hunt them with sticks. Not all the prairie's inhabitants were friendly, however, and the Icelanders were no match for a determined brown bear.

One well-known tale tells of a New Iceland farmer who found a bear rummaging through the rubbish outside his cabin. Taking a shot, he succeeded in frightening it off, but unde-terred, the bear returned the next day. Once again, the farmer managed to scare it off, but after a few days of the same thing, the bear gradually became used to the efforts of the hapless marksman. Finally, while the animal's attention was occupied by a huge fish head, the farmer managed to hit it from close range, but only succeeded in blowing the fish out of its mouth, at which the bear, no doubt somewhat relieved, sauntered casually off into the woods.

Other smaller mammals aroused a variety of emotions. While the countless squirrels and clans of beavers and otters populating the lakes and rivers caused little inconvenience to their immigrant neighbours, other rodents such as rats and groundhogs, were viewed with less tolerance. Most hated of all, however, was the humble skunk, for obvious reasons.

Prairie bird life was also new to the Icelanders, with the pelican and bald eagle adding an exotic touch to the many colourful woodland species, most of which were unknown in Iceland, a country almost entirely devoid of trees.

The sounds of the prairie, too, were strange, particularly in summer when the constant croaking of frogs was surpassed only by the buzzing of mosquitos, hornets, bees and wasps, most of which were new to the settlers. Despite an abundance of spiders and beetles, they faced only two kinds of snakes, neither dangerous.

The vast tracts of forest, which covered New Iceland and still cover thousands of square miles of Northwestern Canada today, featured a host of trees also new to the colonists, who were quick to appreciate their potential. Poplar, maple, birch, oak, ash, spruce, elm, and several other varieties offered a ready source of fuel, building materials and timber.

This vast natural storehouse also offered a ready supply of wild berries and nuts, including strawberries, saskatoons, wild currants, wild plums, hazelnuts, and chokecherries, while crops grew readily in its rich, dark soil.

Lake Winnipeg and the rivers and streams of New Iceland teemed with a variety of fish, most of which the Icelanders had never seen before but were quick to name in their own tongue, with whitefish, goldeye, sunfish, sucker, pickerel, and catfish becoming *hvítfiskur, gullauga, sólfiskur, sugfiskur,* and *kattfiskur.*

For the early colonists, however, exploiting these rich natural resources lay somewhere in the future, for, unlike the Natives who had lived there for centuries, the Icelanders were very much strangers in a strange land.

CLAIMING A HOMESTEAD

As was the case in Manitoba and the rest of the Canadian West, the settlement of New Iceland was subject to the Dominion Lands Act, federal legislation aimed at attracting farmers to the Canadian West.

Under its terms, any male aged 18 years or over, or any woman with a family to support, could apply for 160 acres (64 hectares) of Dominion land, with homesteads allotted on a first come, first served basis. For the prospective homesteader or his authorized representative, filing entry for a quarter section involved a visit to the nearest Dominion Lands Office, where he, or she, registered for the land by completing an application and paying a set fee of $10.

To obtain full ownership, however, the claimant had to fullfil a number of basic conditions, which were soon translated into Icelandic, and this process, known as "proving up," could be accomplished in any one of three ways.

The realities of the Dominion Land Offices did not live up to the imposing title.
Here, a CPR agent concludes a deal somewhere on the prairie.

1. By living on and cultivating the land for 3 years, never being absent for more than 6 months of each year, or:

2. By living for 2 years within 2 miles of the land, then occupying a home on the land continuously for at least 2 months of each subsequent year until a patent was issued; by breaking 10 acres the first year, and 15 acres the second and third years, or:

3. By breaking 5 acres the first year and 10 acres the second, seeding the first 5 the second year as well as building a home, then beginning continuous residence the third year, and being absent for no more than 6 months of any year for at least 3 years.

In short, acquiring land involved occupying and improving it, and those who had acquired a patent for their land before 1887 were also entitled to apply for a second claim.

Central to the system were the teams of government surveyors sent to map and measure the vast prairie, which was then divided into large squares of land, each 36 square miles (about 100 km^2) in area, known as Townships. These were then subdivided into square-mile units known as Sections, each of which accommodated four farms. As a result, each Township contained 144 homesteads, half a mile by half a mile (800 x 800 m) in area, each of which was numbered like the squares on a giant chess board, a feature highlighted by Stephan G. Stephansson in his poem "Kurlý."

> Like a retracted chess board, the ruler was drawn
> Over the wooded, populous countryside
> Every farmer's estate stood close to the road

Logs in place, the cabins were sealed with a mixture of mud and straw applied by hand. Here, a Ukrainian couple put the finishing touches on the universal building style favoured by the early settlers, c. 1905.

A one-and-a-half-storey New Iceland log cabin of the better variety, with large windows, a porch, lean-to kitchen, and cellar, probably just before the turn of the century. The man to the left seems to be steering a horse-drawn hay mower, while the figure to the right sits on a buggy.

Enclosed in a fenced-off square
Each mile-corner a crossroads, a road with no bends
No steep path lay betwixt ridge or gorge
Half of them had been laid by noon
And the rest before evening

At the end of the agreed period, homestead inspectors came to check that all the conditions had been fulfilled, in which case the farmer became the owner. If not, an extension was granted. If abandoned, the land was offered to anyone else who wanted it, not an uncommon event as many of the first settlers moved on.

In the case of New Iceland, the Dominion Lands Act seems to have been interpreted fairly liberally. The settlement was also unique in that, according to the agreement with the Canadian government, no one except Icelanders could claim land there, a proviso that technically remained in force until 1897.

The lie of the land also brought some variations to the pattern, with some of the farms on Lake Winnipeg and the

I was proud of my boys

Sigurður Erlendsson from Aðaldalur in Þingeyjarsýsla, his wife, Guðrún Eiríksdóttir, and their five children arrived in Canada with the "Large Group" in 1876. Writing years later, he describes their trip to New Iceland. After a journey of several weeks, their craft ran aground at the mouth of the Red River on Lake Winnipeg.

"The next morning, we set off for Gimli. Most heads of households were given twin-oared boats known as tubs, little more than a few planks nailed together at both ends, but able to carry 1,400 lbs in a dead calm. I was given one of these, and it carried our chest, bedding, my wife, and four of our children, Stefán, 12, Jóhannes, 8, Kristjana, 5, and Sigfús, 1½. Our fifth, Jakobína, 16, was staying on a farm three miles from Winnipeg. With this load and two oars I set off north and had reached the inlet at Gimli about 3 o'clock, when a sudden thunderstorm soaked us all to the skin. We landed at the north end of the bay and arrived at Gimli on foot, my wife carrying the baby in her arms, wet through and through. I carried the girl, and the two boys walked. I was given a flat-roofed cabin with no door in which to spend the night. It was not a good place for tired, drenched folk to be.

Erlendsson spent the next weeks searching for land for himself and his family. He rowed with another man up river, but the trip went badly due to high winds, and the land they saw was nothing but marshes. Having spent more than a week looking in the area round Gimli, he decided to head for Mikley, where he and Helgi Tómasson finally selected two parcels of land. Erlendsson obtained permission to spend the winter in a shack owned by the island sawmill, and although it was little more

Icelandic River surveyed as "river lots" (longer and narrower than usual), to allow access to water, which was for some time a major means of transportation.

Few sources exist to tell us how the first settlers chose their

---

than a hovel, he considered himself lucky. "It had no chimney, and life inside was nearly impossible due to the smoke." Undaunted, he returned to Gimli for his wife and children, and rowed back to Mikley. "By this time, I was at the end of my tether from a stomach ailment, and the trip took us a week." The family had little in the way of food, but managed to survive on fish. Then, the winter snows began.

Almost every day, my son Stefán, in his 12th year, and I battled our way into the forest through snow halfway up our thighs, or even further, in search of dry wood, which we then had to cut and carry back to our clay stove, kept burning even though we were nearly choking from the smoke or shivering from the cold. Between Christmas and New Year, my stomach was so bad that I thought every day would surely be my last, and I would leave behind a widow and four children.

Despite his hardships, Erlendsson survived, and he and his family escaped the smallpox then ravaging the rest of the colony.

In April, I claimed land a mile from here on the east shore of the island and built a log cabin that wasn't much to look at. Stefán was my right-hand man and, despite his youth, helped me with every task. Jóhannes, then 8, brought us our mid-day meal (fried whitefish), and I thought he did very well, walking north more than a mile without a path to follow through freezing, wintry storms. I was proud of my boys, and believed they would make something of themselves if they lived long enough.

They did. The couple's five children all lived to adulthood, and today their descendants can be found all over Manitoba and elsewhere. And as their father had predicted, Stefán and Jóhannes both became successful.

lands when they arrived in New Iceland in 1875, but they all seem to have been reasonably satisfied. Initially, the best claims probably went to those who arrived first or with "connections," the others having to settle for land further away from Gimli and the lake.

However, with the arrival of the "Large Group" the following autumn, it immediately became clear that the land along the Icelandic River, several miles to the north, was better suited to farming than the Gimli area itself.

A PLACE TO CALL HOME

For the Icelanders, one of the most attractive features of New Iceland was its vast forests, a seemingly endless source of wood for building materials, saleable timber and fuel, and many doubtless envisioned cozy little log cabins in the woods, with fires burning brightly and the bitter winter cold kept firmly locked outside the door.

Dreams aside, what is not in doubt is that when the first group landed at Víðirnes on that freezing October day in 1875, their first priority was to build a roof over their heads. Most of them had already spent a year in Canada, and their time in Rosseau and Kinmount had given them some experience in the construction of housing.

Writing home to Iceland at the beginnning of 1874, one of them, Vigfús Sigurðsson, described how these log cabins were built.

> New houses are built from straight logs piled horizontally on top of one another to form walls, and cut at the corners in dovetails. The spaces between are then filled with moss, and the outside covered with wet clay which hardens like lime. When holes have been cut for the window and door, logs are piled up to form gables, one on top of the other, cut shorter as they ascend. The frame is completed with a ridge pole and rafters just like at home

In the absence of a sufficient supply of lumber, turf was used to roof the most primitive log cabins. The structure on the left awaits completion, as can be seen from the uncut logs at its corners. By the time this photograph was taken in New Iceland, these structures were probably used as stables, whatever their original purpose.

in Iceland, and roofed with branches or turf. The roof and floor are finished with split logs, although some prefer to use spruce for the floor, and smoothed with an adze. The result is a cabin as warm as any timber house. Everyone who can obtains a cooking stove, which also serves as a source of heat. These are expensive, however, costing anywhere from 24 to 40 dollars, and some of the poorer people have to be content with making their own stoves, using stones piled up like bricks.

Crude and simple as they were, the cabins served to keep out the worst of weather and wind, if, that is, they were built by men who knew what they were doing.

As everything had to be carried and shaped by hand tools, the size of these dwellings was dictated to a large extent by the strength of those who built them. Carrying several logs up to four metres long was back-breaking work for even the toughest

A typical log cabin, seen in New Iceland about 1930.

of men and, as a result, the New Iceland cabins were small, averaging only about 15 square metres in size. Built in a hurry and intended only as a temporary measure, they were little more than crudely constructed hovels, poorly lit and badly ventilated. Light was provided by a single window, if any existed at all, and access was gained through a rough, low door. With roofs covered with turf, branches or split logs, fire was an ever-present hazard, and several instances of homes burning are recorded in the colony, although without serious injury to the inhabitants, something of a wonder, given that up to 15-20 people could be packed into a single dwelling at any given time.

Only one building existed in New Iceland when the colonists arrived, but it served them well. A small trading post built by the Hudson Bay Company, it stood on the banks of the Icelandic River and had been used by the traders who purchased meat and furs from the local Natives.

When the first Icelandic families arrived in 1876, the shelter it provided gave Ólafur Ólafsson, Jóhannes Sigurðsson, and Flóvent Jónsson (who will all appear again later in this book) valuable time which they used to construct sturdy structures, each roofed with planks from the barges on which they had travelled.

In his memoirs, Símon Símonarsson from Heiðarsel describes a cabin he built near Gimli, along with Erlendur Ólafsson from Ytri-Brekkur in Blönduhlíð. When they began work at the beginning of November, the pair had lived for several weeks in one of the "miserable tents," where Símonarson had just spent two weeks ill in bed in "this terrible abode of sleeplessness, toil, exposure, and bad food."

Símon Símonarson.

Despite this, he survived, but when the partners began building, most of the best lots between the warehouse and the lake had already been claimed. Forced to move further south, the pair built a rough log cabin, 16 square metres in size. Barely fit for human habitation, this man-high structure was covered with a thatched roof, and the holes between the logs were chinked with clay as best they could.

Entrance to their new home was gained through a door set in the east wall, flanked on each side by a small window. Rough beds were made from rails, and the stove stood in the middle of the floor. Crude it may have been, but compared to the tent they had left, it was a palace.

A graphic description of early Gimli appears in an article which appeared in the *Manitoba Free Press* in the autumn of 1877, describing the visit of Lord Dufferin.

> Gimli is about a mile and a half long and half a mile broad.
> There is only one street, more a cattle track than a street, as
> it lies between two fences in half-cleared prairie dotted with

By the time this photograph was taken of the farm Laufhóll in Árnesbyggð early this century, its occupants had already left.

The landscape of New Iceland is nowhere more picturesque than at Willow Creek. The homestead seen here is Víðirnes, just south of Gimli, built in 1887 by Jónas Jónasson Bergmann from Miðfjörður, Northern Iceland, and his second wife, Kristín Jóhannesdóttir. By then aged 55 and half-blind, Bergmann was the father of 20 children with his two wives, nine of whom survived. Eight were born in Canada, while one of his sons, Guðmundur, was a farmer at Reykir in Iceland.

tree stumps, but it is not as muddy as the main street in Winnipeg after a shower of rain. The inhabitants' houses stand just off the street on both sides. Most are made from logs, with log floors, low doors, small windows and, it appears, no chimneys, so light and air are, for the most part, excluded.

Hewn log structures soon replaced this crude style of building. Log walls and planked roofs, floors, and doors served the colonists well, and one-and-a-half-storey houses quickly became common. The advent of sawmills led to a general improvement in construction methods, and people gradually began moving to bigger, more comfortable frame houses.

A simple number may have been enough for the Canadian government, but not for the Icelanders, who quickly began to name their new farms, although these titles were never recognized officially. The names they chose were based on those they knew from home, and, as had been the case in Iceland, were soon appended to the names of the men who farmed them. While everybody knew Þorgrímur at Akur well, identifying Þorgrímur Jónsson required a bit more thought.

Some of the homesteads such as *Halldórsstaðir* were named

Bjarkavellir, a farm near Riverton on the Icelandic River, seen about 1903. Home of the well-known settler Hálfdán Sigmundsson. The people in the foreground are members of his family.

for the men who first settled them. Others, like *Skógarhöfði* (Bushy Point), *Kelduland* (Bog Land), *Fagranes* (Fair Point), and *Akurvellir* (Acre Fields) took their names from natural features. When the Rev. Páll Þorláksson visited New Iceland in 1878, his relative Hans Níelsson was busy building a house. He asked Páll

Better or Worse?

Following his sojourn in New Iceland, the Rev. Jón Bjarnason returned home to Iceland, where he described his experiences in *Ísafold*. By then, *Framfari* had ceased publication, and no news had been received from the colony for some time.

The soil is fertile, the forests more than plentiful, and the waters teem with all kinds of fish. Indeed, it was fish more than anything else which first attracted the Icelanders to the area. However, the colony has so many drawbacks that there is a very real danger that the vast majority will give up and leave. Among these is the fact that it is so full of marshes, that the cost of building passable summer roads would be so high that I fear the poor settlers could not afford it. In addition, the winters are long and bitterly cold.

Despite this, the conditions of the colonists are nothing like as bad as some have claimed here in Iceland. In fact, I am convinced that conditions here are worse, and certainly no better, than in New Iceland in recent times. And housing there is better than anything I have ever seen here. Last New Year, the settlers had 1,400 cattle, even though they themselves number just over 1,000.

As the prosperity of the Icelanders grew, so too did their houses. Flugumýri, on the Icelandic River, was the home of Þorvaldur Þórarinsson and his wife, Helga Tómasdóttir, seen outside at their front door in 1894. Helga is holding Tryggvi, an infant. Þorvaldur's daughter Steinunn stands beside them, as does Jakob Briem, while the ox-drawn mower is driven by the poet Guttormur J. Guttormsson, with "Steini" from Selkirk by his side. Built on extremely marshy ground, the house was moved to a nearby site six years later.

to name it, who after gazing for a few minutes at the thick forest surrounding it, suggested *Grenimörk*, meaning "spruce wood." And *Grenimörk* it was.

Some christened their land after farms or estates in Iceland, and while names such as *Möðruvellir*, *Skriðuland*, and *Grund* served to remind them of their former homes in Eyjafjörður, *Skálholt* and *Hólar* were named in honour of Iceland's two episcopal sees. Others chose to compromise, *Reykjavellir* in Skagafjörður becoming *Bjarkavellir*, Manitoba, while *Víkingavatn* in Þingeyjarsýsla became *Víkingsstaðir* in Canada. Others looked to Norse mythology for inspiration, their choices reflected in *Ásgarður*, *Bifröst*, and, above all, in *Gimli* itself.

The homesteads named *Reykhólar* in New Iceland, however, had nothing to do with the geothermal steam of the settlers' native land. One such homestead was named for smoke sighted rising up from a Native camp.

THE GOVERNMENT LOAN

To encourage and accelerate the settlement of the vast wilderness of the Canadian Northwest, the Canadian government occasionally approved financial assistance for would-be settlers in the form of loans, to be repaid with interest at a later date.

The Icelanders benefited from this policy, Sigtryggur Jónasson and John Taylor having applied for such a loan on their behalf before they set off from Kinmount for New Iceland. The pair also supervised the purchase of supplies and equipment and in this, as in everything else, they were ably assisted by Friðjón Friðriksson.

The intial group of 1875 received $15,000, intended for the purchase of food, seed, cows, and for transportation west. Purchase of the cattle, however, was postponed until the following spring, as there was little point in buying cattle in autumn when there was no hay to feed them.

When the "Large Group" arrived the following year, almost penniless and with little in the way of possessions, it also enjoyed a significant level of government assistance. With Jónasson again acting as go-between, it obtained three loans worth a total of $22,000 to see it through the journey from Quebec City to Winnipeg, and to purchase food, tools, nets, and boats.

In October 1876, the group received a further loan of $18,000 towards the purchase of 100 stoves, a variety of utensils, and 40 cows, and a further $25,000 in April, 1877, to buy desperately needed supplies, particularly cows. All in all, the

Icelanders received $80,000 from the government, which they began repaying on January 1, 1879, at 6% interest, the intention being to pay it off in ten years.

There is no doubt that it was the generous assistance of the Canadian government that kept the New Iceland colonists alive, a fact made clear by Skafti Arason in this short extract from his autobiography.

> It should be added that few of us had any money. Most depended entirely on the government loan supplies, on which they lived for most of their first two years in the colony.

Sigtryggur Jónasson

Known as the "Father of New Iceland," Sigtryggur Jónasson was without doubt the most influential of the Icelandic settlers in the New World. During a long and eventful life, he occupied a number of key positions, working at various times as editor, farmer, M.L.A., ship's captain, government agent, and entrepeneur, to name but a few. Although he was a complex, controversial figure, he was undeniably imaginative, courageous, and remarkably energetic, and his involvement was ongoing throughout the history of the colony.

Sigtryggur Jónasson was born in 1852 at Bakki in Öxnadalur, in the Eyjafjarðarsýsla region of Northern Iceland. His parents were Helga Egilsdóttir and Jónas Sigurðsson, and his paternal grandmother was a first cousin of the poet Jónas Hallgrímsson. As early as the age of 12, the young Jónasson showed

The loan also formed the basis of commerce in New Iceland for the first two years of the colony's existence. It paid for the necessities which Friðjón Friðriksson, John Taylor, and Sigtryggur Jónasson distributed among the colonists as fairly as possible, a thankless task, but well worth the trouble for the influence it brought. For the two Icelanders, it brought the added problem of being agents of a foreign government among their own people, and the tensions this created later surfaced in a series of quarrels that broke out among the settlers, culminating in the religious dispute that reached its height in the summer of 1878 and sparked a large exodus from the colony.

promise, and was sent to work for Pétur Hafstein, sub-governor of the North, on his estate at Möðruvellir in Hörgárdalur. At first a servant, he later became Hafstein's secretary, receiving an education in this home which saw him become fluent in Danish and English, and acquire a smattering of law along the way.

When Hafstein lost his post in 1872, Jónasson decided to emigrate, and he arrived in Quebec City in September of the same year, alone in the world and still only 20. Despite his relatively humble roots, he did well, not least thanks to his knowledge of English, and quickly found work in Ontario, first as a worker in a carriage factory and later in a logging operation. The following spring, he formed his first company in partnership with a Canadian, providing railway ties to a railway company in New York. The venture proved profitable, and within the space of a few months it made him $1,100.

By this time, the first group of immigrants from Iceland had arrived in Rosseau, and as he knew many of them from his youth in Eyjafjörður, Jónasson went to greet them. His compatriots welcomed him warmly, desperate for all the assistance they could get in a strange land,

As a result, Ottawa soon found itself dragged into what had begun as a seemingly local issue, as the question now arose as to who was responsible for the loans received by the colonists who had left, and the cattle and equipment they had been allotted. Some of the Icelanders simply left without a word to anyone, while others were more honest, announcing their impending departure to Jónasson and Taylor, who were obliged to have cattle and equipment impounded. In most cases, it appears that some kind of compromise was reached, but concerns over loan repayments would not seem to have hindered many from leaving the colony.

The upshot was that the loan was never repaid in full. The later settlers refused to assume the responsibilities of their predecessors for land that was barely cultivated and housing that was barely habitable, and at the end of the day, much of the debt was simply written off.

---

and he spent the winter with them. Although he had no way of knowing it at the time, this decision would have a profound effect on the rest of his life, because when news reached the Canadian authorities that another group of Icelanders was expected the next summer, he was appointed as their official agent.

Jónasson did his best for the 350-member group, accompanying them to Kinmount, where he shared in the dreadful hardships of their first winter and opened his own store. And so it was that he assumed the triple role he would play for most of the rest of his life—social and political leader of his people, government representative, and shrewd businessman.

Although he played an active part in planning the journey to New Iceland in 1875, Jónasson himself did not accompany the first group of settlers, as the Canadian government sent him back home to Iceland to coordinate prospective emigrants. After wintering in Iceland, he returned to Canada in the summer of 1876, bringing with him 1,200 of his countrymen, the so-called Large Group.

By then, Jónasson himself was no longer alone in the world, having married his childhood sweetheart, Rannveig Ólafsdóttir Briem, who, like

AN EXPERIMENT IN GOVERNMENT

As has been mentioned, a five-man council was elected shortly after the arrival of the first settlers in Gimli in the autumn of 1875, its initial brief responsibility being the distribution of loan supplies. The hardships and smallpox epidemic of the following months left little time or energy for politics, however, and it was not until the beginning of 1877 that the colonists had recovered sufficiently to turn their attention once again to internal affairs.

Following two preliminary meetings, a public meeting was held in Gimli on February 5, and a set of interim laws was adopted. Initially, New Iceland was not part of Manitoba, but of the District of Keewatin in the Northwest Territories, which

him, had spent some years in the sub-governor's house at Möðruvellir. Along with Rannveig came a companion, the poet Torfhildur Hólm, who stayed with the couple for a few years.

Jónasson and his wife first claimed land in the North of the colony by the Icelandic River, which, conscious of their mutual roots, they named *Möðruvellir*. At first, they lived in the same primitive conditions as the rest of the settlers, while Jónasson remained in government service, supervising the distribution of the loan to his fellow colonists. At the same time, he was one of the leading figures in formulating the colony's draft constitution, and was elected governor of its first assembly.

Sigtryggur Jónasson and Rannveig Ólafsdóttir Briem.

was under the direct jurisdiction of the Governor-General of Canada and the Lieutenant-Governor of Manitoba. The colony's constitution was then sent to Ottawa for direct parliamentary approval in 1878, as part of the Keewatin Municipalities Bill, an act for which there was no precedent in Canadian history. Although this bill was defeated, the government of New Iceland proceeded as planned.

For administrative purposes, the colony was divided into four districts, bounded on the south by *Víðirnesbyggð* (Willow Point) and *Mikleyjarbyggð* (Big Island) to the north, with *Árnesbyggð* (River Point) and *Fljótsbyggð* (Icelandic River) in between. On February 14, 1877, each district elected a five-man council, with one representative from each being chosen as district head, or reeve. Víðirnes chose Björn Jónsson from Ás in Kelduhverfi;

Despite his many duties, he immediately began laying plans for the newspaper which eventually emerged as *Framfari*. As the scheme's chief financial backer, he supervised the formation of the company which purchased the press and other equipment, and when the first edition appeared in September 1877, he was its first editor. Never one to rest on his laurels, he was also responsible for organizing the first school at Icelandic River.

When religious conflict came to New Iceland in 1878-79, Jónasson emerged as the chief supporter of the Rev. Jón Bjarnason, and used every means at his disposal to make his views as public as possible. In the difficult days that followed, he remained behind, strongly opposing those who left.

In the autumn of 1880, in partnership with Friðjón Friðriksson, he purchased the steamboat *Victoria*, and assumed the responsibility for its operation, quickly earning the title "Captain." The following year, the pair opened a sawmill on the Icelandic River in partnership with a German American named Osenbrugge, which provided so much

Árnes, Bjarni Bjarnason from Daðasstaðir in Skagafjörður; Fljótsbyggð, Jóhann Briem from Eyjafjörður, and Mikleyjarbyggð, Jón Bergvinsson from Múlasýsla.

On February 21, the four councils assembled at Sandvík, at the northern end of New Iceland, to elect a governor. The choice fell on Sigtryggur Jónasson, with Friðjón Friðriksson as his deputy.

Within less than a year, a permanent constitution had been formulated, which came into force on January 14, 1878. A remarkable document, it was composed of 18 chapters in all, and its terms, laid out in some detail, prescribed the social, administrative, and constitutional framework of New Iceland.

Minor judicial functions fell to five "public supervisors," and the powers of the districts, which formed the basic units of the

employment for the remaining settlers that it has since been seen as the most important single factor in saving the colony from abandonment.

Despite his initial stubborn refusal to move, Jónasson and his wife left New Iceland in 1881, first moving to Selkirk, and later to Winnipeg, where

A steamboat circa 1905, similar to the Victoria.

they lived for many years. Until 1890, most of his business activities remained centred on Lake Winnipeg.

colony, were similar to those of the poor law districts in Iceland. Elections were to be held annually on January 7, with male property owners over 18 and all males aged over 21 eligible to vote.

Democracy brought with it responsibility, and each male aged over 21 was required by law to contribute two days of statute labour each year to road work, or pay a two-dollar fee instead. The head of each district was responsible for recording deaths, births and marriages in his area, along with census records and other statistics.

A detailed report on all aspects of the economy of each household had to be submitted to the reeve before the end of December each year, and the residents of each district were responsible for the support of widows and orphans in accordance

In 1893, Jónasson was sent once again to Iceland on behalf of the Province of Manitoba due to the large number of emigrants then expected. Despite the briefness of his visit, he found time to dabble in the politics of his homeland, and he returned to Iceland in 1894 via England, this time acting for himself. Like most others, he disliked intensely the system used for transporting emigrants across the sea, and pressed for radical change. In many ways ahead of his time, he attempted to have a bill presented to the Althing proposing the establishment of an Icelandic railway and steamship company, but failed. Nevertheless, he succeeded in igniting the first sparks of a public debate which would culminate in the formation of Eimskip in 1914.

On his return home to Winnipeg in 1894, Jónasson became editor of *Lögberg*, and as his interest in politics grew he stood as a candidate for the Manitoba Legislature in the election of January 1896. His chief opponent was his cousin Baldvin L. Baldvinsson, whom he defeated by 78 votes to become Canada's first Icelandic M.L.A. As things turned out, however, his seat was by no means safe, and in the with regulations agreed by the majority. A 25-cent poll tax was also levied annually on all those eligible to vote, payable before the end of September. Responsibility for road building, health, poor relief and the building of meeting houses was also placed firmly in the hands of the districts.

Supreme authority in New Iceland lay with the five-man executive assembly, known as the *Vatnsþing*. Composed of representatives from each of the four districts, with an extra member chosen from their ranks, its duties included the setting of laws, building of the colonial road, and the adjudication of disputes. The assembly was chaired by the governor, whose prime ministerial-like duties also made him the colony's official representative outside its borders.

What made the New Iceland constitution most remarkable

next election he was forced to surrender it to Baldvinsson by a narrow margin of 7 votes.

Jónasson resigned as editor of *Lögberg* in 1901, but continued to work for the government, travelling widely throughout Canada in the course of his duties. Now in his fifties, he gradually became tired of these long absences from home, and when he was returned to the Legislature again in 1907, he retired from his official post. Three years later, he retired from politics as well and moved from Winnipeg to Árborg, then a growing town created by the coming of the railway, a development for which he was in large part responsible.

Although successful in so many walks of life, Jónasson and his wife never had any children of their own, but the couple adopted a boy, Percy, and fostered two other children. Born to Scottish parents but brought up by Icelanders, Percy Jonasson himself married an Icelander and left a large family.

One of Sigtryggur Jónasson's foster children was Rose, daughter of an Icelandic couple in New Iceland with 17 children. John of all was that it was a unique combination of British-Canadian and Icelandic laws, ideas, and customs. Responsible directly to Ottawa, the government of New Iceland pursued policies aimed at attracting useful industries, "expanding the colony," and deciding whether settlers other than Icelanders should be allowed to live within its borders.

This curious state of constitutional limbo relative to the rest of Canada would persist for 12 years after the arrival of the first settlers, and a decade after the constitution itself was drawn up. It was not until 1887 that municipal government was formally adopted, although in reality New Iceland had been a municipality of Manitoba since 1881. As a result, New Iceland maintained its unique identity among other Icelandic settlements in Canada

Taylor and his wife, Elizabeth, had fostered this child until Taylor's death in 1885. It was always considered something of a joke in the Jónasson household that, although she was Icelandic, she could speak only English, while the Anglo-Saxon Percy spoke Icelandic. Rose, however, did not stay long, and was reared mainly by Elizabeth Taylor in Ontario.

Jónasson's other foster child, Matthías, was the son of Einar H. Kvaran and Maren Mathilde Petersen, and was fostered on the death of his mother in 1888, when he was only nine months old.

When Sigtryggur Jónasson moved north in New Iceland in 1910, Rannveig, whose health was now failing, remained in Winnipeg, where she died in 1916. She had never cared for life on the colonial frontier, and it was mainly due to her that the couple had moved to the city. Her husband, on the other hand, had always longed to be a farmer, and in 1912 he took a new homestead north of Árborg.

The last 25 years of his life he spent alternately with his brother's people in Riverton or at Árborg near Percy and his family. In 1942, and the U.S. for several years after the focus of Icelandic activity had shifted to Winnipeg, where the Icelandic presence, although much stronger in terms of numbers than in the colony, adapted more quickly to Canadian ways.

While the foundation of this settlement tells us much about the pride, dreams, and ambitions of the settlers, as well as their strong sense of nationalism, it actually made life more difficult for them in many ways than if they had immediately adapted. The reluctance of the older ones in particular to learn English and adapt to Canadian ways hindered development, and the wheels of progress began to turn much more slowly in New Iceland than they did in other similar parts of Canada.

Sigtryggur Jónasson died, then into his 91st year, and almost 70 years to the day from the time he had first set foot in Canada. In later life, he received many honours, but perhaps the greatest of these is his place in Canadian history as the undisputed "Father of New Iceland."

Pioneer reunion on the 50th anniversary of the founding of New Iceland: from left, Sigtryggur Jónasson, Jóhann and Guðrún Briem, Jón Guðmundsson, Steinunn Stefánsson, Flóvent Jónsson, and Guðrún Jóhannesdóttir Jónasson, Jónasson's sister-in-law.

A settler's cabin sketched 15 years after it was first built. Signs of progress are evident everywhere. A second story has been added to the house, along with a substantial stable, the creek has been bridged, and the fields stand fenced off and under cultivation.

They lost ten children

A native of Marbæli in Skagafjörður, Northern Iceland, Páll Pétursson was born in 1828. When he was only a year old, his father drowned, and a short time later, his mother took her two children to the farm of Flugumýrarhvammur, where she became a servant. Pétursson was brought up there, but was working as a labourer at Hegranes when he met Margrét Magnúsdóttir, whom he married at Glaumbær in 1857. Born at Páfastaðir in 1834, she was also a native of Skagafjörður and Pétursson's first cousin, the pair sharing a common grandmother, Björg Björnsdóttir, a local woman who had married three times.

When the couple married, Margrét was pregnant with their second child, and for the next 17 years, they struggled to exist on a tiny holding at Reykjarhóll, near Varmahlíð. In June 1876, they left for Canada aboard the steamship *Verona*, as part of the "Large Group." By that time, they had already had 11 children, five of whom had died in infancy, and by the tme they left Iceland, Margrét was already eight months pregnant with their 12th, a girl, who was born immediately after the family landed at Quebec City on July 23.

Delayed by the birth, the family were left behind when the rest of the Icelanders set off for Winnipeg, but by September had joined them in New Iceland, where they claimed a homestead they called Húsafell, by the Icelandic River. There, the couple planned to build a new future for themselves and their seven children. They had barely settled there, however, when the smallpox epidemic broke out. By the time it was over, it had claimed five of their offspring.

Devastated by their terrible loss, Páll Pétursson and Margrét Magnús-dóttir somehow managed to struggle on, and in the spring of 1877, Páll built a cabin for them and their two remaining children. Two years later, when he was 50 and she 44, the couple had their 13th child, a daughter who survived. The rest of their lives were spent at Húsafell, which they farmed successfully until Páll's death in 1900. Margrét lived on to see her 85th birthday before she died in 1918. Their children were:

Magnús, b. 1855, died at birth in Iceland.

Jóhann Pétur, b. 1857, died aged two weeks in Iceland.

Sólborg, b. 1858, died aged one year in Iceland.

Jóhann Pétur, b. 1859, died aged 17 from smallpox in Canada.

Sólborg Pálína, b. 1860, died aged two weeks in Iceland.

Margrét Guðrún, b. 1862. First of their children to reach adulthood, she
 later married Jóhann Briem and had 6 children of her own.

Sigmundur, b. 1863, died aged 14 from smallpox in Canada.

Margrét Pálína, b. 1866, died not yet aged 2 yrs in Iceland.

Jón Sigurður, b. 1868. Survived to become an adult, married in New
 Iceland and reared two foster children.

Páll Magnús, b. 1871, died aged 4 from smallpox in Canada.

Margrét Ingibjörg, b. 1873, died aged 3 from smallpox in Canada.

Sigríður Rósa, b. 1876 in Quebec City, died aged 3 months from
 smallpox.

Elín Jóhanna, b. 1878, New Iceland, survived to have 4 children of her
 own.

THE NATIVES OF NEW ICELAND

For centuries, the land on which New Iceland stood had been the home of the Cree and Salteaux, who, like First Nations peoples elsewhere in North America, lived by hunting and gathering. When the Icelanders arrived in 1875, the Cree and Salteaux had already had over 200 years' experience of contact with the white man, beginning with the French fur traders Radisson and Groseilliers, who journeyed north to Hudson Bay in 1668.

Two years later, in 1670, a few English merchant-adventurers formed the Hudson Bay Company, which for centuries to come would have a major influence in the lives of Natives all over the huge North West Territory, which included what later became Manitoba.

As a result, a few of the Natives encountered by the Icelanders generations later spoke English well enough to be able to trade, and some of them even had English names. One such man was John Ramsay, whom the Icelanders came to know best of all.

Many of the Icelanders, of course, feared the Natives, having heard tales of their dreadful deeds during their sojourn in Ontario, but as later became clear, the Salteaux were a peaceful people, who offered little resistance when the white man came and took their land. Like the animals they hunted, they were a semi-nomadic people, seldom settling for long in one place and stopping only to trade with the fur traders who had set up isolated trading posts close to the lake.

The Icelanders were aware of the Salteaux from the outset, their boats having become accidentally entangled in their nets as they sailed down the Red River from Winnipeg. It was on its banks that the colonists saw their first Natives. One old woman in particular berated the new arrivals for damaging the tribal nets and, although the Icelanders could not understand a word she said, it was obvious to all that she was not offering them a warm welcome.

Little is said of the dealings of the colonists with the Salteaux during their first winter in New Iceland. Contact

The native Cree and Salteaux around Lake Winnipeg were excellent boat builders, and, as the straw aboard the canoe in the foreground of this photograph, taken sometime between 1870-80, shows, their craft were skillfully constructed and almost completely watertight.

between the two races was probably coloured by mutual curiosity and some suspicion, and while the Icelandic women were said to fear the Natives more than the men, the Salteaux were probably no less shocked by the blond hair and pale skin of some of their new neighbours.

The only major conflict between the Icelanders and the Salteaux came in the summer of 1876, when three settlers, all from Eyjafjörður, moved north from Gimli to the Icelandic River. They were Jóhannes Sigurðsson from Árskógsströnd, his wife, Guðrún, and three children, Flóvent Jónsson from Skriðuland, his wife, Bergrós, and son, and Ólafur Ólafsson from Espihóll, and his foster son, Friðrik Sveinsson, who was a brother of the well-known clergyman, author and poet Jón Sveinsson.

A First Nations family outside their tepee. Their clothing, tools and other equipment were largely derived from the animals they hunted, and materials gathered from the surrounding region.

The early Icelandic settlers, particularly the women, were often frightened by the formidable appearance of the native Cree despite their peaceful demeanour. This photograph was taken in Manitoba just before the turn of the century.

The group found a vacant Hudson Bay Company log build-ing on the banks of the river and moved in. All three claimed homesteads on the west (north) bank of the river. Although aware of the presence of Natives, some of whom lived close by in tepees and cabins, the Icelanders began building. What hap-pened next was later described by Friðrik Sveinsson, then still only a teenager:

At the mouth of the creek where Ólafur settled lived a Native named Ramsay with his wife and 5 children; he had a well-cultivated potato field and soon began to object to the presence of white men from whom his people had always been forced to retreat. This continued for some time without any developments of note, and the walls of Ólafur's log cabin began to rise. One morning, however, when the three men rowed up the creek in a boat to go to work, there stood Ramsay. He pushed the boat away from shore, and made it clear that he was forbidding them to land, though he spoke very little English. They then tried to land a second time, but the same thing happened. At that, Ólafur moved to the prow of the boat with an axe in his hand and told the others to row ashore, which they did. They then set to work on the cabin, and Ramsay paddled off downriver in his canoe in a bad temper. The Icelanders worked until nightfall and returned home. About the same time, we boys, Gunnlaugur, Pétur, and I, were rowing on the river a short distance away. Suddenly, we heard some shots coming from further down the river, and saw several canoes full of Natives who were either shooting birds or trying to scare us.

We hurried home with this news, and soon after, the Natives arrived and entered the cabin without permission. They sat down in a half-circle round the door at the south end with their guns, while the Icelanders remained at the other end of the house, and made it clear they could not understand English. As suddenly as they had arrived, the Natives disappeared, but we children in particular had had enough of this unwelcome visit.

When dusk fell, Ramsay returned with a Native interpreter, and informed the Icelanders that the Natives considered the settlement to be an illegal infringement on Native lands, as they had believed that the land assigned to the Icelanders would not extend north of the river.

The Icelanders themselves were unsure as the land had never been surveyed, and it was agreed to obtain the judgement of a government official as soon as possible. At that, the Natives took their leave, and it was decided that Ólafur, Jóhannes, and Friðrik would travel downriver to meet Sigtryggur Jónasson, who was expected with a new group of immigrants . . .

By happy coincidence, the group was accompanied by a Dominion Government Indian agent, travelling north on the lake in search of Natives. The agent assured us that the site of the Icelandic settlement extended north of the White-Mud (Icelandic) River. Soon after, we returned north and made it clear to the Natives that they had no claim to the land there, and they made no further attempt to hinder our settlement. Agreement was reached between Ólafur and Ramsay, and he permitted Ramsay to continue growing his potatoes and camping on the land. After that, they lived in peace.

The poet and playwright Guttormur J. Guttormsson was one of the Icelanders who saw John Ramsay first hand. He is pictured here in 1935 at the grave of Ramsay's wife, Betsey, who perished in the small-pox epidemic of 1876, along with four of their children. The grave stands at Sandy Bar, subject of Guttormsson's most famous poem.

Trapping animals such as rabbits was one of the many skills the Icelanders learned from the Natives, an ability which in winter could mean the difference between survival and starvation. This photograph is much more recent, taken in 1962.

Ramsay, a striking figure, lived well by Native standards. An expert shot and hunter, he was honest, trustworthy, hospitable and helpful, and he proved the best of neighbours. Although he appeared to be pure Native, he was very light-skinned, straight-backed, thin, and well-proportioned, and exceedingly quick and lithe in his movements. His wife was particularly good-looking, as were his children, and the cleanliness of the family was admirable. The writer often enjoyed Ramsay's hospitality in his tent, where a pure white cloth was spread on the ground, and the dishes, cups, and knives they used were sparklingly clean. The food was excellent, unlike that found among other Native families we met, who were rather dirty.

When the smallpox broke out, it is well known that it killed more Natives than white men, and Ramsay suffered the terrible sorrow of losing his wife and four children. They were laid to rest at Sandy Bar, and Ramsay placed a marble tombstone, which he bought in Winnipeg, on his wife's grave.

One of the more prominent members of the Salteaux band associated with Sandy Bar, Ramsay had the closest dealings with the Icelanders. While the tribe as a whole was unhappy with its new neighbours, any potential conflict disappeared with the onset of the epidemic of 1877, which almost wiped it out. Ramsay, however, maintained his close ties with the Icelanders, and his daughter lived for a time on the upper floor at Ós with Benedikt Kristjánsson and his wife, Hólmfríður.

After the first few years, no Natives, Ramsay excepted, lived near the Icelanders, although they often visited New Iceland en route from their tribal lands in the north to trade in Winnipeg. By that time, alcohol was beginning to have a debilitating influence on the lives of the Natives. Sometimes they frightened the Icelanders when they entered unan-nounced and uninvited into their houses and made themselves at home, but in actual fact, they had only come to take a closer look at their new neighbours and to accept any gift that might be offered.

CULTIVATING THE LAND

Apart from letters and memoirs, the main source on farming in the early days of New Iceland is the first report of the *Agricultural Survey of New Iceland*, which appeared in 1877.

Published in *Framfari* the following year, it reveals that the colony had 260 homesteads and a registered population of about 1,000, who shared their new home with some 500 cows, 50 oxen, and 320 calves and heifers, along with a few sheep, pigs, and chickens. Most of the farms were under some form of cultivation, potatoes were fairly plentiful, and fishing nets and rough boats were becoming an increasingly common sight.

A losing battle with the marshes

Gísli Árnason and Dýrunn Steinsdóttir were two Icelanders from Skagafjörður with sharply contrasting backgrounds. The illegitimate son of poor parents, Gísli was raised for the most part by his maternal grandparents at Álftagerði in Seyluhreppur, while Dýrunn was the daughter of a wealthy farmer at Stóra Gröf. When they married in 1877, he was 26, she was 21.

Although very different in temperament, they made a good couple. She is described as an unusually small, likable woman with a ready sense of humour and open manner, always ready to open her house to guests. By contrast, he was silent and reserved, handsome, strong, and very good with his hands.

Writing in *Framfari* on March 28, 1878, Sigtryggur Jónasson reported that the average log house in the colony measured 6 x 4 metres in size, and was 2.5 m high, with a cellar 6 square metres in area and 1.80 m deep.

The New Iceland colonists quickly realized that farming was a more complicated business than they had thought. First, the forest had to be cleared, and any open ground often proved to be grass-covered marshland, as the flatness of the land and heavy clay nature of the soil made it impossible for water to drain off. Where there was no marsh, bush proved an obstacle to cultivation.

After some initial attempts at grain growing, the settlers confined their activities to raising cattle, an activity to which the northern part of the colony was particularly suited due to an

The first years of their marriage were spent at Litla Seyla, a small farm owned by Dýrunn's parents, but in 1883, they set off for Canada along with two of their children, Guðrún, 5, and Árni aged 3. A third, Steinunn, not yet a year old, was left behind with her grandparents.

After spending their first winter in Gimli, the couple moved north to Mikley in the spring of 1884, settling on the west shore of the island on a small point of land which they named *Skógarhöfði*. Extremely isolated, and bordering on extensive marshes to the south, it could only be reached by boat, and the nearest homestead was some kilometres away. In winter, when the marshes froze, the journey could be made on foot through the forest.

In this lonely place, Dýrunn gave birth to another five children, but lost two of them at birth, both boys. In addition, another son, Árni, who had accompanied them from Iceland, died at 15. Despite their loss, the pair continued farming,

The brothers Gunnsteinn, Þorsteinn, and Sigurður Eyjólfsson from Unaland on the Icelandic River were known throughout New Iceland as highly innovative farmers. This photograph of Gunnsteinn and his neighbours was taken during the harvest of 1910. Gunnsteinn can be seen third from left, wearing a hat.

abundent supply of hay. While animal husbandry proved successful, the farmers were also quick to realize that the ways of the old country were totally unsuited to life in the heavy bush of the Interlake, where there were no mountains to graze

but after a 14-year struggle against flooding and isolation, they were forced to abandon their land, by then almost totally under water.

In 1898, they moved with their six surviving children to the mainland, and settled on a low-lying farm called *Viðirhóll*, which had itself recently been abandoned. Within the space of only five years, however, it too flooded. Realizing that life near water was definitely not for them, Árnason and his wife moved further inland to a farm in the Framnes district which they also named *Viðirhóll*.

The link between the two places involved rather more than just the name, however. Using his skills to the full, Árnason dismantled their former home log by log, plank by plank, and carefully sheep, and the thick forests made it nearly impossible to keep an eye on the ewes. Cattle, by contrast, thrived on the marshy ground.

The cattle of New Iceland were the descendants of the so-called government loan cows brought from Winnipeg between 1876-78. Bigger than their Icelandic cousins, they were usually brown or reddish-brown, horned, and they produced large quantities of meat and milk. As in Iceland, the colonists fully appreciated the value of their beasts and tended them well. In best Icelandic tradition, they also named them, and the meadows along the shores of Lake Winnipeg were soon filled with *Skjalda, Rönd, Lukka, Búbót*, and a host of others.

As had been the case at home, the cattle grazed outside in summer but spent the winter indoors, although not in the settlers' houses themselves, except in dire emergencies. Instead, they were housed in crudely constructed stables made of logs and roofed with turf and manure. Initially, the cattle were tethered in summer, but this practice disappeared as fencing became more common.

numbered each piece before transporting it in its entirety to their new farm where he rebuilt it.

Finally free of the marshes, the couple prospered for several years, until aged almost 60, Árnason was struck down by a sudden illness, probably a stroke, which robbed him of his power of speech. Although he never fully recovered his strength, he continued to work, communicating by signs and in writing until his death five years later, in 1919.

Dýrunn outlived him by many years, and by the time she died in 1953 at the age of 96, she had become a local legend for her intelligence, wit, kindness, and hospitality. Her declining years were spent with her children, several of whom had large families.

A family and some local farmers harvest hay at Víðimýri, near Riverton, in the early years of this century. Using ox-drawn mowers and given the right conditions, hay cutting was a swift process, although fall flooding sometimes inundated the meadows and ruined a summer's work.

In the early years of the colony, the settlers devoted their energies to establishing herds large enough to support them and their families. At around $30, a cow was an expensive item, costing about the same as a stove or ten sacks of flour. Cattle were bought and sold, as were their products such as milk, cream, and butter. When a farmer had developed a reasonably large herd, he could then sell a few head for cash to the buyers who arrived from places like Selkirk each spring. Profits from this trade varied wildly, however, and a drop in prices in the years after 1890 hampered development in the settlement.

Being Icelanders, however, the colonists missed their sheep. After all, what is Christmas without that traditional smoked lamb delicacy, *hangikjöt*? The ewes also produced wool, which could be sold or used both for making clothes. Some of the farmers bought a few Canadian ewes of British descent, but

Technology aside, the scythe remained a common sight until well into this century, as seen here in Gimli in 1912.

A flock of New Iceland sheep enjoys a breath of fresh air following a blizzard. Although common for years, sheep farming in the colony disappeared almost completely after the Great War.

Pictured here in 1887, a hay market stood at the corner of Albert, Arthur, and King Streets in Winnipeg for many years, and was a focal point for farmers from the surrounding region.

their crude fences proved inadequate to pen them, and the same system of marking sheep as had been used in Iceland was soon adopted. Sheep farming, however, never became a significant part of the New Iceland economy, and the number of sheep declined as more and more land was planted with grain.

Hay cutting was at first conducted in the same way it had been in Iceland, using scythes, the main difference being that the marsh and meadow grasses grew much taller and more readily, but the summer of 1879 was a landmark year in haying with the introduction of a mechanical mower bought by Sigtryggur Jónasson the previous year. Drawn by a pair of oxen, it was steered by one man who could cut a level field four times faster than even the best scytheman. The honour of driving it the first year fell to Stefán Eyjólfsson.

As the colony grew, wooden rail fencing became an increasingly common sight, and although the material used in its construction may have been very different from the rough, dry stones used in Iceland, the endless round of replacing it was the same.

As the Red River Valley is recognized as one of the best, if not the best, grain growing regions of the world, growing cereal crops eventually became an important activity in the lives of the New Icelanders. Although they knew little about it, a few had gained some limited experience in farming during the months spent in Ontario, and seed grain was one of the first things purchased with the government loan.

Most cultivation was done by hand with "grub hoes," and the cutting and threshing of grain was first done with hand tools as well. The initial attempts at growing grain went badly, however, as the settlers had little or no experience in preparing the ground and seeding the grain.

"Litli Mundi" is the title of this entertaining portrait from the Manitoba Archives. He was Guðmundur Kristjansson of Víðir, a native of Skaftafellssýsla.

Indeed, these problems became a significant factor in the exodous of many of the early settlers from New Iceland in search of better land elsewhere, lured by tales of phenomenal success enjoyed by settlers on the open prairie. Behind them, their lands lay empty, claimed once again by bushes and scrub until the arrival of the next wave of immigrants from Iceland who, little by little, acre by acre, painstakingly changed the bush of New Iceland into the rich fields of golden grain it had become by the mid-20th century.

Gunnlaugur Hólm with his ox, Sörli. Manitoba Archives, date unknown.

Clippings from *Framfari* provide a wealth of information on agriculture during the early years of New Iceland. The July 1878 edition contains news of wolves and bears which had killed some cattle in the Víðirnes district, where two bears had been shot, and a letter from the district in the same edition states:

> Our general health is good, which is just as well as we have enough to do. A few farmers started cutting hay on July 1, and most have now begun. The wheat and potatoes are doing well, and the worms have damaged little aside from the seedlings. Catfish is plentiful.

By contrast, the news from Mikley around the same time was not so good.

> The seedlings have all been eaten by worms, and many have sown twice or even oftener, but it looks as though the last attempt may succeed.

In the autumn of 1878, Sigurður Jónsson of Borðeyri on Mikley harvested 30 kilos of beans, a yield of more than a hundredfold more than he had sown, and others quickly followed his example with the same results. Potatoes also grew well, producing yields of twelve to twentyfold, but they proved very difficult to store. On November 30, 1878, Friðjón Friðriksson of Gimli wrote the following article in *Framfari*:

> The autumn was very stormy and wet, and little fish was caught here or in Árnesbyggð. The potatoes were damaged in several places, as the cellars of the dwellings where they were stored filled with water, making it impossible to keep them there. Instead, they were piled up outside and covered with hay and earth, but the frost got to them and the harvest, which looked so promising, has for many shrunk greatly. Food supplies are low, especially in Árnesbyggð, where some of the families have almost nothing to eat except potatoes. Men now fear that this source will fail them, and they will have no food for the winter. The outlook for them is undeniably bleak. Many here in Gimli are becoming tired of the struggle and wish to leave, but this is easier said than done if they are to do so honestly, having settled their debts. Most of the talk is

of Dakota, and migration from here to there is now as common as emigration from Iceland to America. While such movement is natural and may prove of benefit to some, it provokes a sense of restlessness and discontent

The position of children in the early hierarchy of New Iceland is made clear from this advertisement, which appeared in the pages of Framfari *on June 28, 1878, offering work to youngsters as young as 11.*

staðar orðið 2—3 kvartil á hæð.

20. þ. m. skaut Sveinn Björnsson í Sandvík elgsdýr, skammt frá Víkingsstöðum hjer í Fljótsbyggð.

AUGLÝSING.

Nokkrir menn í Manitoba, sem vilja taka íslenska pilta í vinnu:

James Fullerton í Cookscreek vill fá 11 eða 12 ára gamlan pilt til að gæta 2 ungbarna úti, sjá um að þau fari sjer ekki að voða, bera inn eldivið o. fl. fyrir kaup.

Donald Bannerman bóndi í Kildonan skammt frá Selkirk vill taka að sjer munaðarlausan pilt 12 eða 13 ára, mennta hann og halda hann hjá sjer uns hann er 21. árs.

Dóttir hans, sem er gipt kona, vill einnig taka að sjer munaðarlausa stúlku 13 eða 14 ára með sömu kostum.

William Nimmon, bóndi á Little Mountain nálægt Winnipeg vill fá 1 eða 2 pilta 18 ára að aldri til að vinna vanalega landvinnu og keyra hesta til bæjarins.

Rev. Rupert E. Washer prestur í Headingly vill fá 15 eða 16 ára gamlan pilt í 3 ár eða lengur og gjalda honum $ 4—5 á mánuði og föt að auki. Hann verður látinn gjöra alls konar smávik, þjóna að borðum, höggva eldivið. Kaupið verður aukið á hverju ári; hann fær einnig tilsögn í ensku, og í öllu tilliti góða aðbúð.

Þeir hjer í nýlendunni, sem kunna að vilja sæta þessu, geta snúið sjer til Mr. John Taylors à Gimli.

FRAMFARI.

Eigandi : Prentfjelag Nýja - Íslands.
Prentaður og gefinn út í Prentsmiðju fjelagsins, Lundi, Keewatin, Canada. — Í stjórn fjelagsins eru :
Sigtr. Jónasson. Friðjón Friðriksson.
Jóhann Briem.

among the rest of the populace. For the past three weeks, the weather has been the best possible, warm and calm, but fishing has been limited as the lake has sometimes been frozen. The roads are very bad, and it is impossible to move things from Winnipeg until the snow comes. This is very bad, because like other merchants in the colony I am rapidly running out of many goods.

TAMING THE GREAT FOREST

Many of the Icelanders were unprepared for what they saw when they first arrived in New Iceland. Years later, in 1925, Eggert Jóhannsson, who arrived as a youngster with his parents in the summer of 1876, recalled his experiences.

No one who was not there can imagine the difficulties we faced, even though the overland journey was no more than half a mile. Obviously, there was no road, and up from the sandy shore stretched nothing but empty forest . . . No tracks or paths existed to guide us from our landing place on the banks of the river or lake shore. Everyone awaited the coming of the Natives. Most of us who had left home that summer of 1876 had never seen a forest tree until we arrived in the West, and then only from a distance, either from the deck of a ship or speeding railway carriage.

As the marshes did not reach as far as the shore, our route up from the riverbank was high and steep to walk, especially in Árnesbyggð. But whether it was high or low, it was difficult to traverse. High, imposing poplars grew so thick on the slopes that it was barely possible for a man to squeeze between them, but difficult as they were, it quickly became clear that the dense undergrowth was "seven times worse," as Bólu-Hjálmar once said. Tangled stalks of brushwood, as hard as leather and taller than a fully grown man, grew so densely between the trees that you couldn't have got a needle between them, and those

Children began work at an early age, moving on to heavier tasks as they got older. From an unknown farm in Manitoba, about 1900.

who forced their way through them had to take the greatest care not to damage their eyes or faces.

This was the New Iceland forest of which we had heard so much on the journey, but could not possibly imagine until we saw it for ourselves. Nothing we had ever seen at home in Iceland could possibly have prepared us for a sight such as this, or the tools we would need to hack a way through it, even to clear a small field. But this is what we had come for, to clear the forest and give the earth an opportunity to provide us with our daily bread, in one form or another. Here we would stand or fall, but one thing was clear. There was no shortage of materials from which to build, and we would never fear lack of fuel, both undeniably invaluable resources.

As Jóhannsson makes clear, the Icelanders always viewed the forest as more of a resource than an obstacle, despite its formidable appearance. The first settlers had already spent at least a year in Ontario, and they realized the great potential of forestry as a source of work. All over Canada, sawmills were springing up, and some of the Icelanders had already worked in a number of them. The timber market was booming, with vast quantities of lumber required to satisfy the needs of the

Friðsteinn Sigurðsson, seen here about 1890 with his wife, Sesselja Sigurbjörnsdóttir, and their children, Vilberg, Clara, and Sigurður. Brother-in-law of Friðjón Friðriksson, he was also an employee at his Möðruvellir sawmill, but on his first day at work lost part of his left hand in an accident. As was not uncommon among the settlers, the couple was closely related, although their case was slightly unusual in that both sets of parents were first cousins from Iceland's own "prairie," Melrakkaslétta, in the Northeast.

Cutting timber in spring near Árborg. The steam engine powers a circular sawblade mounted on a wagon.

The saws used in New Iceland may have been primitive compared to modern tools, but they served their purpose. This photograph, taken in winter, is probably from the Bændamylla sawmill near Ós, which operated from 1905-06.

hundreds of thousands of immigrants streaming into towns and cities all over North America.

When the first Icelanders arrived in New Iceland, a small sawmill already stood on Mikley, but it was not in operation at the time. Later, however, another mill was set up nearby, and for a few years some of the islanders worked there and in a logging camp on the island.

When the exodus from New Iceland reached its height in 1881 and the outlook for the colony was at its bleakest, Sigtryggur Jónasson and Friðjón Friðriksson opened a sawmill on Jónasson's property at Möðruvellir on the banks of the Icelandic River. A year before, they had purchased the steamboat *Victoria* to transport the timber, and they also built a lumber camp along the river. For a time, the business went well, and this probably did more than anything else to save the colony at a time when settlers were deserting in droves.

The sawmill provided work for many of the colonists, both those who supplied it with raw timber and the 20 or so who are said to have hired out their services as lumberjacks on short-term contracts. Life for these labourers was often easier in winter, when the logs could be dragged out on the Icelandic River. When the ice melted, they were carried downstream by the current, all the way to the mill. Sawmills of this type could not last long in the same place, however, and it took only four years to exhaust the best supplies of timber closest to the river.

Dangerous in the extreme, sawing heavy logs was very much a team effort, as can be seen from this crew of workers at Ashern, on the eastern shore of Lake Manitoba, in 1915.

In 1886, the mill was transferred to Manigotogan on the eastern shore of Lake Winnpeg, but this operation quickly landed in difficulties, and a new company was formed in 1888, with a number of new shareholders, among them some Englishmen. By that time, however, Jónasson had become a successful businessman in Winnipeg, Friðriksson had moved to Glenboro, and the sawmill closed completely in 1891.

Poets and Readers

The Icelanders of North America did not live by bread alone, which in many cases was probably just as well. As had been the case at home, literature, particularly poetry, played a large part in their daily lives. Initially, it was published in newspapers such as *Framfari*, *Leifur*, *Lögberg*, and *Heimskringla*, and in the years leading up to 1900, no fewer than 20 such publications saw the light of day, although their lifespans varied widely.

In 1887, just over a decade after the first immigrants had arrived, Jóhann Magnús Bjarnason, then just 20, published the first book of Icelandic poetry in the New World. Before the century was over, it had been followed by more than 20 others, and by the dawn of the new century, the literary portfolio of the Icelanders in America extended to 25 books by 17 authors, as well as several new plays performed by a range of amateur dramatic groups. All in all, about 100 of the immigrants saw their work committed to print in some form or another during these early years, enough to earn them a chapter of their own in vol. 3 of the *History of Icelandic Literature*.

In it, its author, Viðar Hreinsson, contends that the literature of the immigrants can be divided into three distinct schools, beginning with those who preferred to view the migration in a romantic light.

The first school could be classed as a kind of pastoral romanticism. This type of verse is usually characterized by an extremely narrow, blinkered

Others tried their luck with sawmills, particularly around the Icelandic River, and for a time some were successful, but the difficulty of proper land communications and shipping may have hindered further development.

Timber remained one of the staple industries of New Iceland until the middle of this century, providing farmers with a ready source of income as they cleared their land for grain.

view of life and deals with the entire immigration issue in a superficial, uncritical manner, the new world tinged with sorrow for the old. This view of life defines a kind of public self-image held by many of the immigrants, and often found its expression in the adoption of radically opposing opinions in matters of politics or religion. Later, this gradually developed into poetry of the nationalistic-heroic variety.

The second variety was by definition diametrically opposed to the first, and being deeply critical of life in the New World was at direct odds with the public image the immigrants held of themselves. As a result, several attempts were made to deny its proponents a voice, but although this school produced many interesting works, they could hardly be said to bear the mark of artistic maturity.

The third school is that in which the new experiences of its authors served to produce both originality and fresh insights. Often, it was characterized by its sharply critical tone, and ability to encompass a new perspective on life in a traditional Icelandic form.

The most noted writers and poets among the early immigrants were Jóhann Magnús Bjarnason, Torfhildur Hólm, Undína, Káinn, Kristinn Stefánsson, Guttormur J. Guttormsson, Gunnsteinn Eyjólfsson and, towering above them all, Stephan G. Stephansson. Although a homesteader and farmer all his life, with a large family to feed, Stephansson's stunning literary output extends to some 2,300 pages of poetry and 1,400 pages of prose, and although he wrote only in Icelandic, he is not only celebrated as a literary giant in Iceland, but is considered by scholars as among the first great poets of North America.

GONE FISHING

In the report compiled in the wake of the scouting party's reconnaisance of a site for New Iceland in 1875, Sigtryggur Jónasson and Einar Jónasson state:

> We can describe fishing on Lake Winnipeg from personal experience. Its waters teem with fish of various kinds. Indians fish there all the year round, although it seemed to us that their gear was poor and they only fish inshore. In the autumn, there are schools of whitefish, which in winter are fished up through the ice. This fish will undoubtedly prove a valuable commodity for trading. The main species of fish found in the lake are whitefish, sturgeon, pike, goldeye, sunfish, catfish, pickerel and sauger. These are all good to eat, and, whitefish excepted, can all be caught in spring when the ice melts.

As the Icelanders knew in advance that those who lived near the lake would fish, many of them brought their own nets with

Fishing craft such as this were a familiar sight on Lake Winnipeg. Twin-masted, they handled well even in a light breeze. In the background can be seen one of the many fishing stations which dotted the shores of the lake.

The vast, lonely expanse of Lake Winnipeg was like no other stretch of water the Icelanders had ever seen, apart, that is, from the ocean itself.

them from home. The day after the first group arrived in the colony in the autumn of 1875, some of the settlers began attempting to fish, encouraged by John Taylor, whose $5 prize is mentioned in the previous chapter. To begin with, the Icelanders laid their nets too close to shore, and none of them had any real knowledge of ice fishing. Soon, however, they began achieving results and, thanks to a combination of trial, error, and some practical advice from the local Natives, they quickly became expert in the ways of the lake.

Lake Winnipeg was unlike any body of water the Icelanders had ever seen before, apart, that is, from the ocean itself. Some 500 km long and 100 km broad at its widest, it is the 11th largest inland lake on Earth, and many kilometres separated New Iceland and its opposite shore, which lay just in sight, across its heaving waters.

While the prevailing current runs from south to north, it is the wind which is the strongest natural feature, and the Icelanders soon learned that when it blows from the north, the level of the lake rises significantly at its southern end.

Locked in over a metre of ice from November to April, the lake served the early settlers not only as a source of food, but as a vital means of transport and, as the Icelanders became acquainted with its ways, they learned to harvest it for profit, as the following article, which appeared in *Framfari* in December, 1877, describes:

> As was recently reported in *Framfari*, a few young men from Gimli went in search of whitefish north of Little Grindstone. Initially, they tried a few places, but caught no fish and were running seriously short of food for their sled dogs. Undaunted, however, they kept trying until they found whitefish to the southwest. Within about 10 days, Magnús Stefánsson, Jósef Schram, and Jón Guðmundsson, who had found the fish to begin with, had caught 500 mature, prize whitefish, and the two first-mentioned returned to Gimli before New Year's with 300 fish, well pleased with their trip. Claiming there were still plenty of fish left, they declared their intention to head north again immediately, adding that while some of their nets had proved too small, those with a mesh over 6 inches on each side were ideal. The schools of

As soon as they had learned the necessary skills, the Icelanders took to the ice on ox- or horse-drawn sleighs which carried them to the distant winter fishing grounds far to the north of the colony. Along with the provisions necessary for their long trip, many also carried crude portable stoves for cooking.

A small steamboat was sometimes used to help the fishing fleet on its way north to the fishing camps on Lake Winnipeg.

whitefish they found lay about 20 miles north of the Icelandic River, at a depth of around 7 fathoms. The current was very strong when they began, but had died down by the time they left. One of their party stayed behind, and another of the group, Pétur Pálsson, later returned with 100 fish. The discovery of this site, which was due entirely to the dogged persistence of these bright lads, is truly of great value, both as a source of sustenance—which many in the colony certainly need—and as proof to those sceptics who doubted the feasibility of fishing in winter. The exploits of the lads has breathed new life into the colonists. Around 20 have now followed them from Willow Point, 12 from River Point, and 10 from Icelandic River. With them they have taken the nets of those who have stayed at home, a sign of cooperation, and we wish them well and every success on their trip.

Shortly after New Year's of 1878, another *Framfari* article describes a fishing trip on Lake Winnipeg near the Icelandic River, in which the brothers Halldór and Þorgrímur Jónsson are mentioned as being the most successful. Halldór is said to have caught 150 pike through the ice at a spot where it was over two feet thick and the water four feet deep, and for the rest of that winter the paper's pages were filled with tales of similar successes, with fish so plentiful that "men hardly paused to draw breath between trips."

Travelling light would seem to be the rule for these fishermen, pictured near New Iceland in 1925.

Spurred on by their new-found success, several of the colonists made long trips the following winter north on the lake beyond Big Island and Black Island, but they did not venture further than Little Grindstone, as the vast expanse of fresh water which lay beyond had been little explored, and they had only a vague idea of its size.

As the Icelanders ventured further out onto Lake Winnipeg, the risks they ran grew, as Tómas Jónasson of Engimýri, brother of Sigtryggur Jónasson, discovered.

> About eight years after I arrived here [c. 1884], I set off in a boat to catch whitefish east across the lake at Sandy River, which runs west into Lake Winnipeg opposite Mikley. Our leader was Árni Andrésson from Syðri Bægisá in Öxnadalur, whose father Andrés, and Egill Tómasson, my grandfather, were brothers. The rest of the crew was made up of Dínus Jónsson from Þingeyjarsýsla, Antoníus Eiríksson from Steinaborg in Suður-Múlasýsla, and me. We set off on October 8, and by nightfall had reached our destination,

where we waited for a week until the fish began to come inshore. We got a good catch, about 1,600 fish, which we loaded on board, and set off for home in fine weather on the 25th. As we were late in lifting our nets that morning, we were not ready to leave until about midday, but had fine weather as we headed west. When we reached the middle of the lake, however, the wind suddenly began to blow from the northwest, with frost and sleet. After a while the boat began to ice up, and it was cold for us as we headed east. As darkness fell, we were utterly helpless, and could see no sign of land. Árni steered, and told us to look lively and keep rowing into the wind, which we did as best we could. And so we carried on, with no idea where we were heading until we suddenly saw a light. This gave us renewed strength, and we reached land between Borðeyri and Reykjanes, Borðeyri being the southernmost tip of Mikley. If we had set course just half a mile to the south, we would have missed the island completely, and would have faced nothing but open water. But the Lord looks after his own, and the light we saw was a cabin occupied by some fishermen from further north on the island. In it we found Pétur Bjarnason from Harastaðir, whom many know well and who lived for a long time at Ísafold. Being also well known for his willingness to help others, he gave us all the help and sustenance possible.

The following day was calm but cold. We rowed west past Mikley, intending to head for the Icelandic River, but couldn't reach it because of the ice. Instead, we landed in the marsh east of Fagriskógur where, drained by our efforts, we left the boat and walked towards home, which we reached later that evening, soaked through and utterly exhausted. Three days later, we returned for the boat and sailed upriver, reaching home in good health and in one piece.

A plentiful source of food and profitable source of commerce in winter, whitefish were caught in temperatures as low as -30°C, ensuring they reached market in prime condition.

It was necessity more than anything which drove the colonists out onto the lake in search of fish, which was an excellent source of food for them and their families. Soon, however, it also became a means of trade, and in December of 1877, only two years after the arrival of the first settlers, an announcement appeared in *Framfari* stating that Friðjón Friðriksson was offering 8 cents a piece for whitefish. Friðriksson was not alone, however, and another article which appeared in February stated that a fisherman had sold his catch in Winnipeg for 20 cents a

Antoníus Eiríksson, pictured here with his wife, Ingveldur Jóhannesdóttir, and foster son, Jón, was one of New Iceland's most celebrated hunters and fishermen.

fish, and that the going rate was 16-20 cents. Preserving catches, of course, was no problem, as they froze as soon as they were pulled from the water and arrived in the rapidly growing Winnipeg market in perfect condition.

Following this initial boom, the price of whitefish dropped to just under 10 cents a fish as the market became more settled. Like other traders, Friðriksson purchased his fish from the settlers in exchange for goods, and by the winter of 1879-80, whitefish exports from the colony had reached 15,000-20,000 fish. By no means limited to Winnipeg and the surrounding area, some of these went as far as the U.S., and sources suggest that New Iceland whitefish went as far as St. Paul, Minnesota, 600 kilometers away.

At first, fishing was conducted only in winter, as catches spoiled quickly in the summer heat, and as an activity it involved much more than a quick boat trip out onto the lake. Initially, the Icelanders set off on their expeditions carrying provisions stored in wooden boxes mounted on large horse- or ox-drawn sleds, but the intense cold quickly taught them to add a canvas shelter in which they slept. This was later supplemented by a canvas awning joined to the main tent, which also provided shelter for the horses, and in crude conditions such as these they spent up to several weeks out on the ice.

By 1880, the loosely structured fishing industry had become much more organized, and a number of fishing companies entered the Lake Winnipeg scene.

Soon, however, it became clear that Lake Winnipeg whitefish was by no means an inexhaustible natural resource, and even before 1890 fishermen were beginning to express serious concerns over rapidly falling stocks. The following year, the Canadian authorities imposed a total ban on fishing in the south basin of the lake where the Icelanders fished for their own need, but allowed it to continue in the north basin, where the commercial companies operated.

Not surprisingly, the Icelanders objected strongly to what they perceived as a gross infringement of their rights, but despite a number of attempts to break it, the monopoly enjoyed by the commercial companies would continue for decades to come.

The Icelanders themselves formed several commercial fishing companies around Lake Winnipeg, the first being formed in 1885 by two Gimli merchants, the brothers Hannes and Jóhannes Hannesson. Some of these operated independently, others as subsidiaries or branches of larger companies. Around the same time, two small companies were formed in Mikley.

As an 8-year-old boy Jóhannes Sigurðsson once trudged a kilometre-and-a-half through bitter winter cold to bring his father some cooked fish, but he lived to become a prosperous businessman and the first mayor of Gimli.

One of these, owned by the brothers Stefán and Jóhannes Sigurðsson, grew rapidly, and soon moved south to Hnausa, where its operations later expanded into passenger and freight transporation and included ownership of the pride of the Icelandic fleet on Lake Winnipeg, the *Lady of the Lake*.

THROUGH LAKE AND FOREST

A turning point in the lives of the New Icelanders came on a balmy summer day at the end of July 1889, when two representatives of the Canadian government, Messrs Colcleugh and McDonald, drove a horse-drawn buggy all the way north from Selkirk to the Icelandic River. Fourteen years after it was first settled, New Iceland finally had a passable road.

Known as the Colonization or Icelanders' Road, its route had, in fact, been cleared in the autumn of 1876, only a year after the first settlers arrived. That summer, the authorities had surveyed a road of 50 km and 8 metres wide running the length of the colony, and work began immediately on the arduous task of felling trees and cutting a route through the forest—tough, physical labour, all of which was done by axe.

When work began at Gimli, moving both north and south at the same time, the closest road to the colony extended no further than to Netley Creek, about 30 km from New Iceland's southern end. Through time, this gap was closed by the Icelanders, bringing the total length of the Colonization road to some 80 kilometers.

Paid for by the Canadian government, which also provided the engineering expertise, the road provided many of the Icelanders, particularly the younger ones, with a much-needed source of employment. Although the pay was poor, the food was free and unusually good. The women who worked as cooks received the same wages as the men, and all seem to have enjoyed their work, which also gave them an excellent opportunity to learn how to use an axe. At the day's end, there was the opportunity for some home-spun entertainment, and songs, games, and dance rang through the rough tent camps which housed the work crews.

Work for women in Canada, unlike Iceland, was usually readily available and well-paid, such as in this laundry.

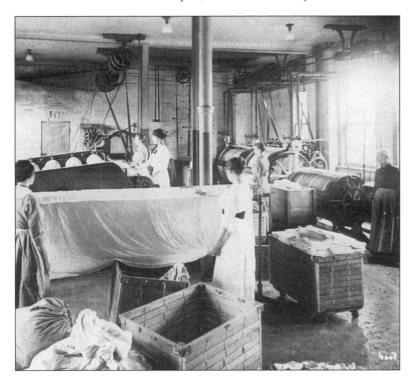

For years, however, this vital artery, through which the lifeblood of the fledgling colony was intended to flow, remained only half completed. In March of 1877, when tree felling had been completed, the Icelanders had returned home to care for their loved ones, then in the grip of the smallpox epidemic, and government funds, erratic at the best of times, had dried up completely. Totally lacking in bridges, embankments, or any form of surface, the rough trail was passable only in winter when it was sealed by snow and ice, until the sun and rain of spring, summer, and autumn turned it into a treacherous quagmire.

Rough as it was, the crude road was better than nothing. When open, it made it possible to journey by horse and sled from Gimli to the Icelandic River in the space of a single day, without making the often hazardous detour out onto Lake Winnipeg. Badly maintained, however, it later became criss-crossed by fences and gates as the colony expanded in the years following 1880, a lack of traffic giving the local homesteaders little incentive to bypass it when fencing off their claims.

As the Icelanders became more at home in their new environment, novel solutions were adopted to protect them from the winter cold, such as this caravan-cum-sleigh pictured at Gypsumville, Lake Manitoba.

At times, long convoys of sleighs formed on Lake Winnipeg. The one seen here is preceded by a snowplough drawn by two teams of horses.

Gradually, the delays and inconvenience caused by this haphazard collection of man-made obstacles became unacceptable, particularly to the postman who traversed the road regularly. Following several complaints, the government finally released the funding necessary to finish the road properly, and the summer of 1889 brought a fresh wave of activity to the colony, as bridges were laid, potholes filled, fencing removed, and a gravel surface laid. By the time Colcleugh and McDonald made their historic trip, New Iceland had its first main road.

The state of the colony's other roads was a different matter. When the government surveyors had surveyed the area, they carved rough, straight paths through its natural features as a means of marking out section lines. Often mere lines through the dense undergrowth, these served the Icelanders as walking paths between farms, and in some places were supplemented by trails through the forest cut by the Natives. Trodden by men and animals over the years, this network of crude trails eventually became wide enough to accommodate a horse- or ox-drawn buggy, and the settlers could now travel about their daily business in relative comfort.

Despite the improvement in land-based transportation, the lake and rivers remained the principal means of transport for the New Iceland colonists, just as they had been for the Natives. In summer, they travelled in row boats, in winter on sleds drawn by horses, oxen, or dogs, and in this way they could travel all year round, weather, of course, permitting.

When the Icelanders arrived in New Iceland, they had no boats apart from the flat-bottomed barges which had brought them and their possessions down the Red River. Soon, however, they learned to build their own boats, developed by local craftsmen to include additions such as sails. The better off among them, such as Friðjón Friðriksson and Samson

At War With the Métis

The Métis were the descendants of French and Scottish fur traders and native Americans.

The descendants of French and Scottish fur traders and native Americans, the Métis, played a major role in the history of Manitoba in the years between 1870 and 1885, the time during which the Icelanders were first settling in the West.

Able hunters, whose numbers extended to several thousand, most Métis preferred the ways of the Natives to those of the settlers. Although they followed the buffalo, they did live in permanent homes. This did little to endear them to the European immigrants, however, who viewed them, as they often did the Natives, with a mixture of disdain and fear.

By 1870, one of the Métis, Louis Riel, had succeeded in uniting his people into a coherent military force, with which

The long arm of the law as represented by this pair of Mounties in winter mode was a rare sight in New Iceland.

he intended to fight the white newcomers, but this short struggle ended with a peace agreement, after which Riel was outlawed. Like many of his brethren in the American West, however, he emerged from these events with semi-legendary status, and by the time the Icelanders arrived in New Iceland, his name was known to every settler in Manitoba.

By 1885, many of the Métis who had inhabited the lands around the Red River had moved west to Saskatchewan, driven by the relentless tide of immigrants and drawn by the rapidly shrinking buffalo herds. Tired of having their rights ignored by bureaucrats in Ottawa, they recalled Louis Riel from his exile in Montana, and he immediately returned home to present demands for independence, which the Canadian government failed to acknowledge. As a result, Riel and his force occupied the village of Batoche, turning it into a fortified headquarters.

Louis Riel

Bjarnason, who both traded on the lake from the colony's inception, had their own York boats, each capable of carrying up to seven tons. This type of craft remained in use until after 1900.

The first steamboat acquired by the Icelanders was the *Victoria*. Built in Ontario in the spring of 1878, it had already spent two summers carrying goods and passengers on the Red River when it was purchased by Sigtryggur Jónasson and Friðjón Friðriksson in partnership with a Scotsman named Walkley. Later, they added a barge, the *Aurora*, but this spent most of its working life elsewhere and was sold in 1891.

The pride of the Icelandic fleet on Lake Winnipeg, however, was the sturdy *Lady of the Lake*, custom-built for the brothers Stefán and Jóhannes Sigurðsson at Selkirk in 1896 to carry passengers and freight.

This time, the government response was swift. In mid-March, 1885, a force of 5,000 regular soldiers was dispatched to deal with the uprising, accompanied by 120 volunteers from Winnipeg, among them several Icelanders whose names appeared on a muster roll published in *Leifur*. They were Jóhann Pálsson, Þorsteinn Pétursson, Þorvarður Jóhannesson, Stefán Guðmundsson, Magnús Jónsson, Jón Dínusson, Runólfur Runólfsson, Jón Júlíus (Jónsson), Jón Blöndal, Björn Blöndal, and Sigurður Árnason. They were joined by Jón Jónasson, who took care of the packhorses, and who long after his death would serve as one of the inspirations for the character of Jens Duffrin, son of Ólafur fíolín, who appears in the novels of the present-day Icelandic writer Böðvar Guðmundsson.

The pride of the Icelandic fleet on Lake Winnipeg, the Lady of the Lake, *seen here just before the turn of the century, was a vital link with the outside world for the New Iceland settlers.*

Jón Júlíus, brother to the poet "K.N." Júlíus, was one of those who served with the forces in the Northwest. He later described these events at a banquet held in Winnipeg upon the army's return.

The army marched northwest to meet the Métis, and after a siege which cost several lives, finally succeeded in bringing its massive numerical superiority to bear on the rebels in an easy victory at Batoche. Riel was captured, and later hung.

Among the Icelanders wounded in the battle was Magnús Jónsson, struck by a bullet which passed through his upper left arm, narrowly avoiding the bone. Apparently nothing daunted, he is said to have stood and fought for an hour before being dragged off to a field hospital for treatment.

The farmer poet Björn Hjörleifsson enjoys a leisurely buggy ride with his wife,
Guðrún Jóhanna Einarsdóttir, and one of their 12 children in the summer of 1908.
After a short stay on Willow Point, this pioneer couple settled near Riverton. Of their
large family, one of their sons, Gunnlaugur, died in the trenches of France during the
First World War. He was one of the 1,245 Icelanders who fought in the conflict, 144
of whom perished.

The army returned to Winnipeg on July 14 to a welcome so
rapturous that its like had never before been seen in the city. The Icelandic
Progressive Society staged a special celebration in honour of the men
who had upheld the ancient warlike traditions of the race from the
North, and after two of the veterans, Jón Júlíus and Jóhann Pálsson, had
regaled their audience with tales of their experiences, everyone settled
down to the serious business of having a good time.

As for the Métis, they were gradually absorbed into the general mainstream of modern Canada but, like many of the immigrant groups, have
succeeded in preserving their own special identity.

Although a variety of other vessels were a regular sight on the lake, the common problem facing them all was the short operating season which, as elsewhere on Canada's major waterways, lasted less than six months of the year. When winter closed the lake, communications ceased altogether for the few weeks it took the ice to harden, and even when it had, the sudden, strong winds which frequently whipped across its surface could make travel a hazardous business. The first recorded Icelander to die in such conditions was Anna Sigríður Guðmundsdóttir from Steðji on Þelamörk, who perished from exposure in the winter of 1876, and in the years that followed, many others would lose fingers, toes, or whole limbs due to frostbite.

The growth of the Winnipeg fish market around 1880 brought with it a pressing need for a proper system of transport across the ice in winter, but as late as 1893, it still took up to three weeks for fish transported by horse- or ox-drawn sleighs to reach Selkirk from the fishing grounds at the northern end

The Canadian Army, Icelanders included, approaches Batoche just before the battle.

of Lake Winnipeg. By then, these travelled in convoys of up to 24, while for those travelling on foot, ice skates offered an alternative means of travel, a method favoured by the postal service at one time.

At the time of the colony's inception, the site of New Iceland was chosen for its promise of access to a proposed coast-to-coast railway running the breadth of Canada. When the railway came, however, the route of the CPR ran not through Selkirk, but Winnipeg, which came as a disappointment to the Icelanders. It would take several years of struggle before New Iceland finally became linked to the rest of the system by means of a rail extension opened at 11 a.m. on the morning of November 27, 1906, when the first steam engine puffed its way to an enthusiastic welcome at Gimli—thanks to the energetic lobbying of two local Committees under the exceptional leadership of Sigtryggur Jónasson.

The advent of the railway was of greater significance than even people at the time realized. As was also the case for the inhabitants of Árborg in 1910, and Icelandic River in 1914, this event changed their lives forever, removing as it did for all time the colony's sense of itself as an isolated settlement of pioneers on the edge of the frontier. As the region became an increasingly popular destination for visitors, the railway brought with it growing prosperity for the descendants of the settlers, accompanied by a change in their attitude towards the outside world. External influences grew stronger, diluting forever the colony's uniquely Icelandic identity. The long years of isolation were finally over, and New Iceland was now more closely linked with the rest of Canada.

Old meets new at Gimli: the coming of the railway in 1906 revolutionized communications throughout New Iceland and changed the life of the settlers forever. This photograph probably dates from the years 1910-15.

TRADING PLACES

As has been mentioned earlier, one of the first entrepreneurial ventures in New Iceland was the opening of a store at Gimli, shortly after the arrival of the settlers in 1875. The site of this venture was a log storehouse, built with the government loan money and overseen by Friðjón Friðriksson.

As most of the colonists had arrived with little more than what they could carry or wore on their backs, disposable income was in short supply, and early trade, such as it was, was primitive, based on a system of barter by which his customers were credited by Friðriksson for fish, milk products or other commodoties in exchange for necessities such as flour or other staples.

The cornerstone of trade and commerce in New Iceland was at first the Canadian government loan, which Friðriksson, John Taylor and Sigtryggur Jónasson distributed among the

Harvesting ice on Lake Winnipeg at Gimli in 1922. The Icelanders quickly learned how to store ice by collecting it in piles buried well below ground or kept in insulated buildings. Broken into smaller pieces, it was used to chill fish and other foodstuffs during the hot summer months.

colonists in the form of supplies, according to need, as best they could. This was later supplemented by income derived from fishing on Lake Winnipeg and, as commercial fishing grew, the jingle of hard cash in the settlers' pockets became an increasingly common sound.

As accounts and advertisements of the time show, fishing was, initially at least, a profitable business, with an average of 10 cents per whitefish being paid at the same time as a 40-kilo sack of flour cost $3.50, giving a rate of 40 fish per bushel. Using the same system of calculation, two whitefish could buy a metre of linen cloth or a pound of sugar, while five could purchase a whole pound of tobacco.

For the first years, Friðriksson's position as owner of the colony's only store gave him a virtual trade monopoly in New Iceland, although a few others, mainly intinerant traders from

Winnipeg, also occasionally visited. Sometimes, enterprising settlers travelled to Winnipeg or Selkirk, and shortly after New Year's, 1878, Árni Sigvaldason and Jón Júlíus Jónsson, arrived from Winnipeg and sold 115 sacks of flour.

At around the same time, another Icelander, Samson Bjarnason, opened a small store in the Árnes district, where he sold flour and other wares in exchange for fish. In late April, 1878, he travelled to Winnipeg on his York boat, taking with him a few of the colonists. Friðriksson was in Winnipeg at the same time, and the pair returned to New Iceland the following week with two boatloads of goods. On their arrival, Bjarnason headed straight back north, and by mid-May he had sold his entire cargo.

This arrangement continued until 1880, with the pair sailing to Winnipeg on their York boats and returning to sell their wares to the eager colonists, but when Friðriksson and Sigtryggur Jónasson purchased the steamboat *Victoria*, its increased capacity gave them the lion's share of the New Iceland trade. In 1881 they also formed the Jónasson-Friðriksson Company at Icelandic River, which, as well as the sawmill, included a store run by Friðriksson until his departure from New Iceland in 1885.

After a few years in New Iceland, Samson Bjarnason was one of the colonists who left for North Dakota with the Rev. Páll Þorláksson.

Home deliveries, as offered by the Tergesen store after the turn of the century. Formed and owned by Hans Pétur Tergesen, an immigrant from Akureyri, the store was based in Gimli.

Although shallow and relatively current-free, the Icelandic River formed a vital com-munications link by boat in summer, and sleigh in winter. This photograph was taken at Lundur (now Riverton) the home of Kristjón Finnson, an important local businessman. To the left stands the building he used as a store, and, as can be seen, the forest has already been cleared for some distance.

The products brought in by these early merchants were mainly goods which they knew the colonists needed, such as flour, sugar, and salt, all of which were sold by the sack. Bacon, oatmeal, and fresh meat were also popular, as were everyday items such as linen, dry goods, shoes, soap, tin buckets, stovepipes, paraffin, and, of course, that greatest of life's necessities, tobacco.

One of the time-honoured traditions which the Icelanders brought with them to the New World was a mistrust of merchants, storekeepers, and traders of all types, and no doubt Friðriksson suffered as much from this as his commercial brethren at home. Collecting payments could be difficult, and this was a particularly sensitive business when it involved friends or family. Contemporary sources reveal, however, that Friðriksson eventually closed his store at Gimli without collect-ing large sums of money owing him.

Writing in the publication *Landnemi*, published in Reykjavík by Baldvin L. Baldvinsson between 1892 and 1894, Gunnar Gíslason had the following to say about commerce in New Iceland:

Many still remember how things were with regard to trade during the 10 years after the arrival of the first settlers, and how there was a monopoly on most of life's necessities, while some could not be obtained at all. Proof of the latter lies in the fact that farmers journeyed to Selkirk and Winnipeg in small boats, or overland using axes and sleighs, to seek what they needed rather than dealing with those storekeepers who cheated them so badly. Since then, however, things have gradually got better, commercial practices in the colony have improved, and supplies are now obtainable at a price that is acceptable, given the circumstances.

BREAKING NEWS

While the early settlers may have arrived in Canada sadly igno-rant of agricultural methods and working practices in their new home, there was one area at least in which the Icelanders stood head and shoulders above their neighbours—newspaper publishing.

From the very beginning, newspapers or newsletters would appear to have been considered a basic necessity in the daily lives of the colonists, and they had barely settled in when the first appeared during the winter of 1875–76. Entitled *Nýi Þjóðólfur*, it was edited and handwritten by Jón Guðmundsson, a native of Þingeyjarsýsla, who produced three editions, all of which have now unfortunately been lost.

Although the idea of producing a newspaper deep in the Canadian wilderness, given the crude conditions under which the Icelanders lived, might appear faintly ridiculous to the modern eye, this proved to be one of the colonists' most endur-ing dreams.

On January 13, as soon as the smallpox epidemic began to show the first signs of abating at the beginning of 1877, a meet-ing was convened under the chairmanship of Sigtryggur Jónasson to discuss just such a project, and over the next days, a company was formed with 100 shares, each priced at $10.

Native Icelandic wrestling, glíma, remained a popular sport in New Iceland until well into this century, and this pair, pictured about 1915, clearly still knew all the right moves. Later, however, it was replaced by more "traditional" Canadian sports, and the country's Olympic ice hockey team of 1920, apart from one member, consisted entirely of Icelandic Canadians.

The front page of the first edition of Framfari, September 10, 1877.

Although this sum was equivalent to a third-share of a cow, 73 of the shares had been spoken for by February 5, and by April, over $300 of the $1,000 startup capital required had been raised. A board of directors comprising Jónasson, Friðjón Friðriksson, and Jóhann Briem then contacted the Rev. Jón Bjarnason in Minneapolis, himself involved in publishing, and asked him to obtain a printing press, typeface, and other necessary equipment. Acquiring Icelandic typeface took time, however, and this did not arrive until June, and then only in part.

The result of these labours was *Framfari*, the first edition of which appeared on September 10, 1877. From the beginning, the paper was published at Lundur on the Icelandic River, where a log printshop was built for the purpose, and the printer was Jónas Jónasson, a brother of Sigtryggur, who had learned his trade in Akureyri. Some 300-400 copies of each edition were produced, and the vast majority of the colonists were subscribers. At the same time, copies were sent home to Iceland, as well as to Icelanders elsewhere in Canada and the U.S., and its subscription network reached as far as the U.K. and France.

On the front page of the first edition can be found the articles of incorporation of the publishing company, along with a leader addressed to its readers and subscribers.

The settlers had to learn a variety of new skills, among them how to address a letter.

> As soon as Icelanders began emigrating to this continent, they immediately began to fear that they would lose their language and national identity unless they did something to preserve them. They have always agreed that two things were necessary in order to preserve these priceless inheritances. One was the establishment of a colony of their own, the other the publication of a periodical in Icelandic, two factors now so closely linked that it is barely conceivable that one could prosper without the other. Much discussion has been held on the establishment of an Icelandic colony, and attempts were even made to achieve this in various parts of this country, but nothing really came of this until the establishment of this colony. However, no attempt has been made to publish a newspaper, although this was one of the intentions of the Icelandic Society in the New World, which staged a National Celebration in Milwaukee in 1874.

The names of the editors are not mentioned in the first edition, but it is known that Sigtryggur Jónasson steered the paper to begin with. In January, 1878, this duty was assumed by Halldór Briem, who served as editor until the paper's eventual demise on January 30, 1880.

The advent of *Framfari* undoubtedly also served to encourage the opening of a post office at Gimli on December 1, 1877,

One of the three directors of Framfari *and a prominent figure in local government, Jóhann Briem lived at Grund on the Icelandic River with his wife, Guðrún Pálsdóttir. Guðrún, the daughter of Páll Pétursson and Margrét Magnúsdóttir, had lost 10 of her siblings by the time she was 14— under the tragic circumstances recorded earlier in this chapter. Jóhann and Guðrún themselves had six children, four of whom survived, the other two dying in their first year.*

with Friðjón Friðriksson serving as postmaster during its early years. However, the mail carried much more than the paper. As much of the source material for this book clearly shows, the New Icelanders were enthusiastic letter writers, and what flowed from their pens was carried by the colony's weekly postal service. When it became properly established, what had begun as a trickle became a stream, and letters, newspapers, and a colourful variety of other material flowed between the colonists and their friends and relatives back home, among them the Norwegian-American newspaper the *Decorah Posten*, from which some of the settlers gleaned their news.

Keeping *Framfari* rolling off the presses was always difficult. Subscribers were few and collecting subscriptions was a difficult business at best. Sharp differences of opinion among the colonists also quickly became apparent, and the paper was soon dragged into the deep religious strife which would divide the colony deeply. As the Rev. Jón Bjarnason and Rev. Páll Þorláksson became increasingly bitter opponents, many of the subscribers and shareholders who supported the latter withheld their subscriptions in protest and demanded a complete restructuring of the paper and its board of directors. These demands were not met, and *Framfari* continued to contribute to its own demise by becoming deeply involved in what was becoming an increasingly bitter debate. When it eventually ceased publication at the beginning of 1880, Sigtryggur Jónasson in particular lost a great deal of money.

The first postmaster at Gimli was Friðjón Friðriksson. His successor was Pétur Pálsson, who was followed by Guðni Þorsteinsson, pictured here in the sorting office around the turn of the century, when correspondence between New and old Iceland was at its height. A respected figure and a member of Gimli town council for many years, Þorsteinsson served as postmaster until his death in 1948.

Despite the unfortunate circumstances of its demise, *Framfari* survives as a remarkable source of information on early life in New Iceland, occupying as it did a major place in the hearts of the first settlers. Its disappearance coincided with a time of great hardship, during which many of the poorer colonists abandoned the colony, and no new Icelandic publication appeared in Canada for the next few years.

As the population of New Iceland was declining, however, the Icelandic presence in Winnipeg was growing steadily, but while many of the immigrants there had been discussing the need for a newspaper of their own for some time, the funds necessary for such a venture could not be found. One of the scheme's most enthusiastic proponents was Helgi Jónsson from Suður-Múlasýsla. A rather reserved and private individual who was stubborn in the extreme, he tired of the endless discussions and started his own newspaper, *Leifur*, which first appeared in the spring of 1883. He also appointed himself editor, which would seem to have been something of a miscalculation, as it has been stated in all seriousness that a worse publication has seldom appeared in the Icelandic language. Determination aside, Jónsson knew nothing of publishing, and as a writer was said to be barely able to compose a letter. To make matters worse, the printer was also a novice, and the paper always lacked subscribers. Amazingly, however, it survived for three years, and, like *Framfari*, is now considered an invaluable source in its own right.

Although said by some to be barely capable of composing a letter, Helgi Jónsson managed to edit the newspaper Leifur *in Winnipeg for three years.*

The mail must get through: an early CPR mail wagon.

"Get your latest Heimskringla!" An imaginative flyer, c. 1895.

The end of 1885 saw the launch of another Icelandic publication, the aptly named *Sameiningin* (Unity). Although the mouthpiece of the Icelandic Synod, it was a quality periodical edited by Friðjón Friðriksson, Baldvin L. Baldvinsson, and the Rev. Jón Bjarnason, who by then had returned to Winnipeg. The first religious publication ever published in Icelandic, it was highly influential, not least back home in Iceland, where a comparable work, *Kirkjublaðið*, soon appeared in Reykjavík.

Even before the final edition of *Leifur* rolled off the presses in June of 1886, plans had been made for a new, improved newspaper. Drawing its inspiration from the classic work of Snorri Sturluson entitled *Heimskringla,* it first appeared on September 9, 1886. Like its medieval predecessor, its goals were ambitious. Not merely written for local readers, it was intended to take an active part in the growing political and cultural debate then in progress back home in Iceland.

In short, *Heimskringla* aimed to become the largest Icelandic-language newspaper in circulation anywhere, and to do so, it employed a journalistic team composed of Einar Hjörleifsson, later known as Einar H. Kvaran, and Eggert Jóhannsson, who had previously worked at *Leifur*. Publication proved difficult to begin with, however, and Frímann B. Anderson, the paper's founder-editor, resigned after only two years in office.

By that time, *Heimskringla* had been joined by a competitor, *Lögberg*, whose roots lay in *Framfari* and *Leifur*, not least through Sigtryggur Jónasson, who was one of its founders and a principal investor, and also due to the fact that it was printed on the old press from New Iceland, brought to Winnipeg and renovated for the purpose. One of its journalists was the poet and writer Jón Ólafsson, who had gone on the expedition to Alaska in 1875, and its editor was Einar H. Kvaran, who had by then left *Heimskringla*. The latter responded by acquiring the services of Gestur Pálsson, a well-known poet and journalist brought from Iceland for the purpose, and, as a result, three of the most influential Icelanders of their generation all found themselves working as journalists in Winnipeg at the same time.

The years which followed proved extremely fruitful for both papers, although neither succeeded in becoming the major power it would have wished. Both published news from Iceland, the Icelandic settlements scattered all over North America, and the world at large, while serving as platforms for debate on a wide variety of issues. Each also offered a wide range of material, both poetry and prose, and in the last decade of the century, when Jónasson edited *Lögberg* and Baldvinsson *Heimskringla*, these weekly papers also served as stages for fierce political debate, with the former espousing the views of the Liberals, and the latter those of the Conservatives. But while the colour of a man's politics might be seen from his choice of paper, *Heimskringla* always remained more liberal than its competitor in matters of religion.

Both publications enjoyed a wide circulation in Iceland, where they served as an important source of information. Until after the turn of the century, they were better than anything produced at home, both in terms of content and design, and they served as a model for future publications in Iceland.

A variety of other newspapers and magazines appeared in the years immediately leading up to 1900, but all were short-

The title pages of four Icelandic publications in Manitoba: Leifur (1883-86), Sameiningin (1885-1964), Heimskringla (1886–), and Lögberg (1888–).

lived. Eventually, *Lögberg* and *Heimskringla* were amalgamated into a single publication, *Lögberg-Heimskringla*, which still appears today, providing a variety of news, mainly in English, of the Icelandic community in Canada and the rest of the New World.

RELIGIOUS SCHISM AND SECULAR STRIFE

The Lutheran church was a powerful social force in Iceland in the latter half of the 19th century, and its pastors exercised a strong influence on their flocks, but when the first group arrived in New Iceland in the autumn of 1875, it did so without benefit of clergy, as did the so-called "Large Group" the following year.

Although the ongoing war against "Bacchus" formed a major part of the work of the many missionary and temperance societies all over North America during the 19th and early 20th centuries, their efforts met with varying degrees of success. Gimli in 1907.

Included in this group of worthies pictured at the first meeting of the Icelandic Synod of North America held in Winnipeg from June 24-27, 1885, were delegates from New Iceland, Argyle, and North Dakota, among them some of the leading protagonists in the bitter religious conflict which had wracked New Iceland a few years before (Sigtryggur Jónasson excepted). Back row, from left, Friðrik J. Bergmann, Eiríkur H. Bergmann, Jónas Hall, Björn Jónsson, Páll S. Bardal, Björn Pétursson, Jónas Stefánsson, Benedikt Pétursson, Stephan G. Stephansson, Baldvin L. Baldvinsson. Centre row, from left, Magnús Pálsson, Friðjón Friðriksson, Rev. Jón Bjarnason, Árni Friðriksson, Gísli Jónsson, Þorlákur G. Jónsson, Sigurður Josúa Björnsson. Front row, from left, Kristján Kjernested, Friðrik Jónsson, Guðmundur Björnsson, Jón Ólafsson, Þorsteinn Jóhannesson, and Ólafur Guðmundsson.

As a result, almost as soon as the settlers had settled in their primitive cabins, discussions turned to acquiring a pastor to minister to the colony, christen its infants, confirm its youngsters, marry its couples, and bury its dead.

Back home in Iceland, religious life had continued almost without change or interruption since the advent of the Reformation there in 1550, but amid the upheaval of pioneering life in the West, the colonists found themselves exposed to a bewildering variety of churches and beliefs.

At the time New Iceland was first settled, two Icelandic Lutheran pastors were already living in the New World. Generally popular and well liked by their congregations, they were the Rev. Jón Bjarnason and the Rev. Páll Þorláksson.

Bjarnason, born in 1845 and the son of a pastor at Álftafjörður in Iceland's East Fjords, had graduated with distinction from the country's seminary in Reykavík, where he subsequently became a teacher in 1869. Later, he married Lára Guðjohnsen, thereafter referred to as Frú Lára, herself a teacher, a singer, and an active helper of her husband.

In 1873, the couple emigrated to America, encouraged by Páll Þorláksson, a close friend of Bjarnason's from his student days, who had preceded them the year before. Intitially they headed for Milwaukee, but they later set off on a series of moves which by the beginning of the following year had taken them to Minneapolis, where Bjarnason became editor of a Norwegian religous magazine.

The first pastor of New Iceland, the Rev. Jón Bjarnason found his calling more than he had bargained for.

The leaders of the New Iceland colony were well aware of the Rev. Jón and made repeated requests to him to become their pastor. Heeding their call, he travelled extensively through-out the colony in the summer of 1877, performing a series of religious duties, and he and Lára moved to New Iceland the following year.

Páll Þorláksson, four years younger than his friend, was only 28 in 1877. Born in 1849, he was the son of Þorlákur G. Jónsson from Stórutjarnir who, as was mentioned earlier, emigrated to the United States with his wife and ten children in 1872. Páll, described by his contemporaries as a sensitive young man with a lively intelligence and thirst for knowledge, had therefore spent five years in the U.S. before his arrival in New Iceland in 1877. While in America, he had become attracted to the religious zeal of the Norwegian settlers among whom he lived and, having graduated from a German seminary in St. Louis, he was ordained by the Missouri Norwegian Synod before returning north to Wisconsin where he became pastor to a Norwegian congregation.

A music teacher by profession and known as Frú Lára, Lára Guðjohnsen proved an able assistant to her husband.

Throughout his time in the New World, Þorláksson had maintained close ties with the land he had left behind and served as an invaluable source of information for the Icelandic immigrants who followed him across the Atlantic. As a result, he did not need to be asked twice when requested to head for the wilderness of New Iceland to minister to his pastorless country-men, and reaching Winnipeg in 1876, he joined the "Large Group" around the time of their arrival in New Iceland in the autumn of that year.

During his first two weeks in the colony, Rev. Páll, as he quickly became known to his flock, christened 14 infants, buried 17 colonists, and held an open-air service in Gimli attended by some 500 Icelanders, who, although they may have found his strict religious beliefs somewhat strange, could not deny that as a person, he was extremely likable, helpful, and active. The following autumn, as the colonists struggled to recover from the effects of the smallpox epidemic, he was back again, ministering to the needs of settlers throughout the colony, and before his return to the U.S. he had organized three congregations, which were named the *Vídalíns-*, *Guðbrands-*, and *Hallgríms-* Congregations in honour of three of Iceland's greatest clerics.

One of the first Icelandic immigrants to the New World, the Rev. Páll Þorláksson later led his flock to Dakota Territory.

About the same time as Þorláksson was organizing his new charges, Rev. Jón Bjarnason and Frú Lára arrived in New Iceland, having being chosen by the majority of the colonists as their pastor. Rev. Jón's congregations covered the entire colony and were known as the Steinkirkju-, Bæjar-, Breiðuvíkur-, Bræðra-, and Mikleyjar Congregations. Formally established congregations, they were supposed to pay his salary.

The result of this arrangement was that the New Iceland colonists split into two factions, the so-called *Pálsmenn* and *Jónsmenn* (Páll's Men and Jon's Men), signalling the beginning of a bitter round of religious and secular strife which would divide the colony. Although the issue focused on differences between the fundamentalist dogma of the Norwegian Synod and the more conservative doctrine espoused by the Rev. Jón Bjarnason and the Icelandic Lutheran church, it soon became magnified in the hothouse atmosphere of the colony, at times degenerating into little more than a personal feud between supporters of both sides, which then grew to encompass elements that had nothing to do with religion.

As the conflict deepened, both parties became more intransigent, and their positions became more deeply entrenched. While Þorláksson railed against the liberalism of the Icelandic Lutheran church and the Manitoba secular school system—which he dismissed as a path to Hell and from which he advised his supporters to withdraw their off-spring without delay—Bjarnason raged against the "narrow, dogmatic, and archaic" teachings of the Norwegian Synod, with its preachings on eternal damnation, the impending approach of Judgment Day, and its ambivalent attitude toward women, who had no say in the running of its affairs.

In viewing the controversy with the benefit of hindsight, it is worth remembering that the Rev. Jón Bjarnason's chief sup-porters, and therefore Þorláksson's strongest opponents, included Sigtryggur Jónasson, Friðjón Friðriksson, and Jóhann Briem, all of whom were leaders of the colony's assembly and directors of *Framfari*. Clearly, religious and secular life in New Iceland were closely intertwined, and this served to exacerbate, rather than alleviate, the conflict.

One of the most bitter phases of the religious dispute touched the very heart of the concept of New Iceland, as expressed in the aims, ideals, and self-image of the colonists themselves. In January, 1878, a number of Þorláksson's leading supporters sent a letter to the Norwegian Synod, describing their many hardships and requesting financial help. Answered with a donation in the amount of $1,300, the missive quickly became known as the "Begging Letter" (*betlibréf*) and became a source of deep offence to many of the colonists and their leaders. An article published in *Framfari* castigated Þorláksson and his supporters for their lack of pride, while claiming that the situation was not nearly as bad as they had portrayed it.

During the weeks and months that followed, Jón Bjarnason traversed the length and breadth of New Iceland, encouraging and ministering to his flock, ably supported by *Framfari*. For his part, Páll Þorláksson never lived in the colony, but spent months at a time there, particularly in the Árnes district where he enjoyed the hospitality of his friends and supporters.

Despite a number of attempts to resolve it, the situation continued for the next two years. The first move towards concil-iation came on March 25-26, 1878, when the two protagonists met face to face for the first time at an open public meeting. Although this encounter ended on a promising note, the dispute continued, and at a similar meeting held almost a year later, on March 18, 1879, the pair agreed to continue to disagree.

*By the time this group portrait was taken by Winnipeg photographers Baldwin &
Blöndal in 1891, these women, several of whom had come from New Iceland, had
become models of urban sophistication. Among those known are the pastor's wife Lára
Guðjohnsen (centre) and Guðrún Briem from Grund on the Icelandic River, who
stands in the back row at the far left. Courtesy of the Manitoba Archives.*

Despite grave implications for the colony and its future, religious dispute was by no means a phenomenon peculiar to New
Iceland. It was widespread throughout Canada and the U.S.,
with the Norwegian Synod, of which Páll Þorláksson was undeniably a part, playing a major role. Now in failing health following a bout of scarlet fever, Rev. Páll left the colony for good
following the meeting of March, 1879, and moved to Dakota
Territory with many supporters, who by now had had more
than enough of New Iceland. Together they formed the
Icelandic settlement in Pembina County, but Þorláksson himself

did not live to enjoy it, dying at the age of only 32 in March of 1882.

In the autumn of 1879, Páll's principal opponent, Rev. Jón Bjarnason, announced his intention to return home to Iceland and, accompanied by Frú Lára, he returned to his native East Fjords, where he remained for the next five years. His last act as pastor of New Iceland came just before his departure in 1880, when he consecrated Halldór Briem as his successor. Rev. Jón later returned to Winnipeg, however, and he served as pastor there with great distinction for many years.

Halldór Briem, previously mentioned as editor of *Framfari*,

The Manitoba Melting Pot

Thus lived many immigrant families in Winnipeg during the early days—in a single crowded but tidy room. The photo was taken circa 1915.

When Manitoba became a province of Canada in 1870, its population included only 12,000 people of European descent, their numbers almost equally divided between immigrants of British and French origin. In the years since their arrival, both nationalities had established blood ties with the native Indians, more so the French, the majority of whom were Métis.

In the years immediately after the province was formed, the main wave of immigrants came from Ontario, their origins lying in the British Isles, but by 1880 they had been joined by Russian Mennonites and Icelanders. In 1886, Winnipeg, a town of only 3,000 when the first Icelanders arrived there a decade could see little future in his new calling, especially as so many of the colonists had already left, doubtless reducing his stipend signficantly. After only a year of service, he resigned, and, after trying his luck as an itinerant preacher for a further two years, he returned home to Iceland, where he became a teacher in the school at Möðruvellir, never to return to Canada.

For the next few years, New Iceland had no pastor and no church and the balance of ecclesiastical power now shifted to Winnipeg. The great schism of 1876-79 was by no means the only religious dispute to grip the Canadian Icelanders. In the last decade of the 19th century, Unitarianism, a more liberal sect

before, had grown to a bustling city of 20,000, and by 1888, the population of Manitoba as a whole had risen to 110,000, of which the French, who only 20 years before had formed half of the European total, had dropped to only 7%.

Shortly after 1890, the Manitoba government embarked on a concerted effort to attract even more immigrants, as only a fifth of the land available had then been settled. The policy clearly succeeded, as by 1900 the province's population had more than doubled to 250,000, and, while settlers from British Ontario continued to form the majority, Francophones, Mennonites, and Icelanders formed the three main minorities.

Over the next decade, a further 200,000 immigrants streamed into the province, over half of them from Eastern Europe, among them 12,000 Poles and 14,000 Ukrainians. Temporarily interrupted by the Great War, the human tide later resumed, and by 1930, Manitoba was home to a million inhabitants.

Although this figure has risen little over the last 60 years, it has since been augmented by more recent arrivals from Asia and Africa, who, along with the Europeans and native Indians, have helped give the province one of the most colourful cultural and racial mixes found anywhere on Earth. At the turn of the century, the origins of the main groups of immigrants were as follows:

The general enthusiasm for religious matters in New Iceland was not reflected in a corresponding zeal for building churches. One of he colony's first large churches was built in 1906 at Gimli, most earlier houses of worship being small local chapels and meeting houses. Some 300 members of the Gimli congregation have posed here for the camera.

The British Isles

As the first Europeans to arrive, the Scots, Irish, English, and Welsh formed the controlling majority in Manitoba from the very beginning. Only a few migrated direct from their home countries, most of them arriving via Ontario. As elsewhere in Canada, provincial government in the early days was fairly loose and in no way able to cope with the sudden population explosion. As a result, discrimination flourished and, in the early days at least, settlers from the British Isles tended to treat arrivals from other nations as "foreigners" rather than as neighbours. Evidence of British influence can still be seen in place names all over Manitoba, with the Scots contributing names such as Argyle and Balmoral, the Irish Killarney and Clandeboye, and the English Hartney, Gladstone, Morris, and a host of others.

French

In 1818, decades before the arrival of large numbers of immigrants, a French mission was established at what is now Winnipeg, and as a focus of Catholic influence it later served to attract large numbers of other French speakers, mainly from Quebec and the U.S. Although St. Boniface, once than the Lutherans, became increasingly popular among many of the Icelanders, and as the new faith spread, Unitarian congregations sprang up in New Iceland and elsewhere. Relations between the two churches varied and were occasionally complicated by the fact that orthodox Lutheran pastors sometimes crossed over without informing their congregations.

As a result, the religious question was not formally resolved until 1922, when a compromise settlement was finally reached with the formation of The United Icelandic Synod in North America.

an independent municipality on the east bank of the Red River, is now part of Winnipeg, it retains a strong French culture, and French influence is evident in place names such as Portage la Prairie, Aubigny, and Beausejour.

Métis
Following their defeat in the conflict described earlier in this chapter, the Métis have gradually been reduced to a small minority of the Manitoban whole.

Russian Mennonite
In 1874, just before the first group of Icelanders landed in Canada, a large group of German-speaking Mennonites from Russia arrived in Manitoba, settling in the thousands on the prairie to the south and east of Winnipeg. A strongly orthodox Christian sect with a strict interpretation of the Bible, they accept the divinity of Christ and of the Holy Trinity. Like the Amish, they are strict pacifists, refusing all forms of military service, and as a rule do not mix with outsiders. Their principal centres of population all bear German names such as Steinbach and Altona.

FAREWELL TO NEW ICELAND

From the colony's earliest beginnings, conditions in New Iceland were bad enough to make many of the settlers wonder if they had come to the right place, and it could hardly escape their notice that many of those who had given up on the settlement prospered better elsewhere.

For many of the disillusioned, Winnipeg offered an

Icelandic

Since their arrival in New Iceland in 1875, the Icelanders have mixed widely with other nationalities, and their descendants can now be found all over Manitoba, although their influence remains strongest in the region around Winnipeg and Lake Winnipeg, and in place names such as Gimli, Arborg, Hecla, and Reykjavik.

Ukrainian

Although the first Ukrainians did not arrive in Manitoba until 1896, their numbers had swelled to over 40,000 by 1910, outnumbering the Icelanders who had preceded them by over 20 years. As most of them came from Galicia, the Icelanders called them "Gallar," which explains why Canadian Icelanders find the Icelandic word for jeans, *gallabuxur*, so funny. Place names like Berlo point to their influence.

Natives

For thousands of years, the West was populated by Natives tribes, chief of whom were the Assiniboines and Ojibwa on the prairies, the Cree and Chippewa in the woodlands, and the Inuit north of Hudson Bay. Driven off their tribal lands by the tide of European immigration of the 19th century, they had, and still have, great difficulty in replacing millennia of tradition as hunters with the fixed settlements of the new order. Countless place names in the province testify to their presence, including Winnipeg and Manitoba.

attractive means of escape, and even for those who stayed behind, the thriving city, then as now the urban centre of Manitoba, was the place where many bought their supplies, heard the latest news of their countrymen, or sought work when times were bad.

Those who persevered though the first four or five difficult years in New Iceland emerged with a heightened sense of self-confidence, and their experiences in their adopted homeland made the prospect of leaving and heading for greener pastures much less daunting than it would otherwise have been.

The census of 1901 put the population of Manitoba at 255,211, with the following breakdown:

English	64,542	Polish	1,674
Irish	47,418	Romanian	98
Scottish	51.365	Russian	3,326
U.K., other	914	Icelandic	11,924
French	16,021	Ukrainian	3,849
Austrian	4,901	Other European	223
Belgian	940	Chinese	206
Finnish	76	Japanese	5
German	27,265	Syrian	45
Greek	27	Other Asian	3
Hungarian	186	Indian	16,277
Italian	217	African	61
Jewish	1,514	Others	1,265
Dutch	925		

Of these, 54,778 lived in Winnipeg. Around the same time, Sigtryggur Jónasson conducted his own unofficial census of the Manitoban Icelanders. According to his calculations, they accounted for 5% of the total population, with 2,500 living in New Iceland, 4,000 in Winnipeg, 700 in Selkirk, and over 1,000 in the Argyle Settlement, the rest being scattered throughout the province, most of them around Lake Manitoba.

For many years, ox-drawn wagons were the most common form of transport on the prairie, road conditions, of course, permitting. Filled with their owners' possessions, carts like this, pictured on the outskirts of Winnipeg, also served as shelter during the long weeks on the road.

One of the many settlers who left New Iceland during the colony's darkest years around 1880 was Skafti Arason, who with his wife, children, and all their worldly possessions, pulled up stakes and headed off in search of a better life elsewhere.

A native of Þingeyjarsýsla, in Northeastern Iceland, Arason was one of the colony's original founders. Viewed by his contemporaries as one of their most promising young men, he was one of the original party that had accompanied John Taylor and Sigtryggur Jónasson on their expedition to select a site for the settlement. He was a single man of 25 when he arrived with the first group in 1875.

In 1877, Arason took advantage of the opportunity presented by the first visit of Rev. Jón Bjarnason to marry Anna Jóhannsdóttir, a year his senior. Typical in many ways of those who left New Iceland, he has left behind a telling account of the difficulties a move of this kind presented, whether it was south across the border to Dakota or southwest to the Argyle Settlement.

As Arason makes clear, personal relationships were vitally important when planning such a move, and in his case, it was his friend Everett Parsonage, who had accompanied the first settlers in 1875 and taught many of them the skills necessary for survival in their new home, who loomed large in the preparations for departure.

In his memoirs, Arason states that although the summer of 1877 had been fine, things soon took a turn for the worse.

The men often went ahead of their families as they searched for new land in the vast prairie wilderness, and had sometimes even begun planting before their wives and children arrived. This typical scene of breakfast time on the trail was taken somewhere near New Iceland, date unknown.

The summers of 1878-79-80 were extremely wet; the ground was so sodden as to be virtually impassable, the mosquitoes were particularly bad, and the animals wandered around starving, emaciated, and useless.

In 1880, the level of the lake rose so high that it flooded the lowlying meadows, and even on higher ground the haying went badly as the fields were so wet. In the autumn, the water rose so high that the haystacks were badly damaged and even destroyed completely in lower-lying parts. As a result, men saw little prospect of any improvement in conditions, and as many had by then acquired sizeable herds, including some draught animals, they began to consider whether it might not be better to look elsewhere. That year (1880), many began to leave the colony, most of them for Winnipeg or Dakota, where people had first moved in 1878. But towards the end of July, I headed west to Shoal Lake, acting on the advice of John Taylor. If I liked what I saw there, it was our intention to go immediately and cut hay, and move completely the following winter. I did not think much of what I saw, however, and so our plans came to nothing.

On September 25, I went to Winnipeg with William Taylor, John's brother, and from there to Pilot Mound to visit our friend Everett Parson [sic], who had been a servant of John Taylor and had accompanied him from Ontario. Prior to our arrival, E.P. had joined Sigurður Kristófersson and Kristján Jónsson on a trip to look at land, and they had staked a claim in Township 6, R. 14 W. Everett Parson took Taylor, myself, and his father and brother to the same place, and we all staked claims. The Dominion Lands Office was west on the Souris River, and Everett drove us there and back home with him again. In some places near the site we chose there were a few scattered settlers' cabins, in others nothing. But the farmers we visited were no better off than we were and could not sell us any meat or bread, so when we had done with the food we brought with us from E.P., we had nothing left but potatoes.

While on his travels, Arason encountered some of his fellow colonists on the same errand, and he helped them explore and choose homesteads of their own. At the same time, he also selected land for others, before finally returning to his family on

November 13, after an absence of 50 days, to face a bitterly cold winter.

On March 15, 1881, I left New Iceland for good, along with my wife and two children, one in its third year, the other still in its first. With us, I had four draught oxen and one pony for our four sleighs. One sled was covered by a simple cabin made of planks, 6 feet broad and 10 long. This served as our house while we were on our way, and until July after we reached our journey's end. Along with me were Guðmundur Norðmann, with two oxen and two sleighs (there was always one animal per sled here in Manitoba), Sigurður Kristófersson, who had the same, and Skúli Árnason [Guðmundur's brother] who, along with his two oxen and two sleds, was accompanied by a few cattle, his wife, and four children. Sigurður also had quite a few cattle. One of the sleds was used to carry hay, which we bought where we could get it, and where we couldn't we just had to do without. Once we went three nights without anything to feed the cattle. Sometimes we had little, but most of the time sufficient. We went first to Winnipeg, then on to Portage la Prairie, from where we continued southwest. Finally, after a journey of 17 days, we arrived on March 31 at our own colony, at the eastern end of what is now the Icelandic settlement at Argyle. The day before we arrived, we encountered a fierce blizzard, but as the day wore on, the weather brightened and the snow gave way to sudden squalls. As some of the oxen were by now exhausted, we were forced to lighten their load and leave some of our belongings behind. Our last night on the trail we spent sheltering in a belt of trees not far from the land claimed by the brothers Skúli and Guðmundur. Our animals suffered badly from the terrible cold, and by next morning one of my yearlings was at death's door and died a short while later. The next day (April 1), we got hay at the place where Sigurður Kristófersson had "put up" the summer before. A short distance away, two Englishmen lived in a cabin they had built the previous autumn, but they could offer us neither shelter nor refreshment. Sigurður and I remained nearby until about the middle of the month, and although it was bitterly cold, there was not much snow. During that time, we moved a little timber onto our land, along with some hay. On April 15, Good

Skafti Arason and Anna Jóhannsdóttir married in New Iceland in 1877, but later moved to Argyle, where they remained until their deaths.

Friday, we parted, each for his own land. The weather was
bright that day, with a rapid thaw, and a few days later the
snow had vanished entirely.

It was about three miles between Sigurður and me, and a
little further to the Englishmen. Skúli was about 6 miles
away, and other human habitation a good bit further. The
nearest store, if such it could be called, was about 20 miles
distant, and there was a blacksmith there as well, to carry out
essential repairs. This was also the nearest post office.

And so it was I found myself in this wilderness with a
wife, two young children, a few dying beasts, and nothing to
feed my family but a little over 100 pounds of meal. I had
three dollars in cash and a few agricultural implements. The
rest of our possessions were made up of nothing but the
home-made sleds we had come on, and a poor excuse for a
plough.

Later that summer, we were joined by a few Icelandic
families who moved onto the nearby homesteads, and newcomers from other nations also began to build, so I could see
a few other houses from my own, although the distance
between myself and my nearest neighbours had shrunk little.
Although time passed slowly, we were fairly content, and we

Communication Breakdowns

Although by 1880 English had long been established as the official language of the entire North American continent, large numbers of immigrants could barely speak the language. This account
by Kristján Ólafsson of Hábær in Þykkvabær reveals how, even
after two years in the New World, he had learned virtually none,
having spent most of his time among Icelanders and Norwegians.
His tale also demonstrates the relaxed informality of the labour
market in the days when people simply knocked at a door and
asked for work.

*The following events occurred during my second year in America.
On August 12th, [1894,] I set off in search of work as a*

Taming the land: a lone settler steers his ox-drawn plough as he takes the first step in turning a field of unturned soil into a sea of golden grain.

never suffered from hunger, although everything we had to buy was very dear. Coffee, for example, cost 40 cents a pound and raisins 25 cents, while sugar cost a dollar for 8 pounds and a side of pork 18 cents a pound. But farmers got a good price for their produce, and a labourer's wages were high, between $3.50 and $5 for clearing an acre.

By the following spring (1882), I had made enough

thresher, first at Walhalla, and then south in the Pembina Mountains, in the area then known to the Icelanders as "on the shelf." I'd walked nearly 10 English miles in the blazing heat and was thirsty, so I knocked at the door of a large log cabin. An old woman answered, and I greeted her in English. I then asked her for a drink in my newly acquired, very broken English, of which she failed to understand a word. I then tried Norwegian, which I knew a lot better. "Ja, ja," she answered immediately, "det er velkommet. Er du Norsk?" "No," I replied in the same language, "I'm Icelandic." "And what's your name?" she asked. "Norwegians call me Kristján Islænder," I replied. "Vel da, du kommer inn." She then took me into the house, and having given me a drink, fed me with some fine coffee and bread. I then left after thanking her profusely.

money to buy seed for the 18 acres I had prepared for sowing. The cattle, which had multiplied, were in the best of health, and the cows milked well.

In the late winter of 1882, more settlers began arriving, and although we could not put on any great welcome for them, we did what we could, providing shelter for cattle and humans alike. At one point, 28 people spent a night in my little cabin, which was only 13 feet long and 11 wide, and some nights the stable was just as packed. At times, despite the weather, I even had to put my own beasts out to make room for the horses and draught animals of the new arrivals.

When we began growing enough wheat to sell, we had to haul it 40 miles to the nearest market, a long journey on an ox-drawn cart. In March 1883, however, I bought a pair of horses, which cost me 450 dollars. In 1886, both of them got sick and died, along with a third horse I had purchased that same year.

At various times, I have suffered heavy losses due to fire, losing cattle, tools, and other possessions.

In the summer of 1886, the railway reached Glenboro. By that time, most of the area had been well settled, and I could count about 200 homesteads from my own front door. Schools had also sprung up at several points around the

---

Shortly after noon, I came to a field where grain was being stacked. The farmer was a Norwegian by the name of John Erlend, and I asked him for work, which I got. At mid-day, we went in for something to eat, and I followed my new master into his living room. We conversed together for a while in English, which went pretty badly, but I managed to tell him I was Icelandic and had lived in America for two years.

He continued to address me in English, to which I kept replying to the best of my very limited ability, but as the food was being placed on the table, I began listening to a conversation in Norwegian going on in the kitchen between the mistress of the house and another woman who was visiting. "That's an Icelandic lad," said the mistress. "Oh yes," replied her visitor, "I've heard a lot about them." "Tell me," said her friend. "Well, they claim

The farm of Stefán Eyjólfsson and Guðrún Þorláksdóttir near Garðar, North Dakota. As Stefán sits in the buggy with their son, Þorlákur, and Guðrún holds their daughter, Þórdís, another daughter, Margrét, pulls her sister, "Pearl" Guðfinna, towards the couple's oldest child, Cecilia (foreground, left). One of the original settlers of New Iceland, Eyjólfsson lived for a time with his brothers at Unaland on the Icelandic River.

they're descended from Norwegian Vikings, but, God preserve us, they're a most unpleasant, selfish people."

She continued in this vein, but by this time I'd stopped really listening. When the pair sat down at the table, they all began talking together in Norwegian, most of which I could understand, although I didn't let on. Then John asked me in English to tell them something about Iceland, but I hesitated. "I don't feel comfortable speaking English, but the lady can tell you all about that," I replied. "What makes you think that?" he asked. "Because I heard her in the kitchen telling Mrs. Erlend everything about Icelanders." These last words I spoke in as good Norwegian as I could muster, at which the visitor went as red as a beetroot, finally blurting out the words, "I was only repeating what I've heard. I didn't think anyone else was listening or could understand me."

district, and by 1889 we Icelanders had our own church, which hosted the fifth annual convention of the Icelandic Lutheran Synod that same summer.

Skafti Arason died in 1903, having lived for 22 years in the Argyle settlement, and by the time of his death, he left behind an estate valued at $100,000. Along with his wealth, he left behind six children, and today several of his descendants still live in the Argyle district and beyond.

During the troubled years around 1880, the majority of the New Iceland colonists followed Arason's example and left, most of them for Dakota and Argyle. The exodous to Dakota had actually begun a few years earlier, and to a large extent it can be traced to the religious dispute which then wracked the colony. The Rev. Páll Þorláksson actively encouraged his supporters to follow him across the border, and by the autumn of 1879 some 50 Icelandic families had heeded his call.

Their experiences were much the same as those of Skafti Arason and his fellow settlers in Argyle. Following the desperate hardships of their first winter, they gradually began to thrive amid the rich fertility of their new surroundings, and as the stream of settlers increased and communications improved, their lives moved closer to the vision of the "Promised Land" they had dreamed of years before, far away in Iceland.

To begin with, no schools existed for children on the prairie, and even when they did, attendance was patchy if their family was poor. This photograph from the Manitoba Archives is entitled "Settler child," and is said to originate from New Iceland.

SEATS OF LEARNING

Although education in Iceland in the 1870s was rudimentary, the settlers on Lake Winnipeg were quick to form their own schools. On October 30, 1875, only a week after the first group landed at Víðirnes, John Taylor wrote a letter to the Governor of Manitoba announcing that the New Icelanders intended to open their own school as soon as suitable premises had been built. Already, they had their own teacher, and they now wished to join the mainstream education system in the province.

Without even waiting for a reply, the doors of a schoolhouse were opened for the first time just before Christmas, in the "warehouse," as the colony's only building of any size was then known. The teacher was Caroline Taylor, niece of John and prospective bride of Sigurður Kristófersson, and the chief subject on the curriculum was English, the reading and writing of Icelandic being taught at home.

Almost 30 children were enrolled that first term, along with a few of the adults, and teaching continued until the following spring, when most of the settlers left Gimli for their new homesteads which were scattered all over the district.

Plans to resume lessons in the autumn were postponed by the outbreak of smallpox, as the school premises were required as a hospital. By the time it reopened, Caroline Taylor had been succeeded as schoolmistress by her sister Jane, but as before, the curriculum centred on the three Rs, with a strong emphasis on English. However, although 63 names appeared on the register, attendance was patchy and averaged much less.

In the winter of 1878-79, a second school was formed at Möðruvellir on the Icelandic River. Boasting an initial roll of 27, it was conducted in the home of Sigtryggur Jónasson, a fluent English speaker who, with his wife Rannveig and the author Torfhildur Hólm, also served as one of its first teachers.

As the population drift from New Iceland gained momentum, dwindling numbers forced both schools to close, and formal education would not resume again until after 1886. When it did, it was no longer in an Icelandic school. The teachers may have been Icelandic, but New Iceland was now subject to the Manitoba educational system, with provincial inspections

The schoolhouse at Gimli in 1901. Although the door stands wide open, not a single child is to be seen, and all are probably at work at home or in the fields.

and public funding. Despite this, however, the revival in education came slowly, and it was not until 1889 that public schools were formally opened at Gimli, Árnes, Hnausar, Mikley and Lundur.

Writing years later in 1951, the poet and author Guttormur J. Guttormsson remembered his first years in the schoolhouse at Grund on the Icelandic River. Operating from 1887-89, in the days before public education became freely available to all, it was funded by a mixture of fees paid by the parents and private donations. The schoolmistress was Salín Sigfúsdóttir, a local woman who had studied in Winnipeg, and Guttormsson was 10 years old in 1889 when his tongue-in-cheek account begins:

> The pupils came in various ages and sizes. Some of them were children who had grown and matured as much as they ever would, among them a widow with three children, all younger than she, of course, although she herself was classed as a schoolchild. Newly arrived from Iceland and having no English, she was also "speechless."
>
> One of the schoolboys had arrived from Iceland with his parents as a fully grown man. Six feet tall, he looked older than his father, even as old as his grandfather. Everyone could see he was not exactly a new-born, as he had a beard and frequently had to shave. As he was clearly big for his age and looked promising, Salín also thought he was filled with wisdom and knowledge, and once asked him

Scrubbed, dressed up and armed with suitably solemn expressions, pupils at the Baldur school at Hnausa face the camera in the winter of 1907-08. Their teacher, seen in the centre of the back row, is Guðný Jónasson.

to name the months of the year in English. But this was something he had never heard in his life, so Salín requested that he name them in Icelandic. As the boy-giant rose to his feet, the rest of us waited expectantly for an answer which was not forthcoming. Thinking that he had forgotten how to begin, Salín said, "Janúar," to which he replied, "Janúar." After a long silence, Salín suggested "Febrúar," which, apparently mishearing, he rendered as "Grebrúar," causing the rest of us to burst out laughing. Clearly miffed, he returned to his seat with the words "God-dem," which provoked another burst of laughter in which Salín could not help but join. Normally, of course, she did not tolerate bad language in her school, but she could not bring herself to chastise a lad of his years.

After that one term, the "boy" never entered the portals of the school again, but he later went on to become a great English speaker and one of the finest skippers on the Great Lakes of Canada.

According to Guttormur J. Guttormsson, Salín Sigfúsdóttir was faced with pupils of all shapes and sizes during her time as teacher at Lundur (Riverton).

In the years leading up to the turn of the century, a succession of new schools opened one after the other, each closely resembling its neighbours elsewhere on the prairie. Lessons were conducted in English, the only exceptions being when teachers taught their English lessons in Icelandic. In the schools of Winnipeg, Icelandic children already sat side by side with "Canadian" children, and it was there that some of the youth of New Iceland went in search of further education.

IN SICKNESS AND IN HEALTH

The daily struggle for survival was by no means the only problem faced by the New Iceland settlers. Even before the onset of the smallpox outbreak, the general health of those in the colony was far from good, and although smallpox was by far the most devastating disease to strike, it was far from being the only one.

Because of the Icelanders' poor nutritional state and primitive living conditions, a battery of other infectious diseases, such as scarlet fever, measles, typhus, and whooping cough took a heavy toll, particularly on infants and the very young, as did

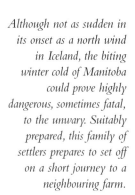

Although not as sudden in its onset as a north wind in Iceland, the biting winter cold of Manitoba could prove highly dangerous, sometimes fatal, to the unwary. Suitably prepared, this family of settlers prepares to set off on a short journey to a neighbouring farm.

tuberculosis, hydatids, hepatitis, and cancer. In most cases, the victims never knew what had hit them, and with the nearest doctor an often impossible journey away in Winnipeg, their chances of recovery were, in most cases, slim.

Accidents were also a daily hazard of life on the frontier, and the forest in particular could be a dangerous place. For those involved, the human cost of clearing land or felling trees for timber could be high, as many of the Icelanders discovered from bitter experience. One such settler was Friðsteinn Sigurðsson, who began work at the Icelandic sawmill on a chilly winter's morning early in 1881. Before the day was out, he had lost his hand to a saw and been crippled for the rest of his life. His was by no means an isolated case.

In a land where timber was everywhere, forest fires were also a continual hazard, and no matter how much care the colonists excercised, nature sometimes took an unexpected turn. Lightning storms, even rarer in Iceland than trees, were a common feature of the long, hot summers, posing a threat to people and animals alike. At least one unfortunate Icelander, Guðrún Högnadóttir of Víðirnes, is recorded as having died when struck by a bolt of lightning as she was closing the window on the upper floor of her log home to shut out a summer thunderstorm.

For settlers of all ages, the waters of Lake Winnipeg were a further hazard, and when they froze in winter, the threat posed by drowning was replaced by that of exposure. In December of 1876, Hjálmar Hjálmarsson from Hofsstaðir in Helgafellssveit and Magnús Magnússon, a labourer, set off on foot from Mikley to Gimli. Lost in a sudden blizzard, they spent three days wandering the frozen expanses of Lake Winnipeg in bitter frost. Finally, they made their way back to Mikley, where by coincidence Dr. Augustus Baldwin was treating the colonists for smallpox. For both, however, survival came at a terrible price. Magnússon lost a foot, and Hjálmarsson part of both feet. After five months recovering on his back, Hjálmarsson spent the next three years working his land on his knees.

When the smallpox epidemic was at its height, three doctors served New Iceland, but when the epidemic was over, the colony returned to a life without medical assistance—a situation which would last for the next 20 years. While the doctors were there, the Icelanders took advantage of their presence to seek treatment for a variety of ailments but, as had been the case in Iceland, medical care was otherwise left in the hands of self-taught homeopaths, individuals without any formal training who had acquired their knowledge from others, but could always be relied on for advice in times of sickness and for treatment of minor sores, ailments, and wounds. Also known as "glass doctors," due to a propensity for mixing all kinds of mysterious potions which they blended with pure alcohol

Jófríður Jósepsdóttir and Hjálmar Hjálmarsson first settled at Fagurhóll, on Mikley. In 1881, they moved to Winnipeg, but they lost their house in Shanty Town to a flood the following year. Undaunted, they embarked on an odyssey which took them far across the prairie to Þingvallabyggð, Saskatchewan, Strathclair, Manitoba, Tantallon, Saskatchewan, and then back to Þingvallabyggð, before they finally returned "home" to settle permanently in the old people's home at Gimli in 1921.

Winnipeg, as seen from the Red River bridge in the winter of 1880. Shanty Town, with its tumbledown collection of rough timber shacks, was home to many Icelanders at the time.

One of early New Iceland's best-known homeopaths was Þorgrímur Jónsson of Akur, seen here about 1890 with his wife, Steinunn Jóhannsdóttir, and twin daughters, Sigrún and Margrét. A familiar figure in the colony, like others of his profession he treated the sick with a variety of home-made potions mixed in alcohol, and also dressed simple wounds.

before dispensing it to their patients, human and animal, in small glass vials, they won confidence or lost it, depending on the results they achieved.

Some of these "medicine men" also attended women in childbirth, though this was traditionally the exclusive province of midwives, some of whom gained their training on the job while others had formal training in Iceland.

Most of all, however, people had to depend upon their own resources. The early colonists brought with them from Iceland a limited understanding of disease and how to avoid it, while most were well versed in the skills of simple first aid, which they had ample opportunity to practise in their new home. In some cases, the remedies they used seem comical to the modern eye.

In his history of the Icelanders in Manitoba, Wilhelm Kristjánsson describes a novel, if slightly unorthodox, way of avoiding smallpox, as practised by one of the colonists who had recently arrived from Iceland. Awakened one night by the movement of an animal in his cabin, he crept to his feet and threw himself and his jacket over the luckless creature, which proved to be a skunk. Although the bold Icelander had never seen such a beast, he now got to know its distinctive odour from personal experience, and it was later claimed that he was one of the few settlers to escape the disease, because the smell drove away anyone tempted to visit him.

A CITY ON THE RISE

When the first Icelanders arrived in Winnipeg in the early 1870s, it was a booming frontier town of around 2,000 souls, and had grown beyond all recognition from its population of 212 just a couple of years before. The years that followed brought no let-up in this spectacular growth, as the city's position as the main service centre for the surrounding prairie saw

In the span of just a few years, Winnipeg rose from little more than a hamlet to become one of North America's fastest-growing cities. When this picture was taken on Main St. in 1883, it was also home to a large population of Icelanders, and, as can be seen, telegraph and electricity were already familiar features of daily life.

its population multiply several times over. Each day, its numbers were further swelled by the arrival of fresh groups of settlers on the Red River steamboats, many of them fairly prosperous former Ontarians, and, faced with this massive population explosion, the city fathers struggled to keep up.

In 1880, the price of real estate in Winnipeg shot to a level higher than that in Chicago and New York, and despite the 45 hotels and 300 guesthouses, many among the colourful assortment of traders, speculators, and swindlers who flooded into the city in the hope of making their fortunes from this "land grab" were forced to sleep in the streets, alleyways and doorways of what was now one of North America's greatest boom towns. And in its banks, bars, and possibly other places of more dubious repute, the Icelanders had their own representatives.

As early as the autumn of 1875, Icelandic could be heard on the streets of Winnipeg, spoken by the sizeable number who chose to stay behind when the rest pushed on to New Iceland. The majority of them were single young women who had obtained employment as servants or housekeepers. The following spring, they were joined by others who returned from the

As was the case with new arrivals from other nations, the first stop for almost all Icelanders in Winnipeg was the Immigrant Hall, where they could spend their first days in Manitoba with free food provided. Those already in the city usually knew well in advance who was on the way, and they visited the newcomers in search of news from home, or to meet family or friends.

colony in search of work, and a few months later, their numbers were swelled significantly by the arrival of the "Large Group."

Employment opportunities for men in Winnipeg were concentrated around the waterfront, where they worked as labourers loading and unloading the steamboats and cutting fuel for their boilers. There was also a variety of public works projects resulting from the city's spectacular expansion, some of which involved sewer and road construction.

Other enterprising individuals equipped themselves with saws and axes, and sold their services door-to-door as wood cutters, an occupation which the author and poet Jóhann Magnús Bjarnason, later a teacher in New Iceland, immortalized in his well-known story, "An Icelandic Sawyer in the West," some of which appears in this extract:

> Trembling with fear, I knocked at a door where little
> kindling was to be seen, and so comes the most difficult
> obstacle of all: stating my errand. For I know no English, my
> friend, apart from one phrase: "kott von kord," and I shake
> my saw as vigorously as I can, so they think I'm crazy.
>
> And if they grasp what I've said, the next stage is to
> agree on my fee. If "dollar" I say for "kott von kord," they
> screw up their noses in contempt: they huff, they puff, and
> dismiss me with a wave, because they must make money,
> these fine men, while I must bear the loss.

Like immigrants everywhere, the Icelanders tended to stick together, and the first Icelandic quarter in Winnipeg, like countless other immigrant sections of the cities of the New World, received the stark title "Shanty Town." Those unable to buy their own houses could obtain scrap wood for next to nothing, which they fashioned into rough dwellings, lined up in such a way that streets gradually began to form. Many of the Icelanders never actually lived in "Shanty Town," and those who did found themselves surrounded by neighbours from various other nations. As the Icelanders became established in the city, many of them gravitated towards the West End, and the houses they built during Winnipeg's golden years still stand on streets such as Sargent, Victor, Spruce, Erin, and Arlington.

From its beginnings, the Icelandic community in Winnipeg differed from that of New Iceland in that isolation was never an

Street life in Winnipeg, about 1909. The general shortage of housing and cramped conditions of urban life soon taught the Icelanders to mix with people from widely differing nations, cultures, and backgrounds.

Recollections of Domestic Service

For Icelandic women, the New World offered prospects of reasonable work at a good wage, something they had never experienced before. The following letter, written from Winnipeg by an anonymous correspondent, appeared on July 20, 1893, in *Landneminn (The Pioneer)*, a periodical designed to promote emigration and published for a time in Reykjavík by Baldvin L. Baldvinsson.

I was born and brought up in Eyjafjörður. During my last years in Iceland I was a servant at Bægisá, and a better place you could not find in the whole country, no matter how far you looked. I worked there doing the usual domestic tasks. In summer, I cut hay, often in wet fields, and along with others I milked the cows and tended a flock of over 200 ewes. In summer I worked from 7 a.m. to 11 p.m., after which I often had to issue. In the city, English was spoken everywhere and, like their neighbours, the Icelanders learned quickly, driven by sheer necessity and a keen desire to be accepted.

As a result, many of them quickly changed their names to more Anglicized forms, Guðmundsson becoming *Goodman*, Sveinsson *Swanson*, and so on. Some of them were quickly absorbed into the mainstream of Canadian society and had no more contact with their brethren in New Iceland than with any other group in the city. Others had more difficulty adapting to urban culture.

How they fared in their new home varied. Broadly speaking, the Icelanders fared better than Winnipeg's other immigrant groups with regard to education. Although much of the first generation worked as labourers or in other unskilled occupations, many of the second generation obtained university education and entered white-collar professions, something that did not happen for most immigrant populations until the third generation.

Although most Icelanders arrived in Canada and North America with little in the way of formal education, almost all

wash clothes and mend shoes or other household effects. For this, I received 35 kr. for the whole year. Here in America, no one would ever dream of asking maids to work such hours, and least of all for such an insulting wage. Since I arrived, I've never earned less than $10 a month, and for the last year have had $20. My working day has never been longer than 10 hours, except when I worked for a family where I usually worked until 8 in the evening and began a little earlier in the morning. Here, I've never had to work outdoors, never had to fetch water, never milked a ewe or cow, and never worked a minute's overtime without being paid, let alone stood in a soaking wet field cutting hay as I so often had to do at home.

For many years, it was much easier for young women to find work in Winnipeg than for their male counterparts, as there was a widespread shortage of servants in the homes of the better-off, and for Icelanders in the surrounding countryside, getting a daughter into service in the city was something to be sought after for the extra money it brought in.

could read and write. As these skills were by no means the general rule among other immigrants of the period, most of them found it fairly easy to find work when it was available.

Some of the Icelandic immigrants were born businessmen, and in the boom years of the early 1880s they began speculating in real estate and the growing stock market. Stories abound of fortunes made during the real estate boom, among them that of one Bárður Sigurðsson. A man clearly blessed with true entrepreneurial vision, he is reputed to have begun with $6 in his pocket, and worked for another $44, the sum total of which he paid as a deposit on a $150 building lot on Jemima St. A month later, he sold it for $250, his $100 profit then being about three times the monthly wage of the average working man. Of course,

Native American culture meets the world of the European immigrant on Main St., Winnipeg, 1883, the same year as the first edition of Leifur *was published. Two wheeled ox-carts such as these were known as Red River carts, and behind the Native family can be seen icons of the new civilization, including a bookstore, watchmaker, and restaurant.*

As they became established in their new home, the Icelanders found themselves involved in a variety of occupations. This photograph, probably taken sometime between 1915 and 1920, shows Arinbjörn S. Bardal at work in his funeral parlour. Bardal accompanied many of his fellow countrymen to their last resting place, and the business he started is now run by Neil Ófeigur Bardal, Icelandic consul in Winnipeg.

those with higher amounts of investment capital than the enterprising Mr. Sigurðsson made correspondingly higher profits.

Although the Winnipeg Icelanders lived among other immigrant groups and were quicker to begin using English than their countrymen in New Iceland, the Icelandic community in the city maintained a strong identity and quickly became the largest in the world, outside Iceland itself. The other communities in New Iceland, Argyle, and Dakota formed a sweeping semi-circle round the city, which soon became their natural centre. A host of Icelandic societies sprang up, ranging from the Icelandic Progressive Society and the Women's Society, to a variety of church, investment, and temperance societies, and a myriad of clubs centred on a whole range of other activities and pursuits.

One of the most remarkable of these was the Icelandic Working Men's Society, formed on April 3, 1890. An independent organization, it was later admitted to the Winnipeg Labour Union, where it was represented by Jón Júlíus. As the roots of formally organized labour in Iceland are generally traced to seamen in the Bárufélag company in 1894, it can be said with some justification that the Winnipeg society was the first example of organized Icelandic labour formed anywhere in the world.

Shortly after the Society's formation, 40 Icelandic labourers employed in the construction of Winnipeg's sewers went on a three-day strike, which ended with them receiving a daily wage raise from $1.25 to $1.75. At its height, the Icelandic Working Men's Society could claim 150 members, but after 1892 interest began to decrease and their numbers dwindled.

In a rather different vein, the Icelandic Women's Society produced a dramatic production in Winnipeg in 1880, staging the play *Sigríður Eyjafjarðarsól* by Ari Jónsson from Þverá. Over the next five years, a further ten works were staged, among them *Útilegumennirnir* (The Outlaws), which opened in 1883 to a warm review from the *Manitoba Free Press*, although the critic did not particularly care for the guttural tones of the Icelandic language, of which he did not understand a word. A music society, Harpa, was also formed, but did not survive long as many of its members moved elsewhere.

The first official Icelandic Day was observed with due pomp on August 2, 1890, with Jón Ólafsson, who had been present at the millennial celebrations in Milwaukee in 1874 and had just returned from Iceland, as one of its leading lights. By now, one in ten of Winnipeg's inhabitants was Icelandic, and almost all of them, close to 3,000 men, women, and children, joined the parade through the city's streets. Their numbers were swelled by many others from the surrounding settlements, and an air of celebration marked the outdoor gathering which followed. The principal speakers were Einar H. Kvaran, Jón Ólafsson, and Eggert Jóhannsson, and, speeches over, it was time for a variety of sports, including Icelandic wrestling, followed by singing and dancing lasting well into the night. Icelandic Day formed one of the high points of the Winnipeg social calendar that year, and it is still carefully observed, although it has long since been moved to Gimli.

At the same time, the custom of the "Mountain Woman," *fjallkonan*, now a central feature of Iceland's National Day celebrations every June 17 and seen by many Icelanders as a native Icelandic tradition, would appear to have originated in Canada. According to Árni Björnsson, Iceland's most respected folklorist, she made her first appearance on Icelandic Day, 1924, but was not seen in her native land until she addressed a gathering in Reykjavík on June 17, 1947.

THE REBIRTH OF NEW ICELAND

By 1881, only six years after the colony had first been settled, three-quarters of its inhabitants had left New Iceland, and its population had plunged to a mere 250 settlers, most of them concentrated around the Icelandic River and south of Gimli. *Framfari* had ceased publication, there was no pastor to look after the colonists' spiritual welfare, education was non-existent, social life had ceased almost entirely, and agricultural development had stagnated.

As was mentioned earlier, an important factor in arresting the decline and almost inevitable death of New Iceland was the enterprise shown by Sigtryggur Jónasson and Friðjón

"Hello there, how are you. Are you not Jón from Hóll? What brings you here?" As the coming of the railway opened up the prairie, it spawned a whole range of related services, including guesthouses and eating places. The two men captured here on film somewhere in Manitoba or Saskatchewan may indeed have been two Icelanders, delighted to see a familiar face on their long journeys.

Friðriksson in establishing the sawmill at Icelandic River and operating the steamboat *Victoria*. Both projects created desperately needed jobs and raised the spirits of the remaining settlers.

The first signs of improvement came in 1883 with the arrival of a number of new settlers direct from Iceland, an upswing borne out by the statistics of the time. In 1879, the population of the Víðirnesbyggð district, of which Gimli was a part, consisted of 80 families, a total of 377 inhabitants. Four years later, in 1883,

The Icelandic Settlements in North America

The term "Icelandic settlements" as applied to North America is not as old as might be expected, mainly due to the fact that the settlers were scattered widely over the continent, and their descendants even more so.

As the map which appears earlier in this chapter shows, most of the Icelanders lived within a 200-km radius of Winnipeg in an area bounded by New Iceland in the north, Argyle in the west, and North Dakota in the south. Outside this area, some moved further west, especially north into Saskatchewan, or all the way to the Rockies, and at the same time as the Manitoba settlements were taking shape, another concentration was forming south in Minnesota. Other settlements in Ontario, Nova Scotia, and Wisconsin did not last long, while, as has already been seen, the settlement in Utah was of a completely different nature, and had little contact with those elsewhere.

Although the Icelandic settlements can seldom be defined in neat geographical terms, the following provides a rough guide to the main concentrations of Icelanders in the New World.

Manitoba
Located about 150 km west of Winnipeg and 40 km north of the U.S. border, the Argyle Settlement is both pleasing to the eye and extremely fertile. The first Icelanders to settle there were Sigurður Kristófersson and Skafti Arason, who arrived in 1880 along with

it had plunged to just 14 families of 60 people in all. By the end of the following year, however, the population of the district had recovered to 54 families, totalling 256 settlers.

The situation in Árnesbyggð was similar, with the six families who had remained being supplemented by a further 20 in 1885. The years 1885-95 saw a recovery in the New Iceland population at the rate of 200-300 settlers per year, and by 1890 the colony's population was higher than it had ever been, exceeding 1,500 souls.

English influences are evident in this picture taken at an unknown location in New Iceland. Here we see smartly dressed young people engaged in a game of croquet, a pastime common among the aristocracy in England. In spite of the clothing, there is no doubt that these are Icelanders.

a few others. By 1888, 430 were said to live there, and a few years later their number had risen significantly. Although by no means the only settlers in Argyle, the Icelanders tended to stick together, particularly in matters of religion and education, and morale among them was generally high. Another settlement, South Cypress, later developed north of Argyle, part of which was known as Hólabyggð. The principal towns of the region are Glenboro and Baldur, and both are still home to many people of Icelandic descent.

However, the newcomers who arrived during this period were among the poorest the colony had ever seen, and New Iceland quickly acquired a reputation as the last resort for new arrivals in Manitoba, with settlers trying everything before opting for a life in the colony.

In New Iceland itself, a belief had persisted from the very beginning that it was possible to drain the marshes which formed a major feature of the region's landscape. Nature herself had played a part in promulgating this idea as, after a few years of uninterrupted rise, the water table had gradually begun to fall to its pre-1875 level, making farming simpler and fishing more productive.

Selkirk

Standing near the mouth of the Red River, roughly halfway between New Iceland and Winnipeg, Selkirk was originally intended to become a city, but its fate changed in 1878 when the CPR bypassed it in favour of Winnipeg. As early as 1888, about 40 Icelandic families lived in the town, and by 1900 the total number of Icelanders had risen to about 700. Despite being ignored by the "iron horse," Selkirk continued in its role as service centre for the surrounding region and offered the services of a blacksmith, shoemaker, butcher, goldsmith, baker, printer, tailor and lawyer, as well as those of a general merchant.

When work became scarce in Winnipeg during the depression years following 1882, many Icelanders turned once again to the land, settling in the area between Lakes Manitoba and Winnipeg. Known as Grunnavatnsbyggð, this settlement later became Lundar with the coming of the railway. Low-lying and difficult to farm, it was prone to frequent floods, but despite this, at its height the area was home to more than 1,000 Icelanders.

North Dakota

Nestling between the rich soil of the Red River valley and the Pembina Hills to the west, Pembina County in the northeastern

An unknown woman and her four children pause for a rest on the pavement at Higgins Avenue, Winnipeg, on a cold day in 1907. Her weariness is obvious, and judging by her luggage, she has travelled a long way. Perhaps she is waiting for her husband to return with news of a place to spend the night.

corner of North Dakota was home to one of the largest Icelandic settlements in North America. The first Icelanders to settle here were Rev. Páll Þorláksson and his followers, who arrived from New Iceland following the religous upheaval of 1878-79. Over the course of the next few years, they were joined by several others, mainly from the Ljósavatnsbyggð district of Wisconsin. As local place names such as Svold, Hallson, Mountain, Eyford, and Gardar indicate, the colony enjoyed a lively cultural life, and it was there that Stephan G. Stephansson chose to form his Icelandic Cultural Society, which enjoyed a short but fruitful existence under the slogan "Humanity, Enquiry, Freedom," much to the chagrin of some local religious leaders.

Wisconsin

Although Milwaukee was one of the first places in North America settled by Icelanders due to the presence of the Danish merchant William Wickmann, who had moved there from Southern Iceland in 1865, its bright lights failed to attract those who followed in any large numbers, probably due to its sheer size. Those who did gravitate to Milwaukee tended to move on quickly, heading north to Washington Island or to Shawano County, known to the Icelanders as Ljósavatnsbyggð, and although the Rev. Páll

At the same time, 1881 saw New Iceland become an official part of the Province of Manitoba, and in 1887 New Iceland adopted municipal status under the name Gimli Municipality, with Jóhann Briem as its first Reeve.

As a result, the following winter brought a spirit of

Þorláksson was the prime mover in this development, by 1880 most of the early settlers had left for greener pastures in North Dakota or Minnesota.

Minnesota

In the summer of 1875, just a few weeks before the first settlers arrived in New Iceland, an Icelander by the name of Gunnlaugur Pétursson set about building himself a cabin in Southwest Minnesota, in what is now Lyon County, next to the counties of Lincoln and Yellow Medicine, and close to the towns of Minneota and Marshall. Thanks to the fertile nature of the land on which it stood, this settlement grew rapidly. By 1884, the Icelanders numbered 575, including 80 farmers, and for many years an English-language newspaper formed part of this community's lively social and cultural life.

Nova Scotia

About the same time as the first immigrants began arriving from Iceland in 1874, the Nova Scotia government embarked on a campaign aimed at encouraging settlement in that province on the country's Atlantic seaboard. The following year, a few Icelandic families moved there from Kinmount, and these were later joined by a few more from Ontario and direct from Iceland. Rough and barren, this region was about 60 km from Halifax, and they named it Markland in memory of the settlers' Viking ancestors who had preceded them by about 1,000 years. Having stayed just long enough to re-name the Mooseland Heights *Elgsheiðar* in their native tongue, the settlers eventually tired of their constant struggle with the barren soil and heavy forests, and within seven years most of them had given up and left for the West.

optimisim to the region not seen for many a day. Several new building projects were launched, trade increased, people were once again on the move, and road building was revived after a break of several years. Improved communications, in turn, led to an expansion of the New Iceland settlement westwards from

Saskatchewan

In 1885 a sizeable group of Icelanders left Winnipeg and headed 380 km northwest across the prairie to a region they named Þingvallanýlenda. Soon, they were joined by several others, some from other parts of Canada, others direct from home. A few years later, in 1891, a few of the farmers set off in search of land further to the west, finally settling 170 km from the colony in a large area which they christened Vatnabyggð. By 1900 they had been joined by some 4,000 of their countrymen, attracted by the rich soil of the area, and although the region has a short growing season, Vatnabyggð became one of the largest Icelandic settlements in North America.

Alberta

In 1889, a number of Icelandic farmers and single men in North Dakota decided to move all the way west to the Pacific Coast. On the way, one of them, Sigurður Jósúa Björnsson, made a detour to visit a few Icelanders who had settled in Calgary. When he arrived, they told him of rich, empty lands north of the city, along the Red Deer River, on the proposed route of the trans-continental railway. Some of the North Dakota farmers followed Björnsson to Red Deer River, and the settlement quickly flourished. It is best remembered as home of the poet Stephan G. Stephansson of Markerville.

Ontario

Although both the first groups of Icelandic emigrants to Canada initially settled in the region north of Toronto, the first at Muskoka and the second at Kinmount, the vast majority soon moved on, most of them for New Iceland. A small pocket of Icelanders remained in Muskoka, however, naming their post office Hekkla.

Lake Winnipeg to areas better suited to farming, and the post office at Gimli opened its doors once more.

Encouraged by these developments, the brothers Jóhannes and Hannes Hannesson opened a thriving new store in Gimli, and in 1887 a new pastor, the Rev. Magnús J. Skaftason, arrived from Iceland. In the winter of 1886-87, schools were once again organized at three places in the settlement, and their number rose to five in 1889, following the granting of provincial funding for public schools in the area. Reading societies formed throughout New Iceland and modest log "meeting houses" appeared in every district. Reading societies formed throughout New Iceland, and modest log "meeting houses" appeared in every district.

In the years following 1887, New Iceland acquired a fresh sense of purpose and direction, and despite the shift from "colonial" to municipal government, its sense of identity as a purely Icelandic settlement persisted until 1897, when the settlement was thrown open to immigrants of non-Icelandic orgin.

For most New Icelanders at the time, this change in policy was a natural development which proved beneficial to the region as a whole. The first chapter in the history of New Iceland was now closed, and the settlement differed little in status, though perhaps it did in essence, from the thousands of others which dotted the great plains of the North American continent.

TELL EVERYONE I WAS ASKING FOR THEM

One of the most influential of the early Icelanders in North America during the years 1885-95 was the poet and author Einar H. Kvaran, who through his work as a journalist and editor of *Heimskringla*, and subsequently *Lögberg*, left an indelible mark on the affairs and opinions of his countrymen. Indeed, such was his status in Winnipeg society that when he left Canada, a large crowd gathered at the railway station to see him off.

Despite his popularity and influence, Kvaran never sucessfully adapted to his chosen land, although he was still only 26 when he first arrived as a young graduate from the University of Copenhagen. On his return to Iceland he resumed his literary career, becoming editor of *Ísafold* and a number of other newspapers, as well as a prolific and well-known writer.

As mentioned earlier, Kvaran's Danish wife, Maren Mathilde Pedersen, bore him a son during their time in Canada, and, following her death, this infant was fostered by Sigtryggur Jónasson and his wife, Rannveig. This child died young. Kvaran later

Changing seasons: the informality for which Icelanders in Canada were deservedly known is obvious from these two rather different photographs of Ketill Valgarðsson and his wife, Soffia Sveinbjörnsdóttir. In the picture on the left, taken in 1920, they have clearly been caught by surprise as they went about their daily chores, while the hymn book Soffia holds in the second, taken about 1912, suggests that they may have been on their way to church. The couple, who had a business and farm at Gimli, were highly active in religious and social life, and their great-grandson, William D. Valgardson, (b. 1939) is today a well-known Canadian author.

The terrible difficulties and dreadful setbacks of the first years in New Iceland firmly behind them, most of the settlers could now look forward to a bright future in their new homeland.

"Discössing" a Thorny Issue

Not long after the arrival of Icelanders in Canada, the influence of English on their native tongue became a matter of great concern to some, and, as peppering their speech with English loan-words became fashionable among some of the Icelanders, the habit became increasingly irritating, as this short news item taken from the July 14, 1887, edition of *Heimskringla* shows.

On June 30 last, the political machine of New Iceland was set in motion. Earlier that day, the council had met at Víðivellir in the River Point district. Although the minutes of that meeting have never been published, being present at such a gathering is an education in itself for a humble member of the general public, for the Icelandic spoken is so frequently mixed with half-baked words of English origin that any listener not in the know has great difficulty in discerning the true meaning of the issue under debate. Many people dislike this, and would prefer the first all-Icelandic political assembly in North America to use the all-Icelandic language.

married again in Winnipeg, and he and his second wife, Gíslína Gísladóttir, had several children.

In 1895, shortly after his return to Iceland, Kvaran held a lecture in Reykjavík on the Icelanders in the West. Later published as a book by the Reykjavík publisher, photographer, and bookseller Sigfús Eymundsson, himself a leading figure in the emigration movement earlier in the century, Kvaran's lecture raises a series of provocative issues, beginning as it does with the question: "How have the immigrants succeeded?"

> It occurs to me to begin by stating that it seems to me that their soujourn in the West has in general made the Icelanders more admirable, impressive men in every respect than there is any reason to believe they would have become had they remained at home.

A few months later, another article by Einar Sæmundsson, which appeared in the same paper, bitterly condemned the language spoken by the Icelandic residents of Winnipeg. In it, he also asserts that some of the young women refused to speak Icelandic together when downtown, being ashamed of their mother tongue.

The practice of mixing languages would appear to have been particularly prevalent in the case of verbs and nouns, and among the examples cited by Sæmundsson are *meika monní, tjarsa, meika mistek, fixa, törna, baulir (boiler), hásklíning, borða (board), mæ goodness, platform, battalíon, starta, tren (train), inkorporeta, taxes á propertíi,* and *discöss.*

In an attempt to demonstrate the absurdity of the habit, Sæmundsson accompanied his article with the following poem, but despite his best efforts and those of others of his ilk, the practice continued unabated, and still persists in Iceland today.

Hér hef ég ása fengið fæv
og fyrsta hross, ó Dæises
Bæ the Móses bet you læf
Ég bit þig ol to píses.

Having offered a variety of arguments in support of his opinion, Kvaran goes on to offer some penetrating insights into the attitude then prevalent in Reykjavík towards those who left.

> Here at home, the majority of emigrants have been dismissed as people of below-average character, and a goodly number as complete and utter wastrels. How are they seen in their new home? In his speech made on Icelandic Day in Winnipeg, the amazement of Rev. Matthías Jochumsson at how noble and free his people in the West had become was clear for all to hear. I know that he spoke from the heart, and that is no wonder, as it can only be said of many of these people, men and women alike, that in their demeanour and speech they have now become what the English call "ladies and gentlemen."

Given his own wide experience of life in both the New and Old Worlds, it is only fitting that the last words in this book should go to Einar H. Kvaran. Although now more than a century old, they echo down through the years with the same crisp freshness as when they were first spoken.

☞ The most famous exponent of the art—if such it may be termed—was the poet Kristján Níels Jónsson (Júlíus) a.k.a. *Káinn*, who emigrated to Canada in 1878, then aged 18. After a time in Winnipeg, he moved south to Duluth, Minnesota, and then to North Dakota. Although possessed of a lightning wit and excellent command of both Icelandic and English, an over-fondness for the bottle meant he sometimes confused the two languages together, a tendency of which he was himself only too aware and to which he alludes in this short verse:

Ef einhver sér mig ekki vera að moka
þetta orða þannig hlýt:
Þá er orðið hart um skít.

All told, almost 20,000 people left Iceland in search of a new life across the sea, each with his or her own individual characteristics. They took with them their own personal hopes and fears, wishes and dreams, strengths and weaknesses, and like any other group of this size, they differed widely.

In his speech, Kvaran mentions that when asked by the Icelanders in Reykjavík about those who had left, their enquiries had centred on their material wealth and prosperity. As he states himself, this was a very difficult question to answer, as some had arrived in their new home desperately poor, even destitute, and many had just recently landed. How the others had fared varied, their condition dictated by a combination of luck and willingness to work, but Kvaran asserts that not a single pauper could be found among the ranks of the immigrants. All were self-supporting, and the majority prospered.

There can be found, for example, in some of the better households here (Reykjavík), and probably not so few at that, conditions so pathetic that it would not occur to even the poorest of Icelanders in America to tolerate them. Of course, the log cabins out in the country are not luxurious, but they are at least clean. There are no earthen walls, no turf roofs, no stench of damp sod, and they don't leak. And in time, they disappear, replaced by sturdy, smart, new houses. In the towns, it is common for merchants, tradesmen, and even ordinary workers to live in houses as well-equipped as the best found anywhere here in Reykjavík. Although living rooms are admittedly seldom as large in the West, they are covered in thick carpets from corner to corner, all the way to the doorstep. The furniture in every room is matching, practical, and tasteful, and I think it's safe to say that here in the capital, you will rarely see such well-made bedroom furnishings.

Other material living standards are in keeping with the houses. Clothes are well made, and the food much better than anything on offer in rural Iceland, with the monotonous varieties of gruel found in most places, not to mention what is common in the fishing areas where farming is almost non-existent. Compared with immigrants of other nationalities, the Icelanders are very fond of their comfort. Here, I would like to mention a

Gimli as it looked from the harbour in the early years of this century. There is no hiding the Icelandic flavour of the houses, and if the landscape were not so flat, the setting could be anywhere in Iceland.

comment made to me last year by a Dakota man, who had an intimate knowledge of the Icelanders in that region, whose neighbours are mainly Norwegians and Canadians who have moved south across the border.

"As soon as he is able," he told me, "an Icelander begins by building himself a fine dwelling house. The Canadian begins by raising a large barn and stable, while the Norwegian does neither. He just scrimps."

As far as food is concerned, what is consumed in many parts of Canada would be considered little short of gluttony here. On my journeys around the settlements last winter, I had lunch at several farms in Minnesota where my hosts took no special trouble on my account. The fare everywhere, however, was superb, consisting usually of two meat courses, roast poultry or some other roast meat, a tasty dessert, and fine cakes with our coffee. The entire household sat at table, husband and wife, children and workers.

Kvaran was also deeply impressed by the standard of education, practical as well as academic, in Canada and the U.S., where people acquired a new perspective on life through their experience of new customs and social organization.

> And then there are the public schools. In this respect, Iceland has much to learn from the West, where the state provides large amounts of money and, except in the most isolated of places, excellent facilities for teachers. All instruction is free, and in more developed places like Winnipeg, youngsters have the right to attend school for 8 years, or even longer if they repeat a class. Prevalent thinking dictates that the state should provide ordinary people with a basic education, a consideration of more importance than any other to the mutual prosperity and well-being of a society as a whole. The provision of private schools or education for a privileged few is a secondary consideration, and many even believe it is wrong to do so from public funds. As you can see, such a philosophy is directly opposite to prevalent thinking here.

Kvaran's words are an excellent example of the messages which were reaching Iceland from across the ocean. For those who had stayed at home, a whole new world was gradually opening up, conveyed in letters, newspapers, and word of mouth from men like Kvaran and others. Attitudes toward work were also very different in the New World:

> I first realized this one Sunday morning when I saw a young, well-off housewife, strikingly beautiful to behold, fetching water in a bucket. It was almost time for church, and she had obviously put on her silk dress before she realized the household had run out of water. Getting water, or tending to horses, stables, cattle, or anything else, are tasks which no man of the cloth, orator, mayor, judge, or rich merchant would consider beneath him, should the need arise. From this, you can see that manual labour in the New World is an honourable occupation. And to honour work is the same as to honour the person doing it. Across the sea, class distinction in business or daily dealings with others is

unknown. In a store line-up, everyone waits his turn, regardless of social status. People address each other as equals, and it would be considered a disgrace to bring up youngsters to treat a maid with such disdain as was customary in the Latin School here in Reykjavík during my years there.

Social customs apart, however, it was the endless news of fresh religious disputes which stirred up the most surprise and offence when it reached Iceland. In a country where worship had remained the same for centuries, it was almost impossible to comprehend how anyone could question religious doctrines, tenets, or form. Although confessing that he found hearing people discussing issues such as God and eternal life in stores

A sketch of the same farm shown in two places earlier in this book after 30 years under cultivation. The forest which almost engulfed it in its first years has now almost completely disappeared, while a watermill has been added to the impressive collection of outbuildings, each more substantial than the original log cabin, which has now been replaced by a comfortable farmhouse. After years of hard toil and struggle, this is clearly a place almost anyone would be proud to call home.

and on the street rather discomfiting, Kvaran did understand the high level of interest in religious affairs among the immigrants.

> The "Dispute," as it is called, results, of course, to a large extent from the concerted opposition which has arisen against the church and Christianity. As a result, people have been forced to defend themselves, their views, and every other aspect of their Christian faith. But everything connected to the church in the West is of greater significance to people in general than it is here at home. As everything connected to it is based on voluntary contributions, these enterprises are incredibly dear to the hearts of those who support them.

Kvaran concludes his lecture by discussing culture and the profound social and cultural changes faced by the emigrants when they arrived in their new homes in Canada and the U.S. To avoid becoming a public laughing stock, the women were forced to dispense with their distinctive tasselled head-gear, Icelandic patronymics were abolished due to the inconvenience they caused, and their language itself found itself under increasing threat.

Kvaran, however, explores the issue at a deeper level, examining it from the standpoint of the immigrants themselves with regard to their own national identity, an identity he has in 1895 no doubt they still strongly wish to preserve.

> The general consensus is that they have realized they love Iceland. It is almost pathetic how concerned they are for this country and everything in it. But the love of Icelanders in America for their motherland is in some ways special, lacking as it is in certain sentiments of a similar nature here at home. For example, it lacks any love of home, as their homes are now in another country. It lacks the strength derived from the mutual drive of a country and its people for improvement, and it lacks any concern for personal gain. And you know what is said about the blind, who, having lost their vision, develop their other senses to a higher degree. The same applies to the love of Icelanders in America for their country. Freed from the practical considerations usually integral to such an emotion, the romantic elements become more

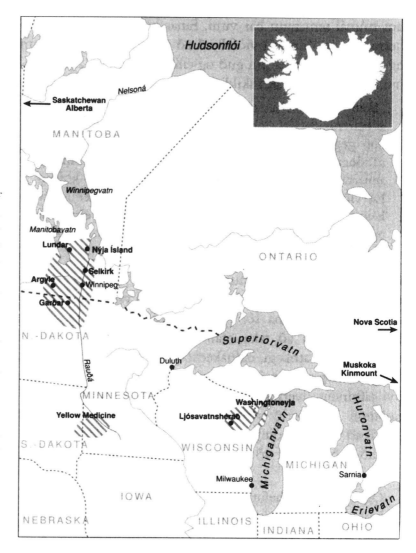

The main concentration of Icelandic settlements in Canada lay along Lake Winnipeg, stretching some 400 km from north to south, about the same distance as separates Reykjavík and Egilsstaðir. As the map shows, two other areas of settlement lay just across the border in the U.S., while there were also significant settlements in two places in Saskatchewan, and a smaller one all the way west in Alberta. Additional attempts were made to establish three others in Nova Scotia, Muskoka, and Kinmount, but these did not last long.

pronounced. As a result, the feeling itself becomes almost wholly romantic in nature. Without fully realizing it themselves, they love Iceland deeply and unquestioningly. Some might call this stupidity, but they themselves realize that in their hearts they do not love their mother more than anyone else because she was the best and most lovable of all women, but because she was their mother. And so it is with Iceland.

The most famous work of the Icelandic-Canadian poet Stephan G. Stephansson is his patriotic panegyric, "From a Speech on

Icelandic Day." Composed shortly after the turn of the century, its opening lines are known to almost every Icelander.

> No matter how far you wander
> Or through how many lands
> Your thoughts and heart bear with them
> The mark of your native strand.

The sense of longing contained in these words was such a common theme in the writings of the Icelanders in America that it must have permeated and coloured their lives for decades.

Einar H. Kvaran expressed this feeling in the closing words of his lecture to the complacent, mainly hostile ranks of the Reykjavík *petit bourgeoisie*, on a cold November day in 1895, himself a returnee from the New World, reclaimed by love of his native land.

Einar H. Kvaran, journalist, author, and returnee from across the sea.

> On my travels through the Icelandic settlements just before I returned home, the last words usually spoken to me were, "Tell everyone I was asking for them." First, they sent greeting to their families and friends. Dear God, if I should meet this one or that one, please would I pass on their message. Then they sent greetings to a host of others—to their native land, its hills and mountains, plains and fields, and its blessed horses—they sent greetings to them all.
>
> It could be said that a common theme of passionate love of their native land ran through every speech, with promises never to forget their native language, the tongue in which the sagas *Njála, Egla, Laxdæla* and *Heimskringla* were written, the tongue in which Jón Vídalín preached, and the tongue in which the author of the Edda, Hallgrímur Pétursson, Bjarni Thorarensen, and Jónas Hallgrímsson wrote; a common theme of promises never to let their children forget their poor, old country, whose blessed summer sun bathed the faces of the older ones, and many of the younger ones as well, and where the sun of the spirit, the sun of charity, blessed them as innocent children, where their mothers kissed them lovingly, held them tightly, prayed for them earnestly, loved them deeply, and taught them to say "Our Father, hallowed be thy name …"
>
> Yes, they all send their greetings.

Dateline New Iceland

1855–60 Emigration from Iceland begins with the departure of a few Mormons for Utah.

1863 A few Icelanders emigrate to Brazil and settle there.

1865 William Wickmann, a Danish merchant of Eyrarbakki, Southern Iceland, moves to Wisconsin and begins writing to his former neighbours.

1870–71 A few Southern Icelanders follow Wickmann to Wisconsin.

1872 A few more emigrants head west, mainly form the North. One of them, Sigtryggur Jónasson, settles in Canada. Emigration becomes an issue in the Icelandic press.

1873 The first in a series of many meetings on emigration is held in the North. The Allan Line begins advertising passages west, and 150 emigrants leave that summer. On arrival, they disperse, some heading for Wisconsin, others for Rosseau, Ontario. At the same time, a further 30–40 leave for Brazil.

1874 365 emigrants arrive at Quebec, most of whom head for Kinmount, Ontario.

1875 The search for a site for an Icelandic colony begins. An expedition is sent from Kinmount to Manitoba. Suitable land is found on the shores of Lake Winnipeg and an agreement is reached with the Canadian government. The first group arrives from Kinmount that autumn and the winter proves unusually harsh.

1876 Almost 1,200 emigrants leave in three stages for Canada. Known as the "Large Group," most of them reach New Iceland by autumn. Later that fall, the smallpox epidemic breaks out, claiming the lives of 102 Icelanders and almost wiping out their Native neighbours.

1877 The first printing press arrives in New Iceland, and *Framfari* begins publication. The constitution is drafted, and district councils and an assembly are elected. Few new immigrants arrive from Iceland, but two pastors, Rev. Jón Bjarnason and Rev. Páll Þorláksson, both arrive in New Iceland, signalling the beginning of a religious dispute which will eventually split the colony.

1878 Several of the original settlers begin to consider leaving in search of land elsewhere. As the religious conflict rages, several others, mainly supporters of Þorláksson, head for Dakota Territory. By now, many Icelanders have settled in Winnipeg.

1879 New settlers arrive, and others leave, leading to significant changes in property ownership in New Iceland.

1880–82 New Iceland is struck by a severe flood in November 1880, prompting many colonists to give up and leave in search of better lives in Argyle, Dakota, and Winnipeg.

1881–83 Conditions in New Iceland begin to improve. A sawmill opens at Icelandic River and commercial fishing takes off, creating new sources of employment. New arrivals from Iceland begin streaming into the colony.

1885–1900 The renaissance of New Iceland is complete. The lives of most of the colonists, their years of hardship now behind them, improve significantly, and 1895 ushers in a period of prosperity which will continue almost uninterrupted until well into the new century.

Afterword and Indices

AFTERWORD — BROTHERS IN CANADA

Now, as the 20th century draws to a close, there are no longer any 'Western Icelanders.' Canadians of Icelandic descent, either partly or completely, on the other hand, now number close to 200,000. They are the descendants of the immigrants, and they are as variable a group as they are numerous. Most, though, are uncomfortable being called 'Western Icelanders'—likely for the same reasons that Icelanders in Iceland would dislike being called 'Western Norwegians.'

Brothers Ryan and Grant are in most ways typical Canadian young people. Though different in temperament and not always in agreement any more than other brothers, their lives have followed a similar course. Both musical talent and a scientific bent have been prominent in the families of both parents, and these two forces—music and science—have competed throughout their lives. They grew up in Edmonton, Alberta, and they lived there with their parents in a beautiful home in a good suburb.

Grant Thorsteinn Sigurdson, the elder of the brothers, is 24 and has completed post secondary studies in biochemistry at the university in Edmonton. He has also played the violin since childhood and now lives in Paris, working and studying music, together with his future wife, who is a cello player.

Ryan Stefan Sigurdson is 19 and is studying biology at the university in Edmonton. Classical music is also important in his life, and like his brother he plays the violin—as well as guitar. He is also a promising singer. The future is undecided—he plans to complete his studies, but music also beckons.

Grant and Ryan are Canadians. They are born in Canada, of Canadian parents, and their *amma*'s and *afi*'s (grandmothers and grandfathers) were also born in Canada. At the same time, they are just as 'pure' Icelanders as those who live in Iceland.

Ryan Stefan Sigurdson   *Grant Thorsteinn Sigurdson*

On pages 172-173 is an account of the great-grandfather of these brothers, Sigurður Erlendsson, dating from the year 1876 when he claimed a homestead on *Mikley* (Hecla Island) under difficult circumstances. Sigurður was a tough pioneer, as revealed by this account, and his children became both industrious and prominent in New Iceland around the turn of the century. He married twice, the second time to Þórunn María Magnúsdóttir in 1901, when he was 70 years of age and she was 32. They had three children, the youngest of whom was born when Sigurður was 76. Þórunn became ill in 1909 and died when the children were young.

One of the children—the *afi* (grandfather) of these brothers) —is Stefán Valves Sigurdsson, born in 1904 and now living at the Betel Home for the aged in Gimli [1997—since deceased]. For years he ran Sigurdson Fisheries in Riverton, which for more than 100 years has been an influential fish company, founded by Stefán's uncles, the Hnausa Brothers mentioned earlier. Stefán's wife, Grant and Ryan's *amma*, was Guðrún, the daughter of Einar Guðmundsson from Hof in Vopnafjörður.

The boys' father, Solberg Sigurdson, is the son of Stefán and Guðrún. Born in Riverton, he has lived for decades in Edmonton, where he is a professor with the Faculty of Education at the University of Alberta. His wife and the mother of the boys is Shirley Thorsteinson, who has managed their home for two decades but previously worked as a researcher in bacteriology. Her parents were Edward Ari Thorsteinsson, a farmer and carpenter at Húsavi(c)k in New Iceland, and Björgveig 'Veiga' Sveinbjörnsdóttir Holm—now both deceased.

Ryan and Grant usually visit their parents' former childhood haunts in New Iceland every summer. They have numerous relatives there, and their parents own property there. The pioneer homesteads, once bush covered and poorly drained, have long since become valuable real estate, now in the ownership of the third, fourth, or even fifth generation. New Iceland is not

Winnipeg on October 21, 1875. This painting is a favourite among the descendants of Icelandic immigrants to Canada—not unlike Iceland's statue of Ingólfur on Arnarhóll— and perhaps it says more about the place this landing occupies in the history and self-concept of Icelandic-Canadians than it does about the event itself.

only an excellent farming area, it is a popular summer resort and residential destination within convenient distance of the city of Winnipeg.

The family visited Iceland in 1988. They rented a car and, among other things, travelled north to see all the farms their forefathers had left over a century before.

Grant and Ryan don't speak Icelandic, they have never lived in an Icelandic community, their friends and acquaintances are of other ethnic backgrounds, and the chances that will find themselves 'pure Icelandic' wives and have 'pure Icelandic' children are minuscule. This does not concern them, however. Their lives do not revolve around Iceland any more than do the lives of most Icelandic-Canadian young people, though they enjoy their heritage and take pride in their forebears—as do most other people. What is more remarkable, their 'history of Iceland' barely extends to Iceland. It begins in 1875 when the first settlers claimed land on the shores of Lake Winnipeg, just as the history of Icelanders in Iceland begins with the first settlement there.

Does this mean that the hopes and dreams of the pioneers are doomed? That their struggle to stick together in order to maintain their Icelandic identity was all for naught? That the warning in the first issue of *Framfari*, that the immigrants would "lose their language and identity here, unless they did something to maintain them," has come to pass?

No. The identity and the language survived the pioneers. There is no doubt that Sigtryggur Jonasson, who wrote these words in *Framfari*, would be proud of his countrymen's accomplishments in New Iceland if he could see them today. He would be proud to discover that New Iceland has produced young men like Grant and Ryan—even though they have lost the language and much of their Icelandic identity.

Sigtryggur and his counterparts wrestled not only with the diverse problems they encountered in the new land. They also had to deal with the apathy and even scorn of those who remained in the old country. In the approximately 12 decades that have elapsed since the settlement, however, something has happened that not even Sigtryggur and his fellow visionaries could foresee—Icelanders in Iceland have also become proud of the fact that there are people like these brothers—in the tens of thousands. Contact and communication with their cousins in North America have now become the topic of much discussion in Iceland in recent years; the books of Böðvar Guðmundsson have opened the eyes of many; an Emigration Museum (*Vesturfarasetrið*) has been established at Hofsós; an official plan to cultivate ties of kinship has been launched; and more could be mentioned—this book for example.

Perhaps the emigrants have now finally had their honour restored.

SOURCES

Primary Sources

The principal primary sources on Icelandic emigration to the North American continent are the first-hand accounts of the settlers themselves, as they appear in the newspapers, magazines, and periodicals of the time, and in personal correspondence. In the following directory, Reykjavík and Winnipeg have been designated the abbreviations "Rv" and "Wp" respectively.

Almanak Ólafs S. Thorgeirssonar. Wp. 1894–1954.

Þorleifur Jóakimsson Jackson. *Brot af Landnámssögu Nýja Íslands,* Wp. 1919; *Frá Austri til Vesturs,* Wp. 1921; *Framhald á Landnámssögu Nýja Íslands,* Wp. 1923.

Þorsteinn Þ. Þorsteinsson and Tryggvi J. Oleson. *Saga Íslendinga í Vesturheimi* I–V, Wp. and Rv. 1940–53.

Andvari 1975.

Magnús Jónsson. *Saga Íslendinga* IX. Rv. 1958.

Nelson S. Gerrard. *Icelandic River Saga.* Arborg 1985. Eyrarbakki Icelandic Heritage Centre, Eyrarbakki, Hnausa, New Iceland, Manitoba.

Wilhelm Kristjansson. *The Icelandic People in Manitoba.* Wp. 1990 (2nd ed, 1st imp. 1965).

Helgi Skúli Kjartansson. *Vesturfarir af Íslandi.* 1976. Cand. mag. thesis, unpublished, University of Iceland. National Library of Iceland, University Library.

Secondary Sources

A Century Unfolds: History of Arborg and District 1889–1987. Arborg 1987.

Arnason, David, andArnason,Vincent. *The New Icelanders*. Wp. 1995.

Arnason, David, and Olito, Michael. *The Icelanders*. Wp. 1981.

Baldvinsson, Baldvin L. *Ágrip af fyrirlestri um bæjalíf Íslendinga í Canada*. Rv. 1893.

Belchem, John, and Price, Richard. *A Dictionary of Nineteenth Century World History*. Oxford 1994.

Benediktsson, Jakob. "Icelandic Emigration to America." *Le Nord. Revue internationale des Pays du Nord* 1 (1942), bls. 35–51.

Bjarnason, Árni. *Að vestan* I–V. Akureyri 1955–83.

Finkel, A., M. Conrad and Strong-Boag, V. *History of the Canadian Peoples* II. 1867 to the Present. Ontario 1993.

Finnbogason, Guðmundur. "Vestur-Íslendingar." *Skírnir* 1917, bls. 68–77.

Guðmundsson, Gils. *Öldin sem leið*. Minnisverð tíðindi 1861–1900. Rv. 1956.

Gimli Saga. The History of Gimli, Manitoba. Gimli 1975.

Hjörleifsson, Einar (Kvaran). *Vestur-Íslendingar*. lecture Reykjavík. 1895.

Hreinsson,Viðar. "Vestur-íslenskar bókmenntir." *Íslensk bókmenntasaga* III, Rv. 1996, bls. 721–66.

Icelandic Canadian. Wp. 1942–.

Jackson (Walters), Thorstína. *Saga Íslendinga í Norður-Dakota*. Wp. 1926 (2. útg. Rv. 1982).

Júlíusson, Árni Daníel, Ísberg, Jón Ólafur and Kjartansson Helgi Skúli. *Íslenskur söguatlas vol 2. Frá 18. öld til fullveldis*. Rv. 1992.

Kjartansson, Helgi Skúli. *Vesturfarar*. Rv. 1995.

Kristinsson, Júníus H. *Vesturfaraskrá 1870–1914*. Rv. 1983.

Kristjánsson, Benjamín. *Vestur-íslenskar æviskrár* I–V. Akureyri 1961–85.

Líndal,Valdimar Jakobsson. "Stjórnarlög Nýja Íslands." *Tímarit lögfræðinga* 1963, 1, bls. 1–14.

Matthíasson, Þorsteinn. *Íslendingar í Vesturheimi*. Land og fólk. I–II. Rv. 1976–77.

Minningarbók íslenskra hermanna. Akureyri 1982. (1. útg. Wp. 1923, "Minningarrit …").

Newby, Eric. *Könnunarsaga veraldar*. Þýð. Kjartan Jónasson. Rv. 1982.

Nýja Ísland í Kanada. Áreiðanleg lýsing á legu og ásigkomulagi lands þess, er Kanada stjórnin hefir afmarkað til Íslendinga byggðar ... í tveim skýrslum. I. Skýrslu herra Jóns Taylors, umboðsmanns stjórnarinnar. II. Skýrslu sendimanna nokkurra Íslendinga, er fluttu út 1874. Ottawa 1875.

Pálsson, Hjörtur. *Alaskaför Jóns Ólafssonar 1874*. Rv. 1975.

Sigurðsson, Páll. "Stjórnarlög og stjórnskipun Nýja-Íslands, nýlendu íslenskra landnema í Kanada." *Úlfljótur* 1984, 4, bls. 219–58.

Saga mannkyns 11. Evrópa í hásæti. Höf. Lars-Arne Norborg, þýð. Gísli Ólafsson. Rv. 1987.

Saga mannkyns 12. Vesturlönd vinna heiminn. Höf. Jarle Simensen, þýð. Jón Þ. Þór. Rv. 1987.

Sealy, Kenneth R., og Henry Rees. *Regional Studies of the United States and Canada*. London … 1968.

Shilliday, Gregg. *Manitoba 125 – A History* 1–3. Wp. 1993–95.

Simundsson, Elva. *Icelandic Settlers in America*. Wp. 1981.

Taylor, Griffith. *Canada*. A Study of Cool Environments and their Effects on British and French Settlement. London 1957 (3. útg.).

Tímarit Þjóðræknisfélags Íslendinga. Wp. 1919–1968.

Þór, Jónas and Tergesen, Terry. *Saga Islendingadagsins*. Gimli 1989.

Þorsteinsson, Björn and Jónsson, Bergsteinn. *Íslands saga til vorra daga*. Rv. 1991.

Newspaper Sources

Copies of the main newspapers of the period can be found in the National Library of Iceland, and news of the settlers can also be gleaned from Icelandic papers of the same period.

Austri. Seyðisfirði and Akureyri 1883–1917.
Framfari. Lundur, New Iceland, 1877–80.
Heimskringla. Wp. 1886–1959 (av. Lögberg-Heimskringla, Wp. 1959–).
Ísafold. Rv. 1872–1929.
Landneminn. Rv. 1891–94.
Leifur. Wp. 1883–86.
Lögberg. Wp. 1888–1959 (av. Lögberg-Heimskringla, Wp. 1959–).
Norðanfari. Akureyri 1862–85.
Sameiningin. Wp. 1885–1964.

Internet

The Internet also offers several interesting sources on the Icelandic emigrants, with sites including:

Britannica Online – http://www.lj.eb.com/
Canada Schoolnet – http://www.schoolnet.ca/
National Library of Canada – http://www.nlc-bnc.ca/
Genealogy Home Page – http://www.genhomepage.com/
Icelandic National League – http://www.helix.net/~rasgeirs/

Sources Cited

The sources mentioned above and listed below are often cited without reference to the author and in abbreviated form, always without the year and place of publication.

7   Einar H. Kvaran. *Vestur-Íslendingar,* p. 3-4.

5-16   From a letter by Björn Kristjánsson Skagfjord, September 1, 1873: *Norðanfari* Dec.3, 1873, p. 133, *Fra Austri til Vesturs,* p. 29.

28   'Ástæður Guðmundur Hjaltasonar' (The Circumstances of Gudmundur Hjaltason: *Austri* Oct. 30, 1891, p. 34.

35-43   'Árferðisannáll' (Weather Annals) (short and sometimes retold): Magnús Jónsson. *Saga Íslendinga IX. Landshöfðingatímabilið.* First part. Þjóðmál - employment, p. 232-235. Emigration figures: *Vesturfaraskra,* p. XX-XXI (1st chart).

44-45   About life in Iceland: Kristján Ásgeir Benediktsson. "Kelduhverfi (Fyrir 40 Árum)." *Heimskringla* July 25; August 1, 8, 15, 29; Sept. 19, 1907.

57-58   Magnús Stephensen's article: *Klausturpósturinn* 1826, p. 57-58, 60-61.

63   Names in caption: *Saga Íslendinga í Norður Dakota,* p. 28.

63-65   From a letter from Washington Island: Árni Guðmundsson: "Some letters to the Sheriff and his wife at Litla Hraun 1872-73" (Finnbogi Guðmundsson prepared for print). *Andvari* 1975, p. 53-54.

67   Emigration Advertisement: *Norðanfari* January 8, 1873, p. 4-5.

72-75   From a letter by Baldvin L. Baldvinsson, Feb.20.1887: *Heimskringla* April 28, 1887, p. 3.

76-77   Report of the meeting: *Ísafold* March 11, 1893, p. 46.

77-78   From a letter by Björn Kristjánsson Skagfjord dated Sept. 1, 1873: *Norðanfari* Dec. 3, 1873, p. 133-134, *Frá Austri til Vesturs,* p. 29.

82-83   "Kveðja" (Farewell of Stefán and Guðmundur (excerpt): *Norðanfari* August 9, 1873; *Saga Íslendinga í Vesturheimi* I, p. 92-93.

85   "On Sailing from Iceland, 1873": Undína (Helga Steinvör Baldvinsdóttir). *Kvæði.* Rv. 1952, p. 5-6.

94   From Jóhann Briem's account of the journey: *Framfari* Dec. 10, 1877; *Brot af Landnámssögu Nýja Íslands,* p. 14-15.

95   From Thorleifur Jóakimsson Jackson's account of the journey: *Brot af Landnámssögu Nýja Íslands,* p. 16.

97-99   From Gestur Pálsson's account of the journey: *Heimskringla* Sept. 11, 1890; *Saga Íslendinga í Vesturheimi* I, p. 196-197.

104-105   Páll Thorláksson's letter, October 14, 1874, about the Icelandic Celebration in Milwaukee: *Norðanfari* Jan. 12, 1875, p. 3; *Frá Austri til Vesturs,* p. 52-53.

105-107   From Thorleifur Joakimsson Jackson's account of the journey: *Brot af Landnámssögu Nýja Íslands,* p. 18-19.

109-110   From a letter by Vigfús Sigurðsson, Jan. 18, 1873: *Frá Austri til Vesturs,* p. 42-44 (p.256).

111-117   From letters by Sigtryggur Jónasson, Oct. 13, 1874 and Feb. 1, 1875: *Norðanfari* Jan. 12, 1875, p. 3, and April 29, 1875, b. 47; *Frá Austri til Vesturs,* p. 49-50 and 54-59.

117-118   Letter by Páll Thorláksson, Oct. 14, 1874: *Frá Austri til Vesturs,* p. 51.

112-123   Skafti Arason's account of the expedition of 1875: *Frá Austri til Vesturs,* p. 71-73.

123-125   Resources of New Iceland; from a report by the Icelandic scouting party: *Nýa Ísland í Kanada,* p. 9-11 and 21-22.

129   The Arrival of the Icelanders: *Manitoba Free Press* Oct. 12, 1875; *The Icelanders,* p. 10.

131-132   Stefán Eyjólfsson's account: *Brot af Landnámssögu Nýja Íslands,* p. 10-11.

137-138   Skafti Arason's account of the expedition of 1875: *Frá Austri til Vesturs*, p. 73-74.

140-145   List of settlers: *Almanak Ólafs Thorgeirssonar* 1899, p. 30-32; *Saga Íslendinga í Vesturheimi* III, p. 13-15.

143-144   Skafti Arason's journal: *Frá Austri til Vesturs*, p. 74.

147-149   Stefán Eyjólfsson's account: *Brot af Landnámssögu Nýja Íslands*, p. 12-13.

151   Skafti Arason's journal: *Frá Austri til Vesturs*, p. 74-75.

154-157   Letter of Augustus Baldwin: *The New Icelanders*, p. 30-31.

158   Magnús Stefánsson's account: *Frá Austri til Vesturs*, p. 82.

158-160   Letter by Sigtryggur Jónasson, May 31, 1877: *Almanak Ólafs Thorgeirssonar* 1926, p. 34-35.

162   From a speech by Lord Dufferin: *Saga Íslendinga í Vesturheimi* III, p. 62, 65 (translation of Þorsteinn Þ. Þorsteinsson, other translations in *Framfari* Nov. 17, 1877, p. 3, and in part in *Lögberg*, May 6, 1893.

167   "October" (second part): Stephan G. Stephansson. *Andvökur* II. Rv. 1909, p. 19.

169-170   Homesteading guidelines: *Heimskringla* Jan. 5, 1888.

171   "Kurly" (first part): Stephan G. Stephansson. *Andvökur*. Sigurður Nordal prepared for print. Rv. 1980 (first edition 1939), p. 327.

172-173   Sigurður Erlendsson's account: *Almanak Ólafs Thorgeirssonar* 1919, p. 82-90.

174-175   From a letter by Vigfús Sigurðsson, Jan. 18, 1873: *Frá Austri til Vesturs*, p. 44 (p.256).

177   Memoirs of Símon Símonarson: *Saga Íslendinga í Vesturheimi* III, p. 7.

177-178   Description of Gimli: *Manitoba Free Press* Sept. 17, 1877; *The Icelanders*, p. 16; *The Icelandic People in Manitoba*, p. 72; *Íslenzk bókmenntasaga* III, p. 730 (translations of V. H. and G. A.)

179   Article by Jón Bjarnason: *Ísafold*, August 14 and 28, 1880, p. 83, 86-88.

182-183   Skafti Arason's journal: *Frá Austri til Vesturs*, p. 74, 76.

190   From the constitution of New Iceland: *Framfari* Jan. 14, 1878, p. 31-32; *Saga Íslendinga í Vesturheimi* III, p. 85.

198-201   Friðrik Sveinsson's account: *Brot af Landnámssögu Nýja Íslands*, p. 33-37.

211   Letters from the Willow Point and Big Island settlements, July 10 and 24, 1878: *Framfari* July 24 and 31, 1878, p. 128, 132; *Saga Íslendinga í Vesturheimi* III, p. 136.

211-213   From an article by Friðjón Friðriksson: *Framfari* Nov. 30, 1878; *Saga Íslendinga í Vesturheimi* III, p. 137-138.

213-215   Eggert Jóhannsson's description of the bush: "Aftur og - fram. Hugleiðingar um Nýja Ísland." *Tímarit Þjóðræknisfélagsins* 1925, p. 12-13.

218-219   About the literature of Icelanders in America: *Íslenzk bókmenntasaga* III, p. 738-739.

220   About fish in Lake Winnipeg: *Nýa Ísland í Kanada*, p. 9-11 and 19-20.

222-223   Fish stories: *Framfari* Dec, 10, 1877 and Jan. 4, 1878; *Saga Íslendinga í Vesturheimi* III, p. 142-143.

224-225   Tómas Jónasson's account: *Brot af Landnámssögu Nýja Íslands*, p. 70-71.

243   Gunnar Gíslason's article about commerce: *Landneminn* October 1892, p. 1.

245   From the first *Framfari*: "To the Subscribers and Readers of Framfari." *Framfari* Sept. 10, 1877, p. 1.

261   Manitoba Census, 1901: *Manitoba 125 - A History:* II, p. 221.

264-270   Skafti Arason's journal: *Frá Austri til Vesturs*, p. 76-80.

266-269   Story about the Norwegians: Kristjan Olafsson. "Two Incidents from Pioneering Times." *Almanak Ólafs S. Thorgeirssonar* 1951, p. 71-75.

271-273   School reminiscences: Guttormur J. Guttormsson. "The First School Year at Icelandic River 1887-1889." *Almanak Ólafs S. Thorgeirssonar* 1951, p. 28-32.

279   "Icelandic Sawyer in America" (excerpt): Jóhann Magnús Bjarnason. *Ljóðmæli*. Ísafjörður 1898, p. 22-25.

280-281 Conditions for hired girls, July 20, 1893: *Landneminn* March 1894, p. 2.

284   About the *fjallkona*: Árni Björnsson. *Saga daganna*. Rv. 1993, p. 152-153.

Photographs

An effort has been made to estimate the approximate year in which undated photographs were taken. These estimates are indicated by questions marks within brackets. If the photographer's name is not indicated, the photographer is unknown.

53   Coffee party. 1890-1893, location unknown. Photo. Tempest Anderson. Reykjavík Photo
       Collection, TEA 66.

57   Magnús Stephensen, Attorney General and 'konferensráð,' Danish lithograph. National
       Museum of Iceland, Mms. 31778.

59   Eiríkur Ólafsson from Brúnir. Photo. Theodór Hansen. National Museum of Iceland, Mms.
       10224.

60   Einar Ásmundsson of Nes. National Museum of Iceland, Mms. 19083.

62   Guðmundur Thorgrímsen. National Museum of Iceland, Mms. 23562.

62   Lefolii Store building at Eyrarbakki. 1884-86. Photo. Sigfús Eymundsson, National Museum
       of Iceland, SEY 836.

63   Icelanders in Leith, Scotland, en route to the United States. 1872. From *Saga Íslendinga í
       Norður Dakota* by Thorstina Jackson, Wp. 1926, p. 28.

65   Guðmundur Lambertsen. Photo. Sigfús Eymundsson. National Museum of Iceland, Mms.
       1056.

66   Tryggvi Gunnarsson. National Museum of Iceland, Tr.G., no number.

68   Vopnafjörður. 1881. Photo. Sigfús Eymundsson. National Museum of Iceland, SEY 538.

69   Petrína Arngrímsdóttir's contract with an agent of the Beaver Line, dated July 29, 1893.
       National Museum of Iceland, Archives of N. Múlasýsla. XXIII. 2.

70   Sigfús Eymundsson. Photo. Sigfús Eymundsson. National Museum of Iceland, Mms. 5391.

71   The *Miaca* in Seyðisfjörður. 1887. Photo. Carl Wathne (?). National Museum of Iceland, 2319 E.

72   Baldvin L. Baldvinsson. From *The Icelandic People in Manitoba* by Wilhelm Kristjanson, Wpg.
       1990 (2nd ed.), p. 252.

74   Seyðisfjörður. Circa 1870. Photo. Fridrik Löve. National Museum of Iceland, Tr.G. 106a.

75   Sheep herded aboard the *Fridthjof* in the harbour at Seyðisfjörður. Circa 1900. National
       Museum of Iceland, Pk. 2329.

76   Sigurður Kristófersson. From *The Icelandic People in Manitoba* by Wilhelm Kristjanson, Wpg.
       1990 (2nd ed.), p. 135.

79   Akureyri 1880-90. Photo. Sigfús Eymundsson. National Museum of Iceland. SEY 617.

80   *Thyra* off Sauðárkrókur. 1895-1905 (?).Photo. Sigfús Eymundsson. National Museum of
       Iceland. SEY 582.

80   *Camoens* in Trékyllisvík. 1887. Photo. Sigfús Eymundsson. National Museum of Iceland. SEY
       669.

81   Aboard a ship off the coast of Iceland. Circa 1876. Photo. Sigfús Eymundsson. National
       Museum of Iceland. SEY 144.

82   Björn Kristjánsson Skagfjörð and Guðlaug Pálsdóttir. From *Saga Íslendinga í Norður Dakota* by
       Thorstína Jackson, Wp. 1926, p. 279.

84   Passengers in the hold. 1910-15 (?), Photo. Magnús Ólafsson. Reykjavík Photo Collection.
       MaO 1631.

85   Undína. From *Kvæði* by Undína, Rv. 1952, opposite the title page (Lbs.-Hbs.)

86   Aboard the *Pennland* en route to America. 1893. From *Seven Centuries of Sea Travel* by Basil W.
       Bathe, New York, 1973, p.172.

87   Emigrants aboard the *Camoens*. Likely 1887. Photo. Sigfús Eymundsson. National Museum of
       Iceland. SEY 133.

88   Below decks on the *Dreadnought*. An English drawing from circa 1870 (?), from *Seven Centuries
       of Sea Travel* by Basil W. Bathe, New York, 1973, p.97.

90   Emigrants aboard the *Camoens*. Likely 1887. Photo. Sigfús Eymundsson. National Museum of
       Iceland. SEY 132.

93   Jóhann Briem. From *Icelandic River Saga* by Nelson S. Gerrard, Arborg, 1985, p. 42, Eyrarbakki
       Icelandic Heritage Centre, Eyrarbakki, Hnausa, New Iceland, Manitoba.

94   Aboard a passenger ship on the English Channel. An English drawing circa 1880-90 (?), from
       Seven Centuries of Sea Travel by Basil W. Bathe, New York, 1973, p. 86.

195   Indians and their canoe. 1870-90. Manitoba Provincial Archives, Indians 96.

196   Indians by a teepee. Date unknown. Manitoba Provincial Archives, Indians 155.

197   A Cree Indian in Manitoba. 1870-90. Manitoba Provincial Archives, Indians 99.

199   Guttormur J. Guttormsson by the grave of Betsey Ramsay at Sandy Bar. Circa 1935 (?). Manitoba Provincial Archives, New Iceland Collection 62.

200   A native trapper. Circa 1962. Manitoba Provincial Archives, Indians 163.

202   Gísli Árnason, Dýrunn Steinsdóttir. From *Icelandic River Saga* by Nelson S. Gerrard, Arborg, 1985, p. 635, 636, Eyrarbakki Icelandic Heritage Centre, Eyrarbakki, Hnausa, New Iceland, Manitoba.

204   Gunnsteinn Eyjólfsson of Unaland and his threshing outfit. Circa 1907. Manitoba Provincial Archives, New Iceland Collection 481.

206   Haying at Víðimýri. Circa 1920. Manitoba Provincial Archives, New Iceland Collection 506.

207   Cutting grass with a scythe at Gimli. Circa 1912. Manitoba Provincial Archives, New Iceland Collection 506.

207   Ewes outside their stable. Date unknown. Manitoba Provincial Archives, New Iceland Collection 11.

208   Haymarket in Winnipeg, Circa 1887. Manitoba Provincial Archives, New Iceland Collection 234.

209   'Little Mundi.' Circa 1920. Manitoba Provincial Archives, New Iceland Collection 330.

210   Gunnlaugur Hólm with his ox *Sörli*. Date unknown. Manitoba Provincial Archives, New Iceland Collection 307.

212   Advertisement from the June 28, 1878 edition of *Framfari*, p. 4 (Lbs.-Hbs.)

214   Children helping with barn chores in Canada. Date unknown. From *History of the Canadian Peoples* II, by Finkel, Conrad, and Strong-Boag, Ontario 1993, p.96.

215   Friðsteinn Sigurðsson and Sesselja Sigurbjörnsdóttir with their three children. Circa 1890. Manitoba Provincial Archives, New Iceland Collection 501.

216   Sawmill near Arborg. Date unknown. Manitoba Provincial Archives, New Iceland Collection 149.

216   Icelandic sawmill. Manitoba Provincial Archives, New Iceland Collection 317.

217   Sawmill near Ashern. 1915. Manitoba Provincial Archives, New Iceland Collection 142.

220   At a fishing camp on Lake Winnipeg. Circa 1920. Manitoba Provincial Archives, New Iceland Collection 32.

221   Whitefish boat on Lake Winnipeg. Circa 1915. Manitoba Provincial Archives, New Iceland Collection 31.

222   Freighters making camp on Lake Winnipeg. Circa 1925. Manitoba Provincial Archives, New Iceland Collection 313.

223   A steamboat hauls whitefish boats north on Lake Winnipeg. Circa 1920. Manitoba Provincial Archives, New Iceland Collection 220.

224   Fishing through the ice on Lake Winnipeg. Circa 1925. Manitoba Provincial Archives, New Iceland Collection 139.

225   Lifting a net through the ice on Lake Winnipeg. Circa 1925. Manitoba Provincial Archives, New Iceland Collection 159.

226   Antoníus Eiríksson and Ingveldur Jóhannesdóttir with their fosterson, Jón. Circa 1890. Manitoba Provincial Archives, New Iceland Collection 307.

228   Jóhannes Sigurðsson. From *Gimli Saga*, Gimli 1975, p.111.

229   At work in a laundry. From *History of the Canadian Peoples* II, by Finkel, Conrad, and Strong-Boag, Ontario 1993, p. 97.

230   Horses hauling freight near Gypsumville. Date unknown. Manitoba Provincial Archives, New Iceland Collection 33.

231   A horse drawn snow plough followed by sleighs loaded with fish. Circa 1925. Manitoba Provincial Archives, New Iceland Collection 326.

232   A Métis. From *Manitoba 125 - A History*, 1, Wpg. 1993, p. 116.

233   "Mounties" travelling by sleigh. Date unknown. Manitoba Provincial Archives, New Iceland Collection 341.

233   Louis Riel, Métis leader. From *Manitoba 125 - A History*, 2, Wpg. 1994, p. 15.

235   *Lady of the Lake*. 1896. Photo. J. H. Clarke, Selkirk. From *Icelandic River Saga* by Nelson S. Gerrard, Arborg, 1985, p. 101, Eyrarbakki Icelandic Heritage Centre, Eyrarbakki, Hnausa, New Iceland, Manitoba.

235   Jón Júlíus Jónsson. From *The Icelandic People in Manitoba* by Wilhelm Kristjanson, Wp. 1990 (2nd ed.), p. 168.

236   Björn Hjörleifsson and Guðrún Jóhanna Einarsdóttir on a buggy with one of their children. 1908. Manitoba Provincial Archives, New Iceland Collection 489.

237   Canadian troops near Batoche. 1885. From *The Canadians* by Ogden Tanner, Alexandria 1977, p 224.

239   Railway station at Gimli. 1910-15 (?). Manitoba Provincial Archives, New Iceland Collection 391.

240   Harvesting ice at Gimli. Circa 1922. Manitoba Provincial Archives, New Iceland Collection 396.

241   Samson Bjarnason. From *Saga Íslendinga í Norður Dakota* by Thorstína Jackson, Wp. 1926, p. 165.

241   Deliverymen from Tergesen's Store. Circa 1910. Manitoba Provincial Archives, New Iceland Collection 207.

242   Lundur on the Icelandic River. Circa 1910. Manitoba Provincial Archives, New Iceland Collection 29.

243   *Glíma* wrestling in New Iceland. Circa 1920. Manitoba Provincial Archives, New Iceland Collection 350.

244-245 *Framfari* September 10, 1877, pages 1 and 4 (Lbs.-Hbs.)

246   Jóhann Briem and Guðrún Pálsdóttir. Circa 1893. Manitoba Provincial Archives, New Iceland Collection 472.

247   Guðni Thorsteinsson in the post office at Gimli. 1900-1910 (?). From *Gimli Saga*, Gimli, 1975, p. 43.

247   Helgi Jónsson. Circa 1885. Manitoba Provincial Archives, New Iceland Collection 461.

248   In a CPR postal car. Date unknown. Manitoba Provincial Archives, New Iceland Collection 249.

248   Promotion of *Heimskringla*. Circa 1890. From *The Icelandic People in Manitoba* by Wilhelm Kristjanson, Wpg. 1990 (2nd ed.), p. 495.

249   The title pages of *Leifur, Sameiningin, Heimskringla*, and *Lögberg* (Lbs.-Hbs.)

250   Outside the 'Bar' in Gimli. 1907. Manitoba Provincial Archives, New Iceland Collection 223.

251   Delegates to the first convention of the Icelandic Lutheran Synod, held in Winnipeg from June 24-27, 1885. Manitoba Provincial Archives, New Iceland Collection 297.

252   Rev. Jón Bjarnason and Frú Lára Guðjohnsen. Manitoba Provincial Archives, New Iceland Collection 469, 470.

253   Páll Thorláksson. From *The Icelandic People in Manitoba* by Wilhelm Kristjanson, Wpg. 1990 (2nd ed.), p. 81.

255   Icelandic pioneer women. 1891. Photo. Baldwin & Blöndal, Wp. Manitoba Provincial Archives, New Iceland Collection 514.

256   Family in a single room dwelling. Circa 1915. From *History of the Canadian Peoples* II, by Finkel, Conrad, and Strong-Boag, Ontario 1993, p. 225.

258   Lutheran Church at Gimli. Circa 1910 (?). Manitoba Provincial Archives, New Iceland Collection 199.

262   Pioneers head out from Winnipeg. Date unknown. From *Manitoba 125 - A History*, 2, Wp. 1994, p. 52.

263   Settlers on the prairies. Date unknown. Manitoba Provincial Archives, New Iceland Collection 259.

265   Skafti Arason and Anna Jóhannesdóttir. *Frá Austri til Vesturs* by Thorleifur Jóakimsson Jackson, Wp. 1921, p. 69.

267   Ploughing. Date unknown. From *Manitoba 125 - A History*, 2, Wp. 1994, p. 36.

269   Farmstead of Stefán Eyjólfsson and Guðrún Thorláksdóttir southeast of Garðar, North Dakota. 1898. From *Icelandic River Saga* by Nelson S. Gerrard, Arborg, 1985, p. 184, Eyrarbakki Icelandic Heritage Centre, Eyrarbakki, Hnausa, New Iceland, Manitoba.

270   Child on a chair in New Iceland. Date unknown. Manitoba Provincial Archives, New Iceland Collection 300.

271   School at Gimli. 1901. Manitoba Provincial Archives, New Iceland Collection 233.

272   Children at the Baldur School at Hnausa. 1907-08. Manitoba Provincial Archives, Hnausa - School 2.

273   Salín Sigfúsdóttir. 1891. From *Icelandic River Saga* by Nelson S. Gerrard, Arborg, 1985, p. 127, Eyrarbakki Icelandic Heritage Centre, Eyrarbakki, Hnausa, New Iceland, Manitoba.

274   Settlers ready to travel. Date unknown. Manitoba Provincial Archives, New Iceland Collection 258.

275   Jófríður Jósefsdóttir and Hjálmar Hjálmarsson. From *Framhald á Landnámssögu Nýja Íslands* by Thorleifur Jóakimsson Jackson, Wp. 1923, p. 7.

275   Winnipeg, circa 1880, looking over the Red River from the Broadway Bridge. Manitoba Provincial Archives, New Iceland Collection 242.

276   Thorgrímur Jónsson, Steinunn Jóhannsdóttir, and their daughters, Sigrún and Margrét. Circa 1890. Manitoba Provincial Archives, New Iceland Collection 496.

277   Main Street (now Lombard Avenue) in Winnipeg, view looking north from the post office. 1883. Manitoba Provincial Archives, New Iceland Collection 240.

278   At the Immigration Hall in Winnipeg. Date unknown. From *Manitoba 125 - A History*, 2, Wp. 1994, p. 55.

280   House in Winnipeg. Circa 1909. Manitoba Provincial Archives, Immigration 22.

282   Indian family on Main Street (now Lombard Ave.) in Winnipeg. Circa 1883. Manitoba Provincial Archives, New Iceland Collection 241.

283   Arinbjörn S. Bardal on the phone at his funeral parlour. 1915-20 (?).Manitoba Provincial Archives, New Iceland Collection 277.

285   Street in a small town in Manitoba or Saskatchewan. Circa 1910. Manitoba Provincial Archives, Settlement 222.

287   New Icelanders playing croquet. Circa 1910. Manitoba Provincial Archives, New Iceland Collection 295.

289   Woman with children on Higgens Avenue in Winnipeg. Circa 1907. Manitoba Provincial Archives, Immigration 16.

293   Soffía Sveinbjörnsdóttir and Ketill Valgarðsson in summer, circa 1920 (?), and in winter, circa 1912 (?). Manitoba Provincial Archives, New Iceland Collection 136 and 135.

294   Child in a basin. Date unknown. Manitoba Provincial Archives, New Iceland Collection 67.

298   Gimli from the pier. Circa 1910. Photo. Kristín Johnson. Manitoba Provincial Archives, New Iceland Collection 410.

300   Pioneer homestead 30 years later. Circa 1882. Canadian drawing by an unknown artist. Manitoba Provincial Archives, Settlement 221.

303   Einar H. Kvaran. Photo. Gunnhildur Thorsteinsson. National Museum of Iceland. Mms. 3212.

309   Ryan Stefán Sigurdson, Grant Thorstein Sigurdson. 1996-97. Family photos from the collection of Terry Tergesen.

310   The Landing at Willow Point, 1875. Painting by Árni Sigurðsson, 1930, owned by the Þjóðræknisfélag Íslendinga í Vesturheimi. From a postcard.

INDEX